RESISTING ILLEGITIMATE AUTHORITY

A THINKING PERSON'S GUIDE TO BEING AN ANTI-AUTHORITARIAN— STRATEGIES, TOOLS, AND MODELS

BRUCE E. LEVINE

RESISTING ILLEGITIMATE AUTHORITY

A THINKING PERSON'S GUIDE TO BEING AN ANTI-AUTHORITARIAN— STRATEGIES, TOOLS, AND MODELS

BRUCE E. LEVINE

AK PRESS

Resisting Illegitimate Authority:
A Thinking Person's Guide to Being an Anti-Authoritarian—
Strategies, Tools, and Models

© 2018 Bruce E. Levine
This edition © 2018 AK Press (Chico, Edinburgh)
ISBN-13: 9781849353243
E-ISBN: 9781849353250
Library of Congress Control Number: 2018932259

AK Press
370 Ryan Ave. #100
Chico, CA 95973
United States
www.akpress.org
akpress@akpress.org

AK Press
33 Tower St.
Edinburgh EH6 7BN
Scotland
www.akuk.com
ak@akedin.demon.co.uk

The above addresses would be delighted to provide you with the latest AK Press distribution catalog, which features books, pamphlets, zines, and stylish apparel published and/or distributed by AK Press. Alternatively, visit our websites for the complete catalog, latest news, and secure ordering

Printed in the USA

CONTENTS

Introduction

Dobbs (Humphrey Bogart): "If you're the police, where are your badges?"

Gold Hat (Alfonso Bedoya): "Badges? We ain't got no badges! We don't need no badges! I don't have to show you any stinkin' badges!"

—JOHN HUSTON'S 1948 FILM
THE TREASURE OF THE SIERRA MADRE

When I was a teenager, my friends and I enjoyed repeating Gold Hat's line. It did not matter that Gold Hat was a "bad guy" attempting to steal from the "good guys." While school had taught us compliance with all those possessing badges of authority and to slavishly work to acquire such badges, Gold Hat's view was liberating.

Authoritarian is routinely defined as "relating to, or favoring blind submission to authority." In contrast, *anti-authoritarians* reject—for themselves and for others—an unquestioning obedience to authority, and they believe in challenging and resisting illegitimate authority.

Anti-authoritarians are a threat to authoritarians who demand unquestioning obedience. Thus, authoritarians attempt to marginalize anti-authoritarians. Anti-authoritarians in the United States have been scorned, shunned, financially punished, psychopathologized, criminalized, and assassinated. While U.S. society now honors a few deceased anti-authoritarians, these same figures were often marginalized, silenced, and dishonored in their own lifetime. Today, anti-authoritarians continue to be under great pressure to comply with the status quo, making their survival difficult.

All noncompliance creates tension, but not all noncompliant people are anti-authoritarians. I will distinguish anti-authoritarians as distinct from other noncompliant individuals—and explain why Gold Hat is no anti-authoritarian.

While all anti-authoritarians do not identify with a political philosophy, all anti-authoritarians do represent a political threat to their authoritarian surroundings, be that a government, school, or family. Anti-authoritarians create tension not simply for authoritarians with power but also for authoritarian followers, who fear that the absence of a strong authority will result in chaos. In contrast, anti-authoritarians believe that what is most dangerous and harmful is an illegitimate authority, and they resonate with scientist and novelist C. P. Snow's observation: "When you think of the long and gloomy history of man, you will find more hideous crimes have been committed in the name of obedience than have ever been committed in the name of rebellion."

Resisting Illegitimate Authority is about bigotry but not about bigotry directed at race, religion, gender, or sexual preference—all of which certainly remains in the United States today. This book is about another kind of bigotry, one directed at certain personalities and temperaments—a bigotry that often goes unnoticed.

One temperament that U.S. society has grown less tolerant of is introversion. Susan Cain's bestselling book *Quiet: The Power of Introverts in a World that Can't Stop Talking* (2012) argues that we undervalue introverts in our culture, doing them and society a disservice. When asked why she wrote the book, Cain answered: "For the same reason that Betty Friedan published *The Feminine Mystique* in 1963. Introverts are to extroverts what women were to men at that time—second-class citizens with gigantic amounts of untapped talent. Our schools, workplaces, and religious institutions are designed for extroverts, and many introverts believe that there is something wrong with them and that they should try to 'pass' as extroverts."

There is even more intolerance for anti-authoritarians—a highly diverse group whose members include people from all genders, races, ethnicities, sexual preferences, and personalities. In 2012, I wrote an article "Why Anti-Authoritarians Are Diagnosed as Mentally Ill" (titled on some websites as "Would We Have Drugged Up Einstein?"), and I continue to receive emails from people feeling validated by it, stating that they believe their anti-authoritarianism—or their child's—has resulted in mental illness diagnoses.

In the 1950s and 1960s, the horrors inflicted by Nazi Germany were still on the minds of many Americans, and the 1950 book *The Authoritarian Personality*, which psychopathologized authoritarian personalities, became popular. In the early 1960s, psychologist Stanley Milgram's studies revealed a frightening obedience among Americans to illegitimate authority, and this became a cause for concern. I will detail these and other examinations of authoritarianism and anti-authoritarianism, as well as controversies surrounding the "authoritarian personality" and the "anti-authoritarian personality."

By the 1980s, U.S. society had changed. In 1980, Americans elected former actor Ronald Reagan to the presidency. Reagan had previously acquired an authoritarian strongman reputation by putting down student revolts as governor of California. By the mid-1980s, the Democrats, wanting to appear as tough as the Republicans, strongly supported "anti-crime" legislation that has contributed to the United States having the highest incarceration rate in the world, caused in large part by hypocritical drug laws.

In my mental health profession during the 1980s, it was noncompliance rather than compliance that became increasingly pathologized. The American Psychiatric Association (APA), politically in step with U.S. society, revised its diagnostic manual, the *DSM-III* (1980), to include "oppositional defiant disorder" (ODD) for noncompliant kids who do not engage in criminal behaviors. The APA classifies ODD as one kind of "disruptive behavior disorder." Disruptive behavior disorders are now the most common classification of children medicated with antipsychotics, among the highest grossing classes of drugs in the United States today. The U.S. antipsychotic drug explosion is largely the result of their use on non-psychotic vulnerable populations—especially foster children, the elderly in nursing homes, and inmates in prisons and jails—as a relatively inexpensive way to subdue and manage these groups.

Between 1978 and 1985, I was in graduate school and in training to become a clinical psychologist, and my embarrassment with the mental health profession increased throughout my schooling and internships. I struggled as to whether I should quit or continue so as to get my PhD "badge." Ironically, this "stinkin' badge," which lacks legitimate authority for me, has provided me with credibility for the mainstream media that for the most part bases its assessment of authorities solely on their badges.

There are certainly societies less free and more oppressive than the United States. However, what makes life difficult for U.S. anti-authoritarians is that Americans are indoctrinated to believe that their society celebrates anti-authoritarianism. And so they are less prepared for the reality of anti-authoritarian life than others who have not been so indoctrinated.

Anti-authoritarians exist in all walks of life and come in all kinds of temperaments—some extroverted, some introverted, some funny, some serious, and so on. To illustrate this diversity, I will profile several famous anti-authoritarians with a lens focused at illuminating their essential anti-authoritarianism and an emphasis on what can be gleaned from their lives. Obviously, I cannot include every famous anti-authoritarian public figure. I will instead talk about those who I have been drawn to because their lives have provided me with lessons about anti-authoritarian survival, tragedy, and triumph.

Readers will sense that I have affection for many of these famous anti-authoritarians who I profile, and that I am sympathetic to all of them, even the ones who have hurt themselves, others, and the cause of creating a more just and free society. Sometimes luck is the only difference between anti-authoritarians having a constructive or destructive life.

Resisting Illegitimate Authority is about valuing anti-authoritarians. My life work has been "depathologizing" noncompliance and rebellion; helping anti-authoritarians survive within authoritarian schools, workplaces, and other environments; assisting those who love anti-authoritarians to better understand them; and helping anti-authoritarians gain hope that while a wise struggle against illegitimate authorities may or may not be victorious, it can lead to a community of fellow anti-authoritarians.

Earlier in Stanley Milgram's life, he was personally affected by the Holocaust and Nazi atrocities, as family members who had survived concentration camps stayed temporarily in his home when he was a child. So when his research on Americans revealed an unexpectedly high rate of obedience to authority commanding subjects to commit cruel actions, this very much troubled Milgram. Moreover, prior to his publishing *Obedience to Authority* (1974), Milgram was shaken by the My Lai massacre and other U.S. atrocities that were committed by American soldiers in the Vietnam War.

Milgram wrote: "The results as seen and felt in the laboratory, are to this author disturbing. They raise the possibility that human nature or—more specifically—the kind of character produced in American democratic society, cannot be counted on to insulate its citizens from brutality and inhumane treatment at the direction of malevolent authority." For Milgram, "the capacity for man to abandon his humanity" so as to comply with authority is what he called humanity's "fatal flaw," which he concluded, "in the long run gives our species only a modest chance of survival."

A small ray of hope is that within the human family there are anti-authoritarians—people comfortable questioning the legitimacy of authority and challenging and resisting where it is seen to be illegitimate.

PART ONE

AUTHORITARIANS AND AND ANTI-AUTHORITARIANS

1

Authorities—and My Path To
Resisting Illegitimate Authority

When I was six years old, I had appendicitis. The pediatrician said that I had a stomachache that would go away. He was wrong. I ended up in the hospital for two weeks due to a ruptured appendix. I remember my family being very angry with this doctor for his misdiagnosis.

Soon after that, like many other children and teenagers, I can recall evaluating whether an authority was a legitimate one to be taken seriously or an illegitimate one to be resisted, and I have never stopped this evaluation process.

One way young children test the legitimacy of adult authorities is by being a smart ass—or disruptive in some manner—to see how the adult reacts. Will the adult reciprocally behave like another kid? Or will the adult behave like an adult should behave, which is not to use their power to take revenge? I certainly tested that out.

Entering third grade, from the first day of class, I carefully observed my teacher, Mrs. Rike. When one of my classmates would talk without her permission, she would command: "Write one hundred times, *I will not talk.*" Or if her directions were not followed, she would order: "Write one hundred times, *I will follow directions.*" A couple of months into the school year, I hatched a plan for her, one that involved writing.

The evening before my big day in Mrs. Rike's classroom, I had privately written "*I will not talk*" one hundred times, and then did it again, so I had two such lists, both which I brought to school the next day. I could hardly wait for my opportunity. That morning in class, I began talking without permission. Mrs. Rike told me to be quiet, but I kept right on talking, and she appeared flabbergasted. While I had often forgotten to raise my hand to get permission to speak, I never had actually blatantly disobeyed her.

Mrs. Rike ordered me to write one hundred times *I will not talk*. This I had predicted, and I immediately pulled out my first prepared list from my desk and handed it to her. My classmates laughed, and I was delighted. Mrs. Rike responded, "You think you are so smart, Bruce. Well, I will have another one-hundred *I will not talks*." Exactly as I also predicted, and I pulled out my second list and handed it to her. My classmates howled. Would she stop there or ask for a third such list which I had not prepared? With a look of disgust on her face, Mrs. Rike threw up her hands and moved on. My victory gave me an empowering buzz, the kind of buzz that one gets from outsmarting an authority figure.

In addition to testing Mrs. Rike's legitimacy as an authority, I was also motivated by a desire to be seen as clever by my classmates. Being viewed as clever, I later discovered, was one of George Orwell's motivations for writing. In his essay "Why I Write," he candidly explained that *sheer egoism* and the "desire to seem clever, to be talked about" is one of his "four great motives for writing." Orwell's other three writing motives were: *aesthetic enthusiasm*, including the pleasure of words and their right arrangement; *historical impulse* for truth and to see things as they actually are; and *political purposes*, including a desire to push the world in a certain direction. At eight-years-old, I did not yet possess these other three motives, but my future writing efforts were encouraged by getting recognition for cleverness from my classmates.

That empowering triumph of outsmarting a teacher was in 1964. Today in many schools, a third-grade teacher, rather than retreating, can call for a *para*—short for *outreach paraprofessionals*—who can escort a misbehaving kid out of the classroom for counseling. These outreach paraprofessionals are supervised by an outreach counselor, who can bail out a teacher who has been overmatched by a kid.

Mrs. Rike did not hold a grudge, and so she maintained her authority for me. Had she taken revenge—which for myself and many other eight-year-olds would have meant telling my parents that I needed to be taken to the psychologist for an evaluation—she would have lost my respect and lost her authority for me.

What would have happened to me if today's rules were in place in 1964? Perhaps authorities would have looked up my records and discovered what my second-grade teacher had written about my *Social Behavior*: "On a number of occasions lately, Bruce had to be reminded about proper behavior in school and his lack of self-control. Bruce tends to speak out in class without first waiting to be called upon." This report in today's world may well have been enough for the school to pressure my parents to have me evaluated by a psychologist. Would I have been diagnosed with attention deficit hyperactivity disorder (ADHD)? Oppositional defiant disorder (ODD)? Would I have been medicated?

I feel lucky. Lucky about not being diagnosed and labeled. Lucky about not being behavior modified or medicated. And lucky about not being deprived of that great feeling of successfully outsmarting a teacher. And I feel sad that many kids today are not so lucky.

I grew up in the New York City neighborhood of Arverne in Rockaway, Queens. It was composed of racially and ethnically mixed working-class and poor people. My friends and I grew up in blue-collar families. My father worked in the post office, and my mother was a part-time "colorist" (coloring in black-and-white photo portraits) and later a part-time bookkeeper. Among my group of friends, none of our parents had gone to college, and since we were all doing well enough in school to go to college, that's pretty much all our parents cared about. And so, outside of school, we were pretty much free to do whatever we wanted to do.

The authorities that most dominated our everyday life were teachers, and our experience of them was not much different than what most teenagers tell me today—that almost all their teachers are excruciatingly boring, and in the unusual cases that their teachers are interesting and fun, they seem to get fired.

As a kid, sports was my greatest passion, and I was keenly aware of legitimate and illegitimate authorities even in this realm. For example, it was clear to me that some sportswriters were honest with fans about what was wrong with a hometown team, and others were shills and flunkies who cared more about gaining approval from team management than being honest with fans. And so by the time I became a teenager, it was clear to me that the world was divided between people willing to risk security in order to challenge and resist authority versus people who sucked up to all authorities so they could get ahead.

I've always loved movies and history, and looking back at my youth, I can see that I was drawn to historical movies from all eras with anti-authoritarian themes—from *Spartacus* to *Serpico*. As a young kid, I recall getting excited by one particular scene in *Inherit the Wind*, the fictional account of the Scopes monkey trial. In that scene, Spencer Tracy playing Henry Drummond (whose character is based on Clarence Darrow) cross examines Fredric March playing Matthew Brady (based on William Jennings Bryan). Challenging his literal interpretation of the Bible, Drummond asks Brady about where Cain found his wife, "If, in the beginning, there were just Cain and Abel, and Adam and Eve, where did this extra woman come from? Did you ever stop to think about that?" And when Brady tries to sidestep the question, Drummond mocks him, "You figure somebody else pulled another creation over in the next county somewhere?" It was exhilarating to see an anti-authoritarian challenge an authoritarian, and deliver a comical intellectual knockout. But it was troubling to see how this intellectual triumph meant nothing in terms of the trial outcome. Drummond, as had Darrow, lost the case.

I grew up during the Vietnam War era when it was common for many Americans to question and challenge their leaders—and even resist them. Lyndon Baines Johnson had won election for president in 1964, and not long after, I remember many young people chanting, "Hey, hey, LBJ, how many kids did you kill today?" I recall watching Johnson on television, always trying to convince everybody that we were winning the war. No one I knew believed him.

Then in 1968, Richard Nixon was elected president. Nixon seemed to be such an obvious liar that I had a sinking feeling about the adult world: Were they blind to the obvious, or were they resigned to their leaders being nothing but self-serving politicians? Later when I found out that Nixon had sabotaged the 1968 peace talks so that he could win the election, then lied to Johnson about his treason, and also that Johnson had evidence to prove Nixon was lying to him but covered it up for his own selfish reasons, I began to understand that as horrible as I had already thought these politicians to be, they were in fact even worse.

As a young kid, I remember that almost all the guys who were a few years older than me were frightened about getting drafted into the military. Toward the end of 1969, the draft lottery began, and I began to worry about what my lottery number would be when I became eligible. I distinctly recall my adolescent years filled with the fear that I was going to get maimed or killed in Vietnam unless I ran away to Canada and became a fugitive.

So by the time I was a teenager, I had discovered the hell that can be created by authorities who are either liars or who don't know what they're talking about but have spent a lifetime perfecting how to appear like they do. The capacity of Robert McNamara (secretary of defense under John Kennedy and Lyndon Johnson) and later Henry Kissinger (Richard Nixon's National Security Advisor and secretary of state) to convey confidence about the rightness of America's Vietnam policies is a major reason for the tragic deaths of more than 58,000 Americans and three to four million Vietnamese. McNamara was a Harvard Business School alumni, and Kissinger received several advanced degrees at Harvard and became a Harvard faculty member and director of the Harvard Defense Studies Program. I learned early in life not to trust prestigious college degree/badges of authority.

By 1974, Nixon was forced to resign, not for his real crimes against humanity but for his cover-up crimes in the Watergate scandal. I remember having an almost sadistic pleasure watching the Congressional Judiciary Committee's impeachment hearings on television, and being disappointed that Nixon quit before he was humiliated by an impeachment.

Every summer of my high school and college years, I had jobs. I have a pleasant memory of only one boss, Spatz, who was my boss one summer working for the New York City Parks Department. In the workplace hierarchy, Spatz was below the much feared general foreman, Charlie "Bags" (short for a last name that I have long forgotten). Charlie Bags would make surprise inspections, seeming to always show up when we were relaxing, and then ruining our day with threats. But Spatz would yell at Charlie Bags and defend us, "The park is clean, so get the fuck out of here." Then Spatz yelled at him in Italian, and Charlie Bags, who was also an Italian American, would get angry but leave. I hadn't seen any other authority assert themselves with their boss to defend their subordinates, and I found myself respecting Spatz.

By my teens, I had become what is now called "depressed," and I started reading psychology and philosophy books. I also listened to a lot of pain-soothing folk-rock music. My musical hero was the anti-authoritarian Phil Ochs (profiled later) who sang about injustices and mocked hypocrisy across the political spectrum. In 1976, Ochs killed himself. He was not the only one of my anti-authoritarian heroes who met a tragic end.

After graduating high school, I went to Queens College at the City University of New York because it was completely free. I became a psychology major but discovered that most of what was in the textbooks was either silly or obvious and in no way illuminating. I was lucky to have one psychology professor, Thom Verhave, who didn't take the psychology department seriously. He had been a big shot in academia and had personally known famous big shots such as Richard Herrnstein, co-author of *The Bell Curve*, which espoused a genetic and racist view of IQ and intelligence. Thom would refer to Herrnstein as "Dickie," poke fun at him, and explain to us the pseudoscience behind IQ testing. Thom combined cynicism about psychology academia with kindness for his students, and he was the only genuinely anti-authoritarian psychology professor who I would ever have.

As a psychology major, it became clear that the only way to assure some kind of career was to get a PhD; and to have options outside of academia, it meant getting a PhD in clinical psychology; and to get a license in that, it was helpful to have gone to a program that was approved by the American Psychological Association. I got accepted in one such program in the New York City area but having been a fairly compliant student much of my life, I thought it was time to "get off the train" for a while. So in 1977 I used all my savings to bum around Europe, which in the days of free or modest tuition was not that unusual even for working-class kids.

After returning from four months of traveling, I moved back with my parents. Feeling lost and trying to avoid life as much as possible, I stayed up late into the night and slept late into the afternoon, doing pretty much nothing for a couple of months. In retrospect, I consider myself lucky that my parents weren't doctors, lawyers, or professional types who sent their young adult kids like myself to psychiatrists. When, later in life, I got to know people who also had been lost in their youth, got labeled with serious mental illness, and shipped off to psychiatric hospitals, I would think of Phil Ochs's lyrics, "There but fortune, may go you or I."

Lost but lucky, I muddled through, eventually getting a ridiculous job taking money from hospital patients who had to pay for TV use. Between my job and being home with my parents, I was ready to get back to school. In 1978, I entered a graduate program at the University of Cincinnati, with free tuition and stipends enough for me to survive without taking out any loans.

In graduate school, much of the socialization and professionalization was directed at convincing us that we were "scientists," as scientists are among the most esteemed of societal authorities. To that end, we were required to take multiple classes on statistics and research design so as to be a higher authority than psychiatrists in evaluating the scientific quality of research. And we took courses on assessment and testing so as to be a higher

authority than psychiatrists in the area of classifying children and
adults with regard to intelligence and mental disorders. It was
clear that a major goal of our program was to establish that we
were authorities that should be given societal prestige.

It didn't take long for the rude awakening that the ticket to
career advancement for ambitious professionals had to do far
less with knowing what they were talking about than appear-
ing like they did. Philosopher Harry Frankfurt, author of *On
Bullshit* (2005), distinguishes between *liars* and *bullshitters*. The
liar knows the truth, and the liar's goal is to conceal it, while the
goal of bullshitters is not necessarily to lie about the truth but to
persuade their audience of a specific impression so as to advance
their agenda. In the case of academic bullshitters, I discovered
that they were especially committed to persuading others of their
importance.

I had already learned from Thom Verhave, my Queens College professor, how these IQ tests conveniently omit areas of
intelligence that most academics are not good at. For example,
these tests do not assess the intelligence it takes to be funny and
not bore an entire class; to read body language; to see through
bullshit; or to stay alive on the streets in a dangerous neighborhood. Psychologist academics routinely have no great intelligence in these areas, and so, of course, these capacities are omitted
from IQ tests.

In addition to IQ tests, it was obvious to me that the psychiatric diagnostic bible—the *DSM*, published by the American
Psychiatric Association—was far more a political than a scientific
instrument. When I began my graduate school training in 1978,
many psychologists did not take the *DSM-II* (1968) seriously,
and even many psychiatrists questioned its scientific value. And
so the APA set about to create a revision, the *DSM-III* (1980),
that professed to have made the *DSM* valid, reliable, and scientific. The APA repeatedly promulgated that the *DSM-III* had
accomplished these goals, but it was not true.

It was obvious to me that the *DSM* was about as scientifically valid as Leviticus. The authors of both *DSM* and Leviticus

simply labeled those behaviors that made them uptight. In Leviticus, these anxiety-producing behaviors were labeled "abominations" and "sins," and in the *DSM* they were labeled "mental illnesses" and "mental disorders." In Leviticus, homosexuality is an abomination; and in *DSM-II*, homosexuality was a disorder. Homosexuality was not listed as a disorder in the *DSM-III* only because gay activists—assisted by a changed cultural climate in the 1970s—had enough political clout to abolish this insult to their sexual identity. However, noncompliant youngsters had no such political clout, and so in the *DSM-III*, "oppositional defiant disorder" was created for them.

Early in graduate school, I discovered that challenging authorities got me labeled as having "issues with authority." This was somewhat amusing for me, as among the working-class kids who I had grown up with, I was considered relatively compliant with authorities, as I had done my homework, studied, and received good grades. But in this extremely compliant environment of graduate training, I was being seen as a "bad boy." In graduate school, the clinical director—who would repeatedly tell us about his days at Yale—accused me of having "authority issues." Since he was an authority, I realized that if I defended myself that would prove his point, so I initially said nothing in response. But finally after he repeatedly baited me, I responded, "I don't have authority issues. I just have issues with authorities who don't know what they are talking about."

It became obvious to me that gaining acceptance into graduate school or medical school and then gaining a PhD or MD to become a psychologist or psychiatrist required an extraordinary amount of compliance to authority. It became clear to me that the selection and socialization of mental health professionals bred out many anti-authoritarians, and this—as I will later detail—has significant consequences in the pathologizing of noncompliant and rebellious people.

After acquiring my PhD and clinical psychologist license, I then hid out in private practice. However, by the early 1990s, I had become so embarrassed by my profession that I felt a need to publicly separate myself from it—first through a letter to the editor, then in articles, and eventually with books and talks. By 1994, I had become aware of a political movement of ex-patient "psychiatric survivors" and dissident mental health professionals. This movement aims at abolishing pseudoscience and coercive treatment as well as providing the general public with "informed choice." I've been involved in this world ever since.

While none of my previous books have been specifically about authoritarianism and anti-authoritarianism, in retrospect, I realize that virtually all my publications have been geared for anti-authoritarian readers. While I had previously written a few articles about anti-authoritarians, I had long thought that this subject required an entire book. When the anti-authoritarian AK Press invited me to write a book for them, I thought that they were the right publisher for *Resisting Illegitimate Authority*.

The Compliant,
the Noncompliant,
and the Anti-Authoritarian

Defining Terms / The Percentage of Americans Who Resist Illegitimate Authority / The Authoritarian and Anti-Authoritarian "Personality" and Left-Right Politics

Lyndon Johnson famously proclaimed his requirements for an appointee: "I want him to kiss my ass in Macy's window at high noon and tell me it smells like roses." Johnson and his ass-kissers were authoritarians.

Defining Terms

Authoritarian is defined by the *American Heritage Dictionary* as "characterized by or favoring absolute obedience to authority, as against individual freedom; of, relating to, or expecting unquestioning obedience." Authoritarians with power demand unquestioning obedience from those with lower rank. And authoritarian subordinates comply with all demands of authorities.

Anti-authoritarians, in contrast, reject unquestioning obedience to authority. Anti-authoritarians question whether or not an authority is legitimate before taking that authority seriously. And anti-authoritarians challenge and resist illegitimate authorities.

Anti-authoritarians oppose the imposition of illegitimate authority not only on themselves but on others as well. This is why Gold Hat is no anti-authoritarian, as while he did not for himself take seriously the state's societal badges, he sought unquestioning obedience to himself.

For anti-authoritarians, evaluating the legitimacy of those in authority includes questioning the legitimacy of societal badges. Anti-authoritarians assess whether authorities actually know what they are talking about, and whether they are competent, honest, have integrity, and care about those people who are trusting them. And when anti-authoritarians determine an authority to be illegitimate, they challenge and resist that authority, whether the authority is their doctor, teacher, parent, or government.

Dissent is different than *disobedience.* A person may dissent with an authority but may still obey. People who are capable of dissent but incapable of disobedience are uncomfortable challenging the very legitimacy of that authority to wield power. Anti-authoritarians are comfortable with both dissent and disobedience, as they are comfortable questioning, challenging, and resisting authority they deem to be illegitimate.

Anti-authoritarian is not synonymous with *noncompliant.* In the 1932 movie *Horse Feathers*, the noncompliant Professor Wagstaff, played by Groucho Marx, is *oppositional*—not *anti-authoritarian*—when he sings: "Your proposition may be good, but let's have one thing understood, whatever it is, I'm against it. And even when you've changed it or condensed it, I'm against it."

Oppositional is defined as the actions of opposing, resisting, defying, and/or combating. Before young people become anti-authoritarians, they are often oppositional; as before they pride themselves on distinguishing legitimate from illegitimate authority, they can pride themselves on their noncompliance. Thus, it is troubling that being oppositional and defiant has been pathologized by the American Psychiatric Association as a mental disorder called "oppositional defiant disorder." This psychopathologizing and resulting "treatment" make it more difficult for young people's prideful noncompliance to mature into this vital societal contribution: discerning an authority's legitimacy, and resisting illegitimate authority.

Contrarian is also not synonymous with anti-authoritarian. A contrarian rejects popular opinions and goes against current practices. Contrarians, for example, are selling their stock when the stock market is rising and when most are buying stock; and they are buying stock when the stock market is plummeting and most are selling. A contrarian may reject a war when it is popular, but also call for unpopular military actions. Contrarians reject popular opinion, while anti-authoritarians reject illegitimate authorities. Anti-authoritarians and contrarians have in common a certain fearlessness around being unpopular, disliked, and ostracized; and so sometimes contrariness and anti-authoritarianism exists within the same person.

All genuine *anarchists* are anti-authoritarians, however, not all anti-authoritarians are anarchists. *Anarchism* literally means "without rulers," and the *Merriam-Webster Dictionary* defines it as: "a political theory holding all forms of governmental authority to be unnecessary and undesirable and advocating a society based on voluntary cooperation and free associations of individual groups." Among anarchists, there is no monolithic view of anarchism though there is generally agreement that the state is an illegitimate authority.

Some anarchists self-identify as *libertarian socialists*, who believe in socialism but oppose state socialism. However, the term *libertarian*, especially in the United States, is now routinely associated with the Libertarian Party and people who oppose state coercions but don't view capitalism as essentially coercive. So for example, Emma Goldman (profiled later), identified herself as an anarchist, while Marilyn Chambers (porn star and the 2004 Personal Choice vice presidential candidate), identified herself as a libertarian. Both Goldman and Chambers opposed state authority and both celebrated sexual freedom, but they differed on the coercive nature of capitalism. For anarchists, both the state and capitalism are illegitimate authorities that are coercively dehumanizing.

One iconic anarchist poster reads, "Fuck Authority," which feels good for many anarchists to say. However, for anti-authoritarians who are not anti-state (such as Thomas Paine and Ralph Nader, both profiled later), it is not "Fuck Authority" but rather: "Fuck Unjust Authority," "Fuck Stupid Authority," and certainly "Fuck Illegitimate Authority."

Authoritative has a very different meaning than *authoritarian*, and the distinction is important. *Authoritative* means being accurate, true, reliable, valid, and thus trustworthy. Part of being a legitimate authority is to be authoritative. For example, my longtime car mechanic has a lengthy history of being authoritative—competent, honest, and trustworthy—and if he tells me that my brakes are unsafe, I take him seriously and comply with his recommendation to replace them.

The idea of taking any authority seriously might upset certain anarchists, however, not those who are familiar with Mikhail Bakunin (1814–1876), one of the most famous anarchists in world history. Bakunin wrote: "Does it follow that I reject all authority? Far from me such a thought. In the matter of boots, I refer to the authority of the bootmaker; concerning houses, canals, or railroads, I consult that of the architect or the engineer. . . . But I allow neither the bootmaker nor the architect nor the savant to impose his authority upon me. I listen to them freely and with all the respect merited by their intelligence, their character, their knowledge, reserving always my incontestable right of criticism and censure."

Perhaps the most well-known modern American anarchist is linguist and political activist Noam Chomsky (profiled later), and he too would not say, "Fuck Authority." For Chomsky, every form of authority has to "prove that it's justified—it has no prior justification." Chomsky gives an example of justified authority: "When you stop your five-year-old kid from trying to cross the street, that's an authoritarian situation: it's got to be justified. Well, in that case, I think you *can* give a justification." However, for Chomsky, "Most of the time these authority structures have no moral justification . . . they are just there in order to preserve certain structures of power and domination." My guess is that Chomsky would be okay with the anti-authoritarian poet Walt Whitman's advice: "Resist much, obey little. Once unquestioning obedience, once fully enslaved."

It is important to distinguish between *anti-authority* and *anti-authoritarian*, as the two terms have different meanings.

Anti-authority means being in opposition to *all* authority. Anti-authoritarian means opposing authoritarians and illegitimate authority. Unfortunately, some social scientists such as Christian Bay in *The Structure of Freedom* (1958) have equated anti-authority with anti-authoritarian, viewing anti-authoritarianism as a syndrome and pathologizing it. The anti-authoritarian, for Bay, "represses awareness of his own weakness and dependency needs. He sees all authorities as bad and wicked, and all weak people as exploited and persecuted." For people who oppose *all* authority, one can debate whether this psychological analysis has any merit; but anti-authoritarians are not opposed to all authority, only illegitimate ones—and so this psychological analysis is irrelevant.

Totalitarianism is an authoritarian system of government that recognizes no limits to its authority, attempts to regulate every aspect of life, and demands complete subservience. George Orwell's novel *1984* describes a totalitarian government, and Orwell is known for having condemned the totalitarianism of both the so-called "Right" and the so-called "Left," from National Socialism and fascism to Stalinism. More later on confusions about Left-Right political battles over authoritarianism and anti-authoritarianism as well as on the political battle about the "authoritarian personality" and the "anti-authoritarian personality."

The Percentage of Americans Who Resist Illegitimate Authority
There is a continuum from extreme authoritarianism to extreme anti-authoritarianism, and at different points in people's lives and under different circumstances, people may be at different points on this continuum. Under periods of great anxiety and fear, an individual, family, society, or nation can become more receptive to authoritarian measures of unquestioning obedience; and anti-authoritarian attitudes have been more normalized in some extraordinary periods of American history.

How many of us obey or disobey illegitimate authority? This estimate will vary depending on the assessment method.

A 2012 Harris Interactive survey asked American adults: "Given the recent reports concerning the threat posed by terrorists who plan to implant bombs within their own bodies, how willing, if at all, would you be to undergo a TSA [Transportation Security Administration] body cavity search in order to fly?" A body cavity search consists of one's mouth, anus, and vagina being probed and inspected by uniformed authorities—an extreme invasion of one's physical privacy, and so one can argue that only an authoritarian who unquestioningly obeys authority would comply. The poll reported that 15% of American adults are "completely willing" to comply, and that an additional 15% are "somewhat willing." And so, a total of 30% would comply with authority and submit to such a privacy violation in order to board a plane. Results were virtually the same with self-identified Democrats and Republicans (15% of both Democrats and Republicans were "somewhat willing," and 15% of Democrats and 16% of Republicans were "completely willing").

Another question on the Harris Interactive survey was: "How reasonable or unreasonable do you feel it is that travelers should be made by law to obey every command given by a TSA agent inside an airport or any other public place given the threat posed by terrorists?" A majority of Americans, 57%, considered a law to obey every command to be either completely or somewhat reasonable.

However, surveys only detect people's self-perceptions and not their actual actions. Perhaps the most famous attempt to discover how rampant authoritarian behavior was in U.S. society was psychologist Stanley Milgram's "obedience to authority" studies. Milgram was deeply affected by how many people complied with Nazi authoritarian directives to commit atrocities, and in the early 1960s, he sought to discover how far ordinary Americans would go in obeying an authority's harmful commands.

In the original Milgram study at Yale University, 40 male volunteers were recruited for an experiment ostensibly investigating learning. They were paid "$4.00 plus 50 cents carfare" for showing up (paid regardless of whether or not they

THE COMPLIANT, THE NONCOMPLIANT, AND THE ANTI-AUTHORITARIAN   25

discontinued participation). These subjects were introduced to another participant, who was actually a confederate in league with the experimenter. The naïve subjects were the "teachers" and the confederate was the "learner," and there was also the experimenter authority. Each teacher subject was given an actual "sample shock" of 45 volts so that they could experience what learners would be receiving in the experiment (though in the experiment, the confederate learner did not receive actual shocks but pretended to be shocked).

In the most well-known variation of the experiment, 26 of 40 teacher subjects (65%) continued to shock the confederate learner to the highest level of 450 volts even as the confederate learner pounded the walls to protest and no longer answered after 315 volts. While 65% never disobeyed the experimenter authority, even the 35% who ultimately disobeyed at higher shock levels showed a significant degree of obedience.

Specifically, in the experiment, the learner confederate was strapped to a chair with electrodes. After the learner was taught a list of word pairs, the teacher subject was told by the experimenter authority to administer an electric shock every time the learner made a mistake, increasing the level of shock each time. There were 30 switches on the shock generator marked from 15 volts (labeled as "slight shock") to 450 volts (labeled as "Danger: severe shock"). The confederate learner purposely gave mainly wrong answers, and for each wrong answer, the teacher subject was told by the experimenter authority to give the learner an electric shock. When the teacher subject objected, the experimenter authority gave a series of orders/prods to ensure they continued (Prod 1: "Please continue"; Prod 2: "The experiment requires you to continue"; Prod 3: "It is absolutely essential that you continue"; and Prod 4: "You have no other choice, you *must* go on"). Milgram reported, "At 75 volts, the 'learner' grunts. At 120 volts he complains verbally; at 150 he demands to be released from the experiment. His protests continue as the shocks escalate, growing increasingly vehement and emotional. At 285 volts his response can only be described as an agonized scream."

Milgram carried out several variations of this study, altering the situation to see how this affected obedience. The authority's "badges" were significant. In the original study, the experimenter authority wore a grey lab coat uniform as a symbol of his authority, but in one variation, the uniformed experimenter authority was called away and replaced by an experimenter in everyday clothes rather than a lab coat; and here the 450-volt highest-level obedience rate dropped from 65% to 20%. In another variation, when the site of the experiment was moved from Yale University to a run-down office, the 450-volt highest-level obedience rate dropped to 47.5%. Proximity to the experimenter authority figure also changed the compliance rate, as when the experimenter authority telephoned orders rather than being in the same room, the obedience rate fell to 20.5%.

Another variation of the experiment shows the importance of modeling disobedience in order to reduce compliance with illegitimate authority. When two other participant teachers were also confederates (sitting next to the teacher subject) refused to obey—one stopping at 150 volts, and the other stopping at 210 volts—the level of obedience was reduced from 65% to 10% compliance for the highest-level shock.

Milgram's studies on obedience to authority have been replicated many times in the United States and around the world with slightly different methodologies but similar results. Milgram believed that the obedient were not without morality but that their morality was an authoritarian morality. He noted, "Although a person acting under authority performs actions that seem to violate standards of conscience, it would not be true to say that he loses his moral sense. Instead, it acquires a radically different focus. . . . his moral concern now shifts to a consideration of how well he is living up to the expectations that the authority has of him."

One criticism of Milgram's conclusions, leveled by sociologist Matthew Hollander, was that obedience and disobedience are more nuanced than Milgram depicted. Hollander analyzed the dialogue from audio recordings of Milgram's study participants, and he found that people classified as obedient tried several different forms of verbal protest saying "I can't do this anymore" or "I'm not going to do this anymore" but they ultimately continued. For Hollander, this was an attempt at disobedience. But for Milgram, these protests were *dissent*, not *disobedience*, and what's crucial is that dissent without disobedience had no value for the shocked "learner."

The Authoritarian and Anti-Authoritarian "Personality" and Left-Right Politics

Within the mainstream American media, the rise of the Republican president Donald Trump energized renewed concern about authoritarianism. While Trump is a caricature of a wannabe strongman, some of the most authoritarian presidential actions in U.S. history have been administered by Democratic presidents—from Andrew Jackson's forced removal of the Cherokees and the ensuing "Trail of Tears"; to Grover Cleveland's use of the army to break up the Pullman Strike; to Woodrow Wilson's incarceration and deportation of World War I resisters; to Barack Obama's prosecution of more government whistleblowers under the Espionage Act than all previous administrations combined.

The 1950 publication of *The Authoritarian Personality*, authored by sociologist Theodor Adorno along with psychologists Else Frenkel-Brunswik, Daniel Levinson, and Nevitt Sanford, stirred up both methodological and political controversies. A large part of the impetus for this work was the then-recent Nazi regime's genocidal atrocities. Adorno in Germany had been an important member of the Institute for Social Research, which came to be known as the Frankfurt School. He fled Germany in the 1930s. In *The Authoritarian Personality*, Adorno and his co-authors hoped to identify personality factors that resulted in anti-Semitic and fascist behaviors.

The Authoritarian Personality included exhaustive research on different populations and was influenced by Sigmund Freud and psychoanalysis. One of its major theories was that the authoritarian personality type was, in part, a result of punitive parenting causing repressed anger with parents along with a fear of them; thus resulting in a fear of questioning and challenging authorities and, ultimately, worshiping punitive authority figures. Adorno and his team measured authoritarianism by the "F-Scale," short for "pre-fascist personality." The F-Scale variables included: conventionalism; authoritarian submission; authoritarian aggression; anti-intraception (rejection of inwardness, the subjective, the imaginative, and self-criticism); superstition; power and toughness; destructiveness; projectivity (perception of the world as dangerous); and exaggerated concern for sexual behaviors. (In 2006, psychologist Bob Altemeyer found that only three of these variables actually correlated together: authoritarian submission, authoritarian aggression, and conventionalism.)

By seeking psychological explanations for authoritarianism and fascism, Adorno angered some orthodox Marxists who viewed human actions purely as a product of economics. And by equating the "authoritarian personality" with the politics of the Right, Adorno also upset conservatives and libertarians who objected to the omission of the authoritarian Left.

People such as Adorno and his co-authors who identify themselves as on the Left routinely associate authoritarianism with the Right, and those on the Right see an authoritarian Left. For the Left, Hitler, Mussolini, Franco and the right-wing ideology of fascism's demand for unquestioning obedience to the state are examples of authoritarianism. However, for the Right, Stalin, Pol Pot and Khmer Rouge communism also demanded unquestioning obedience and are examples of Left authoritarianism.

In *The Anti-Authoritarian Personality*, the Left political scientist William Kreml attempted to establish anti-authoritarian personality attributes. For Kreml, those possessing anti-order, anti-power, impulsiveness, and introspection attributes "will tend toward the acceptance of Left-wing political views." However, there are non-Left, self-identified libertarians who would also claim those attributes.

Libertarian philosopher David Makinson argued that since authoritarians engage in coercion, anti-authoritarianism is synonymous with anti-coercion. *Coercion* means the use of force, threats, and intimidation to break resistance and obtain compliance. However, to equate anti-authoritarianism with anti-coercion overlooks the necessity of coercion as a tool for resisting and removing illegitimate authorities. By definition, anti-authoritarian resistance often requires coercions directed at these authorities. Coercions vary. For example, American colonials used violent revolution in order to remove the illegitimate authority of Great Britain. In India, Mahatma Gandhi used methods such as hunger strikes, which though called "nonviolent," are still coercive.

More recently there have been other efforts to discover what kind of people have authoritarian tendencies and who, when they become insecure and anxious, desire a strongman leader. Leading social scientists in this field include social psychologist Jonathan Haidt and political scientists Karen Stenner, Marc Hetherington, and Stanley Feldman.

Feldman attempted to create a more reliable measure of authoritarianism by unlinking it from political ideology. In the early 1990s, Feldman began measuring authoritarianism by using four questions about parenting, asking respondents to state which they thought to be more important for a child: (1) independence or respect for elders? (2) self-reliance or obedience? (3) to be considerate or well-behaved? (4) curiosity or good manners? Feldman's questionnaire received a great deal of attention for the association of its measure of authoritarianism with a higher likelihood of being a Republican voter and for predicting Donald Trump voters. But political scientist Samuel Goldman believes that these parenting questions are not apolitical—that what is called "authoritarian" by Feldman's scale could be called "old-fashioned parenting values" that are more common among blue-collar than white-collar people, and more common in the South than the rest of the United States.

The conventional Right-Left distinction—especially for many oppressed groups—is not all that useful when examining authoritarianism. For many oppressed groups, the difference between the Right and the Left is only in their techniques used to coerce conformity and gain control.

While the Right favored killing indigenous Americans to steal their land, so-called progressives on the Left favored forced assimilation through boarding schools that prohibited the use of tribal languages and customs, which made it easier to divide and conquer Native people—and then steal their land.

For oppressed homosexuals in the United States, again the Right and Left differed only on the kind of techniques used to coerce conformity and gain control. The Right favored criminalizing and imprisonment, while progressives on the Left favored "treatment" for homosexuality, including aversive conditioning techniques involving electric shock and nausea-inducing drugs during presentation of same-sex erotic images.

The limitations of categorizing anti-authoritarians by Right-Left can be seen in the evaluations of figures like Thomas Paine and Ralph Nader, who are both profiled in the following chapter. There are libertarians who claim Thomas Paine, using his famous anti-government quote "Society in every state is a blessing, but government even in its best state is but a necessary evil." However, Paine was not anti-government or anti-state. He advocated for a government that had a progressive estate tax, social security for the aged, and a government that would abolish inequality, poverty, exploitative taxation, and inadequate wages. But Paine was also no socialist, as he did not call for land collectivizing or redistribution, and he believed in private enterprise. Paine cannot be placed into today's Right-Left spectrum, but he was clearly an anti-authoritarian, a fierce opponent of illegitimate authority. Similarly, there are few more passionate anti-authoritarians than Ralph Nader; and Nader, like Paine, is not anti-state but for a government that promotes social and economic justice and freedom.

PART TWO

THE ASSAULT
ON U.S.
ANTI-AUTHORITARIANS

Great Contributions Do Not Prevent Marginalization:
Thomas Paine, Ralph Nader, and Malcolm X

Today in the United States, it is politically correct to have high regard and even awe for famous Americans who have challenged and resisted illegitimate authority. However, many of these same anti-authoritarians were hated and shunned at their life's end. The extraordinary lives of the following group of anti-authoritarians offer evidence that even the greatest of contributions do not inoculate anti-authoritarians from marginalization in U.S. society.

It may seem odd to see Thomas Paine, Ralph Nader, and Malcolm X in the same group, but they have commonalities. The boldness of actions by Paine, Nader, and Malcolm X separated themselves from their contemporaries, even from those with similar political views. All three, by virtue of their extraordinary talents and some luck, were remarkably successful in positively transforming the lives of millions of Americans. All three cared little about wealth or personally profiting from their contributions. All three were unintimidated by the violence of the illegitimate authorities whom they challenged and resisted. All three refused to tolerate hypocrisy in anyone, and for that, all three were punished severely. Paine was ostracized by a nation that he, in major ways, had helped to create. Nader was shunned by progressives after his unparalleled progressive accomplishments. And Malcolm X was assassinated by members of a religious organization despite his genius for making their institution a large and powerful one.

With respect to their legacies, there are also similarities. Thomas Paine and Malcolm X, hated at the time of their deaths, are now American icons with U.S. postage stamps honoring them both—but with the most radical aspects of their lives and politics largely ignored. And Ralph Nader too will likely share that fate.

Anti-authoritarians' refusal to be intimidated by the political consequences of challenging authority can—at the right moment in time and with some luck—be successful. What can catch anti-authoritarians by surprise is that no matter how important their supporters have deemed their past contributions, if their other anti-authoritarian actions create problems for their supporters, admiration can quickly turn to abandonment and assault. What is especially sad is how previous extraordinary accomplishments in no way mitigates the ferocity of these assaults.

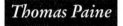
Thomas Paine

"He had faults, like other men; but it was for his virtues that he was hated and successfully calumniated."

—BERTRAND RUSSELL, "THE FATE OF THOMAS PAINE,"
1934

"One by one most of his old friends and acquaintances had deserted him. Maligned on every side, execrated, shunned and abhorred—his virtues denounced as vices—his services forgotten—his character blackened, he preserved the poise and balance of his soul."

—ROBERT INGERSOLL, "THOMAS PAINE," 1892

Thomas Paine (1737–1809) was one of the most influential anti-authoritarians in not only U.S. history but in world history. In *Thomas Paine and the Promise of America*, his biographer Harvey Kaye tells us, "He fought to liberate men and women from the authoritarianism of states, classes, and churches and to empower them to think for and govern themselves." Yet despite

Paine's great talents, unparalleled accomplishments, famous friends, popularity, and admiration, he was, at the end of his life, hated and shunned by virtually an entire nation that he had a large part in creating.

Paine came to the American colonies just before the outbreak of the Revolutionary War in one of the more anti-authoritarian eras in American history, and he took advantage of these circumstances to become—for a time—widely admired. Like the other anti-authoritarians who I profile, Paine was compelled to challenge all illegitimate authorities regardless of political consequences. He would come to denounce and ridicule the most popular man and the most popular belief system in the United States. This resulted in Paine being ostracized and marginalized in U.S. society in the last years of his life—and long after his death. Paine's legacy has had a historical comeback, and he is today honored for challenging and resisting British control over colonial America, and he is admired for his role in fomenting the American Revolution. But his historical comeback has been based on a convenient neglect of his most politically incorrect condemnations.

Born Thomas *Pain*, later changing the spelling to *Paine*, he was to become a major pain in the ass for authorities around the world. As a teenager, he apprenticed to his stay-maker (corset-maker) father. As a young adult, Paine became an exciseman (a government official who inspects and rates articles liable to tax), but he was fired after two years for claiming to have been working while actually studying at home. He became a poorly paid schoolmaster until he was able to get reinstated as an exciseman. Paine and other excise officers asked Parliament for higher pay and better working conditions, and Paine published his first political work in 1772, *The Case of the Officers of Excise*; and in early 1774, he was fired again from the excise service. His other financial efforts failed, and to avoid debtors' prison he sold his household possessions.

Paine's first wife had died in 1760, a year after their wedding; and, by 1774, he was separated from his second wife, and his financial life was in shambles. Paine saw the British system—Parliament, the monarchy, and hereditary authority—as the reason for his failure. Paine's personal pain compelled him to gain justice for himself and others similarly oppressed. He was committed to exposing the illegitimacy of the British system of rule, and there was no better place to do that than in colonial America where Paine would find a receptive audience.

At age 37, Paine was a "societal loser," but he then got a huge break, meeting Benjamin Franklin in London. Franklin was impressed by Paine and provided him with a letter of recommendation (calling Paine an "ingenious, worthy young man"). Franklin's name was gold in colonial America, especially in Franklin's home town of Philadelphia, where Paine immigrated to in 1774, using Franklin's recommendation to great advantage.

"Paine arrived in America," notes biographer Eric Foner, "with a unique combination of resentments against the English system of government and opportunities for immediate self-advancement and self-expression." In January 1775, Paine became editor of the *Pennsylvania Magazine*, and he proceeded to increase its circulation. In March 1775, Paine called for the abolition of slavery, pointing out the hypocrisy of white colonials complaining about British tyranny while being silent about their own slaveholding.

Paine was a working-class guy and thus quite different from most of the elitist "founding fathers." As late as November 1775, Thomas Jefferson wrote that "there is not in the British Empire a man who more cordially loves union with Great Britain than I do," and Kaye also reported that George Washington continued to toast King George III at dinners with his officers. In contrast, Paine viewed the entire British authority—not just Parliament—as illegitimate, and he would voice the then-taboo word *independence*.

Paine sensed that colonial America was craving a down-to-earth writer who could describe why Great Britain was an illegitimate authority. "Paine's importance in history," concluded Bertrand Russell (English philosopher, mathematician, historian, and social critic), "consists in the fact that he made the preaching of democracy democratic." Paine was, Russell noted, "an innovator in the manner of his writing, which was simple, direct, unlearned, and such as every intelligent workingman could appreciate."

In January 1776, Paine published *Common Sense*, at first anonymously, but soon after he became known as its author. In it, Paine made clear that it wasn't just the current bad king or the current bad government leaders but the entire notion of monarchy, aristocracy, and the British system of rule that was illegitimate. *Common Sense* is what most U.S. students are taught about Paine, as it remains his most politically correct work.

In the three months following its publication, 150,000 copies of *Common Sense* were distributed; and including pirated editions, an estimated 500,000 copies were circulated throughout the colonies during the course of the American Revolution. At that time, there were approximately three million free colonial inhabitants, and so *Common Sense* was read by an astonishing percentage of colonial America. No other writer was so widely read, but Paine refused to financially profit by it.

Six months after the publication of *Common Sense*, in July 1776, the Continental Congress ratified the Declaration of Independence. The American Revolution was in full steam by late 1776 when Paine published a series of pamphlets, *The American Crisis*. This was a propaganda effort meant to inspire a dispirited colonial army and prevent George Washington's troops from quitting on him, as well as to help Washington maintain his job as commanding officer. To inspire his soldiers, Washington had the first *Crisis* read aloud to his troops, which begins with these now famous words: "These are the times that try men's souls."

Following the success of the American Revolution, Paine returned to Europe to help incite revolution there. Paine's *Rights of Man* (first part published in 1791) refuted the British conservative Edmund Burke's criticism of the French Revolution, criticized the William Pitt–led government of Great Britain, and objected to hereditary rule. The second part of *Rights of Man*

(1792) described social programs to reduce poverty of the commoners. *Rights of Man* became an international sensation and stimulated reform societies.

In England, Paine became the object of a smear campaign conducted by the enraged William Pitt. The British public was told that Paine had, historian Jill Lepore reports, "defrauded his creditors, caused his first wife's death by beating her while she was pregnant, and abused his second wife almost as badly, except that she wasn't really his wife, because he never consummated that marriage, preferring to have sex with cats." Paine's friend, poet William Blake, convinced him that if he remained in England he would be hanged, and so Paine bolted for France, narrowly missing arresting officers.

Paine had been enthusiastic about the French Revolution, and his *Rights of Man* made him a celebrity in France where he was granted honorary French citizenship. Despite his inability to speak French, Paine was elected to the French National Convention. However, Paine's integrity again got him in trouble with authorities—this time with the authoritarian Robespierre and his fellow Jacobins. While Paine championed abolishing the French monarchy, he opposed capital punishment; and he reminded the French people that King Louis XVI and the aristocrat Lafayette had both helped liberate the American colonies from England. Paine's loyalty to American Revolution supporters and his opposition to their being guillotined incurred the wrath of the Jacobins who had gained power. The Jacobins first expelled Paine from the Convention and then imprisoned him.

Paine fully expected that his friend George Washington would get him released from prison. Paine had dedicated *Rights of Man* to Washington, and Washington remained popular in revolutionary France. The fiercely loyal Paine could not imagine that Washington would not help him. After all, it was Paine's *The American Crisis* that had kept Washington's troops from deserting him; and when the Continental Congress was questioning Washington's leadership, Paine had used his propaganda skills in *The American Crisis* to make Washington appear to be a smarter strategist than he was. Paine also raised money for Washington's colonial army. However, as is common for many anti-authoritarians, Paine was an innocent when it came to political machinations.

At the time of Paine's imprisonment, the American minister to France was Gouverneur Morris, and Morris had a grudge against Paine for exposing Morris's friend's corrupt dealings during the American Revolution; so Morris had no inclination to help Paine. Also, while Paine was in a French prison, Washington was secretly negotiating a treaty with England that betrayed France; and so it was in Washington's political interest to have Paine rot in prison, unable to inform the French of this betrayal. Paine narrowly escaped the guillotine and came close to dying of illness caused by his prison stay. Luckily for Paine, Morris was replaced by James Monroe, who immediately procured Paine's release and brought him into his home in France, where it took well over a year for Paine to recuperate.

Paine, hurt and angered by Washington's disloyalty, never forgave him. In 1796, Paine published his *Letter to George Washington*, a bitter rebuke of Washington that included the following: "And as to you, sir, treacherous in private friendship (for so you have been to me, and that in the day of danger) and a hypocrite in public life, the world will be puzzled to decide whether you are an apostate or an impostor; whether you have abandoned good principles, or whether you ever had any."

Paine, Russell observed, "incurred the bitter hostility of three men not generally united: Pitt, Robespierre, and Washington. Of these, the first two sought his death, while the third carefully abstained from measures designed to save his life. Pitt and Washington hated him because he was a democrat; Robespierre, because he opposed the execution of the King and the Reign of Terror."

Even with his diatribe against Washington, Paine still had political allies, and he would not have been completely shunned and marginalized if he hadn't published another sensational bestseller. That book, *The Age of Reason*, challenged biblical scriptures and organized religion, including Christianity. Many of his fellow Founding Father deists privately agreed with Paine's views about religion but were politically astute enough to not publicize their views and to distance themselves from Paine.

In *The Age of Reason*, Paine challenged the authority of the Bible and organized religion from a moral point of view, just as he had attacked the immorality of the British system of rule and the French Jacobins. All, for Paine, were cruel and thus illegitimate authorities, and Paine, being Paine, could not back off. He wrote that "all national institutions of churches, whether Jewish, Christian or Turkish, appear to me no other than human inventions, set up to terrify and enslave mankind, and monopolize power and profit." While admiring the morality of Jesus, Paine dubbed Christianity as a "species of Atheism" for it "professes to believe in a man rather than in God."

In *The Age of Reason*, part 2 (1795), Paine's refutation of the scriptures and Christianity was written, Foner points out, "in a tone of outrage and ridicule . . . in manner designed to reach a mass audience." Regarding the story of Jesus's birth, Paine wrote: "Were any girl that is now with a child to say, and even to swear to it, that she was gotten with child by a ghost, and that an angel told her so, would she be believed?"

Paine's condemnation of Christianity was shocking at the time and remains shocking today for many people. Paine said: "Of all the systems of religions that ever were invented, there is none more derogatory to the Almighty, more unedifying to man, more repugnant to reason, and more contradictory in itself, than this thing called Christianity. Too absurd for belief, too impossible to convince, and too inconsistent for practice, it renders the heart torpid, or produces only atheists and fanatics." Paine alienated himself from virtually all Christians, including progressive reformers who had been Paine admirers.

Paine's 1796 pamphlet *Agrarian Justice*, unknown to most Americans, endears him today to Left-populists. *Agrarian Justice* is an attack on the sources of inequality and poverty, which Paine blamed on unfair taxation, inadequate wages, and unwise government expenditures. In it, he spelled out proposals for old-age pensions and a basic income. *Agrarian Justice*, especially compared to Paine's previous works, was widely ignored and remains so.

At age 65, in 1802, Paine returned to the United States, as Foner describes, "only to find himself first vilified and then ignored." A Boston journalist described Paine as a "lying, drunken, brutal infidel." Even former friends and allies abandoned him. Benjamin Rush, a close friend in Philadelphia, refused to see him. Samuel Adams, also once a friend, issued a public letter denouncing Paine. Many innkeepers refused him service. Foner notes: "Paine slipped into obscurity. His final years were ones of 'lonely, private misery.' He was isolated from almost all his old associates and friends, and again began to drink heavily."

In 1806, Paine wrote, "My motive and object in all my political works . . . . [has] been to rescue man from tyranny and false systems and false principles of government, and enable him to be free, and establish government for himself." By then, few Americans cared about anything Paine had to say, and in 1809, he died in a rooming house in Greenwich Village, New York City. Six mourners attended his funeral (compared to 20,000 mourners at Benjamin Franklin's funeral), with almost no mention of his death in the American press. Even the peace-loving Quakers refused Paine's request for burial in their cemetery.

John Adams, a longtime fierce enemy of Paine's vision of genuine democracy and of Paine himself, admitted, "Without the pen of the author of *Common Sense*, the sword of Washington would have been raised in vain," and he acknowledged in 1805, "I know not whether any Man in the World has had more influence on its inhabitants or affairs for the last thirty years than Tom Paine." However, an envious Adams was tortured by the prospect that "History is to ascribe the American Revolution to Thomas Pain [sic]." Adams called Paine "profligate and impious," and he wrote to Thomas Jefferson in 1819, "What a poor ignorant, malicious, short-sighted, Crapulous Mass, is Tom Pains [sic] Common Sense."

For many years after his death, Paine was either attacked or ignored by the American political and cultural elite. In *The Life of Thomas Paine*, published a few months after Paine's death, James Cheetham vilified him as "vain," "intemperate," "dirty," "hypocritical," "parasitical," "unpatriotic," "atheist" and a "copier of ideas." Cheetham accused him of seducing and abandoning his friend and housekeeper Madame de Bonneville (one of the six people at Paine's funeral), and she successfully sued Cheetham for libel. However, despite Cheetham's libelous falsehoods, those who hated Paine and what he stood for, "cared little about Cheetham's veracity," Kaye notes, "and his book supplied anti-Paine invective to generations of conservatives to come." In 1888, Theodore Roosevelt called Paine a "filthy little atheist"; yet, historian J. H. McKenna points out, "Paine was fastidiously clean, stood taller than most of his contemporaries at five feet ten inches, and was a professed believer in God."

Paine has come to be admired for *Common Sense* and for his role in fomenting the American Revolution. In 1969, he was honored with a "Prominent Americans" series U.S. postal stamp. But Paine's historical comeback is based in large part on a convenient neglect for his scathing condemnation of Christianity. As Lepore notes, "So wholly has *The Age of Reason* been forgotten that Paine's mantle has been claimed not only by Ronald Reagan but also by the Christian Coalition's Ralph Reed, who has invoked him, and the North Carolina senator Jesse Helms, who in 1992 supported a proposal to erect a Paine monument in Washington, D.C."

Reviewing four books about Paine as well as an examination of the historical view of him, Lepore concludes: "Paine emerges in most academic accounts as a kind of idiot savant; savvy about adjectives but idiotic about politics." Paine is viewed as "hopelessly naïve," and even "an ignoramus," and one of Paine's biographers offers a tentative diagnosis of bipolar disorder.

Among his more anti-authoritarian biographers such as Harvey Kaye, Paine is viewed more sympathetically, as "inquisitive, gregarious, and compassionate, yet strong-willed, combative, and ever ready to argue about and fight for the good and right." For many famous and non-famous anti-authoritarians, their compulsion for truth-telling makes it difficult for compromises and diplomacy. Foner concludes, "Paine was at his best at the very moment of overthrow, when principles of government were called into question and new classes emerged into political life. But Paine was temperamentally and intellectually unsuited for the day-to-day affairs of government."

Similar to many non-famous anti-authoritarians, Paine disregarded cautions from friends; and, though loyal to his friends, Paine was more loyal to his own integrity. His onetime friend Benjamin Rush cautioned him against the use of the then-taboo word *independence*, but he disregarded Rush. His friend James Monroe tried to dissuade him from publishing his diatribe against George Washington, but Paine published it anyway.

Paine was a political ally with Thomas Jefferson in several areas (with slavery being a major exception). However, Paine's friendship with Jefferson became a significant political liability for Jefferson whose enemies used it to attack him, especially with respect to questions of Jefferson's own religious beliefs. Jefferson, after he had become president, risked political capital by offering Paine transportation back to the United States on a public vessel (which Paine declined). However, soon after his return to the United States, Paine composed another series of letters reviving his hostility with John Adams and George Washington during a time when Jefferson was attempting to foster reconciliation. Another of Paine's friends, William Duane, warned Paine not to publish these letters. Duane later said to Jefferson that he had told Paine that he "will be deserted by the only party that respects him or does not hate him—that all his political writings will be rendered useless—and even destroyed." But again Paine was stubborn, and ultimately Jefferson too severed his relationship with him.

Without Paine's personal papers, which burned in a fire, it is difficult to know for certain whether Paine didn't care about the consequences of his attack on Christianity or was naïve about key elements of American society and American politics. Many self-identified American Christians who would have stood with him in his battle for social reforms that he spelled out in *Agrarian Justice* abandoned Paine because of his attack on Christianity. Paine, like many anti-authoritarians, could not back down from challenging any authority that he believed was illegitimate. But his attack on Christianity deprived him of all political capital to create social and economic justice in U.S. society.

So beyond the personal tragedy of Paine's later life, there was a political tragedy. Egalitarian Americans who cared about greater social and economic justice and who could have used a politically powerful legacy of Thomas Paine and his *Agrarian Justice* were deprived of it because of Paine's attack on Christianity. For Paine, Christianity was a major illegitimate authority, and his integrity compelled him to challenge it.

One of Paine's few nineteenth-century admirers, Robert Ingersoll, concluded that Paine had "more courage than politeness; more strength than polish. He had no veneration for old mistakes—no admiration for ancient lies. He loved the truth for truth's sake, and for man's sake. He saw oppression on every hand, injustice everywhere; hypocrisy at the altar; venality on the bench, tyranny on the throne; and with a splendid courage he espoused the causes of the weak against the strong—of the enslaved many against the titled few."

While Paine can be viewed as a compulsive truth teller, he cannot be viewed as compulsively self-destructive. During his early life as a societal "loser," he displayed impressive resiliency. He took full advantage of his lucky break connecting with Benjamin Franklin, and he recognized and used his talent of being a plain-speaking and provocative writer. Despite his sad end, Paine did much right so as to have an extraordinary anti-authoritarian life.

That Thomas Paine's extraordinary accomplishments in no way mitigated the viciousness of the assault on him is a sad reflection on his society. This dark reality about U.S. society continues to catch naïve anti-authoritarians by surprise—as well as to create anxiety and extreme vigilance for other U.S. anti-authoritarians.

Ralph Nader

"Ralph, go back to examining the rear-end of automobiles. . . and don't risk costing the Democrats the White House this year as you did four years ago."

—JIMMY CARTER, DEMOCRAT CONVENTION, 2004

"Outside of Jerry Falwell, I can't think of anybody I have greater contempt for than Ralph Nader. No one in the history of the world is on a bigger ego trip than Ralph Nader."

—JAMES CARVILLE, DEMOCRAT PARTY STRATEGIST, 2006

"The Democrats just totally trashed the guy. . . . They're the meanest bunch of motherfuckers I have ever run across."

—JAMES RIDGEWAY, JOURNALIST, 2006

For Thomas Paine, illegitimate authorities were the British rule over America, hereditary rule, monarchy, the Bible, clerics, and Christianity. For Ralph Nader (born 1934), illegitimate authority is *corporatism*—an oligarchy composed of giant corporations, the super-rich, and elected officials from both the Republican and Democratic Parties who do their bidding.

No American anti-authoritarians rose to greater national popularity than Paine and Nader, and none took larger falls in terms of popularity. Both, buoyed by earlier successes at slaying authoritarian giants, confronted other illegitimate authorities, and this resulted in both being punished with severe marginalization. Both are "radicals" in the sense of confronting root causes of misery and suffering, but neither are anti-state or anti-government. Both fought for genuinely democratic governments that protect and improve the lives of its citizens.

While Paine biographies do not include illuminating child-hood stories of his anti-authoritarianism, Ralph Nader biographies do. In 1938, his mother, Rose Nader, took Ralph and her other three children for a visit to the family's native country, Lebanon. On the visit, the Nader family stood in line to meet an archbishop of the Eastern Orthodox Church. The archbishop stopped in front of each person who bent down and kissed the archbishop's ring. This continued, Nader biographer Kevin Graham reported, "until he came to a small four-year-old boy who looked up at the archbishop and shook his head." The boy was Ralph Nader, who then told the archbishop, "I don't have to kiss your ring."

Nader is an anti-authoritarian but not anti-authority. He grew up respecting and admiring his father and mother. His father, Nathra Nader, emigrated from Lebanon to the United States in 1912. Nathra said, "When I passed by the Statue of Liberty, I took it seriously," resulting in a lifelong passion for speaking his mind and teaching his children that speaking one's mind was part of being an American. Nathra moved around the United States, finally settling in Winsted, Connecticut, opening a restaurant where Ralph would sometimes help out. One day when Ralph was ten years old and had returned from school, his father asked him: "What did you learn at school today? Did you learn how to believe or did you learn how to think?" Ralph Nader proudly tells that story, and he recounts how his father also told him, "If you do not use your rights, you will lose your rights."

Ralph Nader is equally proud of his community-activist mother, Rose Nader. Frustrated by government inaction over flooding and destruction in Winsted, when Rose heard that Connecticut's then-Senator Prescott Bush (George H.W. Bush's father) planned to attend a campaign reception in Winsted, she waited in the receiving line until she could shake his hand. Then she did not release his hand from her strong grip until she exacted a promise from him to build a backup system that would catch water flowing over the existing dam—and that system was in fact built.

As a boy, Nader read biographies about turn-of-the-century muckrakers. At Princeton, he read an average of one book a day *outside* of his required course work. He then went to Harvard Law School but concluded, "From day one I laughed at the game—to prepare corporate lawyers. . . . They made minds sharp by making them narrow." Nader recounted, "I didn't like Harvard Law all that much. . . . It was basically a high-priced factory. But instead of producing toasters or blenders, they were producing lawyers to serve corporations, and that was it."

Not taking Harvard Law School too seriously, Nader periodically left and hitchhiked around the United States, researching and writing about the lack of rights of Native Americans and migrant workers. He also started researching automobile safety after seeing car crashes during his travels. He later recounted, "I hitchhiked so much . . . that on a number of occasions, we were the first on the scene of traffic accidents. . . . I saw lots of terrible sights." He also could not forget about a friend whose car accident resulted in him becoming a paraplegic, and how that could have been prevented by seatbelts. In 1959, at age 25, Nader gained attention with an article in the *Nation* about design dangers of automobiles.

While many idealistic young people in the early 1960s were drawn to the civil rights movement, Nader began working on a human rights issue that virtually nobody was working on—"human body rights." Continuing his auto safety research, Nader would eventually publish *Unsafe at Any Speed: The Designed-In Dangers of the American Automobile*, and he would come under attack by General Motors and the automobile industry.

Unsafe at Any Speed was published in 1965 when Nader was 31. Nader's research showed that death and injuries were being caused by cars designed for style and not for safety. Most famously, the design problems of GM's Corvair caused rollovers and needless deaths. The book provoked Americans to become appalled by automobile executives who were aware of design flaws but did nothing to fix them. *Unsafe at Any Speed* became a bestseller (and is today listed by the Library of Congress as one of the 88 "books that shaped America"). Nader then became an adviser to Senator Abraham Ribicoff (D-CT) for his auto-safety hearings.

Although there was evidence that the public would pay more for safer cars, automakers did not want to be told what to do. Auto executives did not want to put in the extra expenses for auto safety, and they feared that "giving in" here would lead to acceding to pollution controls, fuel efficiency, and other measures for a healthier society. So auto executives at General Motors tried to shut Nader up.

GM communications records showed that GM wanted to get dirt on Nader to smear and marginalize him. Nader recounted that while in a grocery store, an attractive woman walked up to him and asked him back to her apartment to help her, and after Nader declined, he noticed that she did not ask anyone else. A similar encounter with an attractive woman occurred shortly later in a drugstore. Nader believed he was being followed, and he sounded to some friends as if he had become delusional and paranoid. However, detectives following him were ultimately caught when they asked a building's security guard about Nader's location; the guard, himself studying to be a lawyer, got the detectives' names. Nader later said, "The surveillance became so amateurish in the end that it was almost like a slapstick comedy."

Senator Ribicoff, chairing Senate hearings, asked the CEO of GM, James Roche, if GM had hired a detective agency to follow Nader. Roche admitted that GM had done so and apologized. Nader later sued GM, with GM settling in 1970 for $425,000 (after legal fees, $280,000), which Nader used—not on himself— but as seed money for his consumer activist groups. Nader has had few financial needs—famously frugal, buying his clothes at thrift stores, never owning a car or a television, and never marrying and having to provide for a family.

Thomas Paine had taken on Great Britain, the most powerful nation on the planet at that time. Ralph Nader had taken on GM, the largest corporation in the United States at that time with larger gross sales than many nations' gross domestic product.

Both Paine and Nader triumphed. Given these triumphs, it is understandable that both these anti-authoritarians believed that they could defeat any illegitimate authority.

At the auto-safety Senate hearings, Nader was asked about his advocacy motives and responded: "Because I happen to have a scale of priorities that leads me to engage in the prevention of cruelty to humans." For Nader, as was the case with Paine, the practice of cruelty and exploitation most defined an authority as illegitimate. Nader's Senate testimony was crucial to Congress passing the National Traffic and Motor Vehicle Safety Act in 1966, which resulted in the National Highway Traffic Safety Administration.

Ralph Nader may well be responsible for saving more lives from consumer product deaths than anyone in world history. The National Center for Statistics and Analysis concluded that from 1975 to 2004, over 195,000 lives were saved just by seatbelts (and many other serious injuries prevented). In 2015, the *Nation* reported that based on an analysis of deaths per mile driven, the Center for Auto Safety found that, taking into account all auto safety-related measures attributable to Nader, over the past 50 years, he had helped avert 3.5 million auto deaths. Seatbelts are only one of many automobile safety measures that Nader is responsible for, and automobile safety is only one of several "human body rights" that Nader helped bring into existence.

By 1970, Nader and "Nader's Raiders" (the young consumer advocates who Nader came to inspire and lead) were responsible for the following safety and human rights protections: the Occupation and Safety Health Act (OSHA); law establishing Environmental Protection Agency; Natural Gas Pipeline Safety Act; Safe Water Drinking Act; Clean Water Act; Nuclear Power Safety; Wholesome Meat Act; Clean Air Act; Mine Health and Safety Act; Foreign Corrupt Practices Act; Freedom of Information Act; and the Whistleblower Protection Act.

Thus, Americans owe a good part of the quality of their everyday lives directly to Ralph Nader and the consumer advocates who he inspired. In the late 1960s and early 1970s, polls showed Nader was among the most admired and trusted Americans (behind only Walter Cronkite). At the same time, Ralph Nader had become the man that corporate America feared most.

In 1971, Lewis Powell (prior to becoming a justice on the Supreme Court) was commissioned by the U.S. Chamber of Commerce to write a confidential memo titled "Attack on the American Free Enterprise System," and Powell offered a counter attack strategy for corporate America. Powell stated: "Perhaps the single most effective antagonist of American business is Ralph Nader, who—thanks largely to the media—has become a legend in his own time and an idol of millions of Americans." Part of corporate America's strategy was to use their financial power to ensure that Nader and other consumer advocates could no longer count on Democratic Party politicians (who, as with Senator Ribicoff, Nader had previously counted on).

When Democrat Jimmy Carter was elected in 1976, Nader naively believed that with Democrats retaking the White House along with Democrat control of the Senate and the House of Representatives, it would make it easier for the consumer movement. Carter had voiced support for the consumer movement and had even hired some Nader allies. And so Nader was confident of the passage of a proposed bill creating a Consumer Protection Agency (which aimed at providing an ombudsman for consumers and was a popular bill with the general public). The bill passed in the Senate but lost in the House. Nader later said about Carter: "At the critical moment when we needed his lobbying help in the House of Representatives, he did not expend the political capital." Jimmy Carter would ultimately disappoint progressives by cutting social programs and increasing the military budget.

The Democratic Party in the 1980s began aggressively pursuing corporate money, and this further increased in the 1990s. Even more disappointing and frustrating for progressives than Carter was Democratic president Bill Clinton's corporatist agenda (e.g., passage of the North American Free Trade Agreement, passage of the Personal Responsibility and Work Opportunity Act, and repeal of the Glass–Steagall Act). However, Nader still was not ready to completely give up on the Democrats. "From 1980 to 2000," Nader recounted, "we tried every way to get the Democrats to pick up on issues that really commanded the felt concern in daily life of millions of Americans, but were issues that corporations didn't want attention paid to." Clinton and his vice president Al Gore refused to meet with Ralph Nader, and Nader could not convince them to support even the most politically popular anti-corporatist agenda.

Finally, Nader could no longer stomach the Democratic Party's complete betrayal, and he concluded that the United States now has "one corporate party with two heads." What became increasingly clear to Nader was confirmed by former Democratic Party operatives such as Lawrence O'Donnell (later an MSNBC political analyst) who said, "If you don't show them you're capable of not voting for them, they don't have to listen to you. I promise you that. I worked within the Democratic Party. I didn't have to listen to anything on the Left while I was working in the Democratic Party."

Nader previously had declined offers to run for office, and continued voicing a preference that someone other than him step forward to challenge the Democratic-Republican corporatism. However, Nader ultimately came to the conclusion that "this two-party elected dictatorship has turned politics into such a dirty word that the whole idea of elected public service is now distasteful to thousands and thousands of wonderful people in this country. That's when I said, okay, that's the final straw. I have got to step forward." In 1996, Nader ran as the Green Party candidate and got less than 1% of the vote. This did not greatly upset the Democratic Party because Clinton handily defeated a weak candidate, Republican Bob Dole, who was further weakened by the Ross Perot candidacy.

In 2000, Nader ran again as the Green Party candidate for president opposing both the Republican George W. Bush and the Democrat Al Gore. Nader's goal was to get 5% so as to qualify for the federal matching funds for the Greens in 2004. Given the Clinton-Gore pro-corporatist agenda, progressive Americans were even more disgusted with their two major party choices. Consequently, Nader attracted over 10,000 people at several rallies across the United States who paid to attend so as to contribute to the campaign, with over 20,000 at his event at Madison Square Garden in New York City. But the mainstream press gave little mention to Nader's enthusiastic support. Nader was frozen out of the debates by the Democrats and Republicans who controlled them—this despite the fact that polls showed that two-thirds of Americans wanted Nader to be permitted to participate. In order to just be part of the audience at a Gore-Bush debate, Nader got an admission ticket but was threatened with arrest and turned away.

After Gore was narrowly defeated in Florida and lost the electoral-college vote to Bush, Nader not only received the expected rebukes from mainstream Democrats but received even greater scorn from so-called "progressive" former admirers of him. One can get a sense of the vitriol of progressives' attacks on Nader in the 2006 documentary *An Unreasonable Man.*

Eric Alterman, columnist for progressive publication the *Nation*, stated about Nader: "The man needs to go away. I think he needs to live in a different country. He's done enough damage to this one. Let him damage somebody else's now. . . . To me, he's a very deluded man. He's a psychologically troubled man."

Todd Gitlin, former president of the Students for a Democratic Society, stated about Nader's 2000 presidential run: "I find this worse than naive. I think it borders on the wicked."

Since 2000, there has been an ongoing marginalization of Nader by mainstream Democrats and progressives. The progressive website *Salon* in 2004 stated about Nader: "He's made a career of railing against corporate misdeeds. Yet he himself has abused his underlings, betrayed close friends and ruled his public-interest empire like a dictator." This is in contradiction with underlings and friends' on-camera interviews in *An Unreasonable Man*, which show that while Nader, like many anti-authoritarians, has at times lacked diplomacy with associates, he has not abused or betrayed them. The treatment of Nader after he opposed the Democratic Party has very much resembled the treatment of Thomas Paine after he had published *The Age of Reason.*

The politically astute progressive Bernie Sanders has kept his distance from Ralph Nader. Nader reported that Sanders is "obsessed by the way I was shunned. He hasn't returned a call in 17 years. He's told people 100 times he didn't want to run a Nader campaign." Despite Sanders's shunning of him, Nader, supported Sanders's 2016 run for the Democratic presidential nomination. Moreover, Nader showed no ego attachment to his own strategy of attempting to make the Democratic Party more responsive to progressives. In a 2016 *Washington Post* piece, "Why Bernie Sanders Was Right to Run as a Democrat" Nader acknowledged, "Because if he had run as an independent, he would have faced only one question daily in the media, as I did: 'Do you see yourself as a spoiler?'"

After Sanders lost the 2016 Democratic Party nomination, Sanders supported the Democratic candidate Hillary Clinton, who was defeated by Donald Trump (with both Clinton and Trump having historically high unfavorable ratings of over 55%). Both Nader and Sanders attempted strategies aimed at compelling the Democratic Party to become less corporatist. Both Nader and Sanders failed. Yet it is Nader, despite his huge array of accomplishments, who continues to be shunned and scorned by progressives, with many of those who had once admired Nader being the most vitriolic.

For both Ralph Nader and Thomas Paine, actions that resulted in their marginalization are seen by former admirers as "ego-trip" departures from their previous altruistic activities. However, if one examines the arc of Paine's life, his compulsion for integrity could not allow him to avoid *The Age of Reason* without feeling cowardly; and his compulsion for courage would not permit cowardice. Similarly, if one examines Nader's anti-corporatist career, there is also a consistent logic resulting in his integrity compelling him to either challenge the Democratic Party or feel cowardly; and like Paine, his compulsion for courage would not permit cowardice.

Both Paine and Nader were venerated for their integrity and courage by admirers, but when they undertook actions based on integrity and courage that caused their admirers political pain, these same admirers called Paine and Nader selfish, egotistical, and even wicked.

The lives of Thomas Paine and Ralph Nader affirm this: No matter how great anti-authoritarians' contribution to society and how much they are admired, they remain vulnerable to marginalization for a politically incorrect challenge of authority. If such an ostracism can happen to Paine and Nader despite their monumental contributions, no anti-authoritarian is safe. The anxiety that many anti-authoritarians experience is not a symptom of mental illness but a sense of reality.

While both Nader and Paine had extraordinary talents, they never would have had such extraordinary accomplishments had they not benefited from two of the more anti-authoritarian periods in American history. As Ralph Nader stated about his success as a consumer advocate: "Our movement benefited enormously from the hundreds of thousands of people who were fighting [against] the Vietnam War, and fighting for civil rights, who were in the streets. It created the climate, the atmosphere, that made our efforts appear less extreme." However, while doing battle with GM was not seen in the mid-1960s as politically incorrect, challenging the authority of the Democratic Party establishment in 2000 was viewed as so politically incorrect that Nader has been ostracized for it.

Thomas Paine likely would have respected Ralph Nader's reaction to this shunning. In 2006, Nader stated: "I don't care about my personal legacy. I care about how much justice is advanced in America, and in our world day after day, and I'm willing to sacrifice whatever 'reputation' in the cause of that effort. And also, what is my legacy? Are they gonna turn around and rip seat belts out of cars? Are they gonna tear air bags out of cars?"

Malcolm X

"An extraordinary and twisted man, turning many true gifts to evil purpose. . . . Malcolm X had the ingredients for leadership, but his ruthless and fanatical belief in violence . . . set him apart from the responsible leaders of the civil rights movement and the overwhelming majority of Negroes."

—*NEW YORK TIMES* EDITORIAL, FEBRUARY 22, 1965
(ONE DAY AFTER MALCOLM X'S DEATH)

"Malcolm X had been a pimp, a cocaine addict and a thief. He was an unashamed demagogue. His gospel was hatred."

—*TIME*, MARCH 5, 1965

"Malcolm X today has iconic status, in the pantheon of multicultural American heroes. But at the time of his death he was widely reviled and dismissed as an irresponsible demagogue."

—MANNING MARABLE, *MALCOLM X: A LIFE OF REINVENTION*, 2011

We see in the lives of Thomas Paine, Ralph Nader, and Malcolm X (1925–1965) a compulsion to discover truth and assert it, a compulsion for integrity, and a compulsion for courage. We see in all three, a compulsion to not violate their trusteeship with the oppressed—a compulsion to *not* become an illegitimate authority.

Malcolm X psychologically liberated millions of African Americans, validating their anger, encouraging them to assert it, and thus empowering them. For this, he was accused of demagoguery by Americans who did not want to deal with this anger. However, Malcolm X did not exploit his power for personal gain. Ultimately, he was assassinated for maintaining his integrity.

Throughout much of his life, Malcolm X was rocked by trauma in the extreme, and thus the arc of his life is one of the most complex ones among great U.S. anti-authoritarians. As a child, Malcolm was a good student before his family was ripped apart. Then, as a teenager and young man, he became selfish, predatory, and anti-authority. After his religious conversion, he was for a time dutifully authoritarian within an authoritarian organization. But after his break with the Nation of Islam, Malcolm X's essential anti-authoritarianism was clearly seen.

For Thomas Paine, Ralph Nader, and Malcolm X, illegitimate authority was unjust, oppressive, and cruel. In Malcolm X's evolution, he first identified white people as an illegitimate authority; then Elijah Muhammad and his Nation of Islam; and at the end of his life, the entire structure of wealth and power in the United States.

It is perfectly logical for Malcolm X to initially view white people as the illegitimate authority. He was intimately aware of a lengthy history of white violence.

Malcolm X, born Malcolm Little in Omaha, Nebraska, grew up for the most part in Lansing, Michigan. His father, Earl Little, was an organizer and chapter president for the Universal Negro Improvement Association (UNIA). Earl Little believed, Malcolm X told us, "as did Marcus Garvey, that freedom, independence and self-respect could never be achieved by the Negro in America, and that therefore the Negro should leave America to the white man and return to his African land of origin." Malcolm's mother, Louisa Little, also was active in the UNIA, and Malcolm recounts that she "looked like a white woman . . . she had straight black hair" because her father was a white man who had raped Louisa's mother.

Malcolm X reported that among the reasons his father became a disciple of Marcus Garvey was that "he had seen four of his six brothers die by violence, three of them killed by white men, including one by lynching. . . . Northern white police were later to shoot my Uncle Oscar. And my father was finally himself to die by the white man's hands." Malcolm's family home burned in 1929, and his parents believed it was set on fire by the Black Legion, a paramilitary white supremacist group affiliated with the Ku Klux Klan.

When Malcolm was six years old his father was killed and his mother and the African American community believed that the Black Legion was responsible for his murder. But the police ruled it a streetcar accident, and the insurer of the larger of two life insurance policies refused to pay, claiming that his father had committed suicide.

Malcolm also saw other white authorities destroy his family. The death of his father resulted in the family becoming desperate financially, and his family went on relief. Malcolm remembered that the state welfare employees would look at his family like "we were not people," and he saw these welfare authorities "as vicious as vultures. They had no feelings, understanding, compassion, or respect for my mother." He was shamed by peers for being "on relief," and he began stealing and getting caught for it. Malcolm came to feel guilty that his stealing "implied that I wasn't being taken care of by my mother," resulting in her further harassment by welfare authorities. Ultimately, when Malcolm was 13, his mother completely broke down and was committed to the state psychiatric hospital (where she would remain for the next 24 years). At that point, his family fell apart. The children were separated and sent to foster homes. Malcolm X later recounted: "We were having a hard time, and I wasn't helping. But we could have made it. . . . I truly believe that if ever a state social agency destroyed a family, it destroyed ours. We wanted and tried to stay together. Our home didn't have to be destroyed. But the Welfare, the courts, and their doctor, gave us the one-two-three punch. And ours was not the only case of this kind."

In school, Malcolm was also assaulted by white authority. Attallah Shabazz, Malcolm X's daughter, corrected one depiction of her father by the 1992 movie *Malcolm X*, pointing out that the film "shows him learning how to read the dictionary as if he didn't already know how." The reality was that, as Malcolm X later recounted, "in the second semester of the seventh grade, I was elected class president. It surprised me even more than other people. But I can see now why the class might have done it. My grades were among the highest in the school. I was unique in my class, like a pink poodle." When his white teacher asked him about his career ideas, Malcolm told him that he'd like to become a lawyer, and his teacher responded, "But you've got to be realistic about being a nigger. A lawyer—that's no realistic goal for a nigger." Malcolm recalled his reaction to that comment: "I *was* smarter than nearly all of those white kids. But apparently I was still not intelligent enough, in their eyes, to become whatever *I* wanted to be. It was then that I began to change—inside."

In his early teens, Malcolm left Michigan for the Boston area, then returned to Michigan for a short period, then went to Harlem in New York City. During this time, he had menial jobs but also became involved in the world of drug dealers, gamblers, and thieves. He returned to the Boston area, and at age 20 in 1945, he and four accomplices committed several burglaries. In 1946, he was arrested and convicted, and he began serving an eight-to-ten-year prison sentence.

In prison, Malcolm connected with John Bembry, a self-educated fellow convict who Malcolm greatly respected. Under Bembry's influence, Malcolm developed a voracious appetite for reading. Malcolm's siblings wrote to him in prison about the Nation of Islam, which at that time was relatively unknown. The Nation of Islam was a new religious movement that preached black self-reliance and opposed integration with white people and that white people were "devils" and inferior to black people. Malcolm was receptive to that message. He became a member, and while still in prison he began a correspondence with its leader, Elijah Muhammad.

Paroled in 1952, Malcolm immediately became active in the Nation of Islam, initially as an assistant minister in Detroit, and he quickly established himself as its most talented recruiter in several locations. Biographer Manning Marable documents that in 1953, the Nation of Islam had approximately 1,200 members; by 1955, nearly 6,000; and by 1961, it expanded to somewhere between 50,000 and 75,000 members. A major reason for this expansion and its accompanying financial windfall was Malcolm X's breakthrough as a national speaker. He was widely regarded as handsome, eloquent, honest, funny, and charismatic.

In 1957, at age 32, Malcolm X gained attention and admiration throughout black America for standing up to the New York City police following its assault on Nation of Islam member Hinton Johnson. After a large crowd gathered outside of police headquarters, the police backed down, allowing Malcolm to assist Johnson. With tensions mounting, Malcolm gave a hand signal for the crowd to disperse, which it did, resulting in a police officer stating, "No one man should have that much power." Malcolm had won over the Harlem African American community, and he was increasingly the public face of the Nation of Islam.

In the 1965 introduction to *The Autobiography of Malcolm X*, M. S. Handler, one of the few white men and reporters for whom Malcolm had some degree of trust and respect, said: "Although he had become a national figure, he was still a man of the people who, they felt, would never betray them. . . . Here was a man who had come from the lower depths which they still inhabited, who had triumphed over his own criminality and his own ignorance to become a forceful leader and spokesman, an uncompromising champion of his people. . . . Human redemption—Malcolm had achieved it in his own lifetime, and this was known to the Negro community."

As Malcolm's own self-confidence grew, he began to question, challenge, and ultimately resist the leader of the Nation of Islam, Elijah Muhammad. In 1961, Malcolm X was appalled by the lack of response from the Nation of Islam to violence directed at one of its members by the Los Angeles Police Department. Then he confirmed that Elijah Muhammad, in serious violation of the teachings of the Nation of Islam, was sexually involved with several young secretaries of the organization and had fathered children with them (Elijah Muhammad confirmed the rumors in 1963, attempting to justify his behavior by referring to precedents set by biblical prophets). Elijah Muhammad, having come to see Malcolm X as a threat to his leadership, exploited the political opportunity to censure and sideline Malcolm following his comment about John Kennedy's assassination in 1963 ("chickens coming home to roost"). In early 1964, Malcolm X publicly announced that he was leaving the Nation of Islam.

Elijah Muhammad's Nation of Islam was an authoritarian organization that demanded unquestioning obedience, but its initial attractiveness to Malcolm X is understandable. The Nation of Islam validated his feelings about the illegitimacy of white authority, provided him with a strong family (that included his biological siblings who were members), and it provided the previously selfish and predatory Malcolm a spiritual path to care about something larger than himself. Malcolm X believed that he was joining an organization led by someone who truly cared about African Americans. It was only through experience that he came to see that the Nation of Islam was operated by a predatory illegitimate authority.

Malcolm challenged and resisted Elijah Muhammad, knowing full well that the Nation of Islam would strike back. A high-ranking member, Louis X (who became Louis Farrakhan and the leader of the Nation of Islam), stated that "such a man as Malcolm X is worthy of death." Evidence suggests that the Nation of Islam firebombed Malcolm's house and then evicted Malcolm and his family from their home in Queens, New York.

Right after leaving the Nation of Islam, Malcolm X founded Muslim Mosque, Inc., a religious organization more in line with traditional Islam. He also founded the secular Organization of Afro-American Unity, which advocated for Pan-African unity. The Nation of Islam had opposed involvement in politics and rejected voting in elections; but Malcolm X advised African Americans to exercise their right to vote, though he cautioned that this might not be sufficient for political change. Malcolm X had not only left the Nation of Islam but had completely intellectually liberated himself from its policies. He had transformed himself into a political thinker.

Also shortly after leaving the Nation of Islam in 1964, Malcolm X made a pilgrimage to Mecca, resulting in his departing from his previously anti-white racist views of the Nation of Islam. He wrote in his diary: "Islam brings together in unity all colors and classes." Marable documents that Malcolm X had come to believe that God embraced Jews, Christians, and Muslims alike, denied that whites were "devils," and blamed his previous anti-white sentiments on Nation of Islam indoctrination. The central point for Malcolm X had now become, Marable concludes, "the necessity for blacks to transform their struggle from 'civil rights' to 'human rights,' redefining racism as 'a problem for all humanity.'"

When Malcolm X returned to the United States after traveling in the Middle East and Africa, he spoke on college campuses and elsewhere, including events for the Socialist Workers Party and their Militant Labor Forum. Marable notes, "For years, he had preached the Garvey-endorsed virtues of entrepreneurial capitalism," but at the Militant Labor Forum, "when asked what kind of political and economic system he wanted, he observed that 'all the countries that are emerging today from under colonialism are turning toward socialism. I don't think it's an accident.'" Marable notes, "For the first time, he publicly made the connection between racial oppression and capitalism."

After Malcolm X's public split with the Nation of Islam, Muhammad Ali, once a close friend, chose to side with Elijah Muhammad. Ali admitted that part of his calculation was fear, "You don't just buck Mr. Muhammad and get away with it." By 1965, Malcolm X realized his days were numbered, and two days before his assassination, he had told his friend Gordon Parks (photographer and journalist) that the Nation of Islam was trying to kill him.

On February 21, 1965, Malcolm X was murdered by a group of Nation of Islam assassins. The New York Police Department, the FBI, and the CIA considered Malcolm X an enemy, and these agencies may well have used infiltrators to inflame tensions between Malcolm and the Nation of Islam. Marable reported that

there is also evidence that these agencies, through their surveillance, knew of Malcolm X's impending assassination but failed to
protect him, and then, following his assassination, enabled guilty
informants to go free.

Malcolm X was committed to asserting the truth, including
the truth of his mistakes. While his views on illegitimate authority
dramatically changed, he was consistent in seeking truth, asserting it, and challenging and resisting authority that he deemed
illegitimate. It is precisely Malcolm's capacity to self-correct that
makes him one of the most extraordinary anti-authoritarians in
U.S. history.

Near the end of his life, Malcolm X discussed with Parks an
incident earlier in his life when a white college girl had come into
a Black Muslim restaurant and asked him what she could do to
help. He had told her, "Nothing," and she left in tears. Malcolm
X told Parks, "Well, I've lived to regret that incident. In many
parts of the African continent I saw white students helping black
people. . . . I did many things as a [Black] Muslim that I'm sorry
for now. I was a zombie then—like all [Black] Muslims—I was
hypnotized, pointed in a certain direction and told to march.
Well, I guess a man's entitled to make a fool of himself if he's
ready to pay the cost. It cost me twelve years."

Between 1965 and 1977, *The Autobiography of Malcolm X*
sold more than six million copies. In his 2011 *New Yorker* piece,
"This American Life: The Making and Remaking of Malcolm X,"
David Remnick writes, "In 1992, Spike Lee set off a bout of 'Mal-
colmania,' with his three-hour-plus film. In its wake, people as
unlikely as Dan Quayle talked sympathetically about Malcolm.
. . . Bill Clinton wore an 'X' cap."

In 1999, more than three decades after his assassination,
enabled by the U.S. government and applauded by most of U.S.
society, the U.S. post office issued a Malcolm X stamp. This was
not all that dissimilar from Germany in 1961 issuing a postage
stamp for Sophie Scholl, a member of the White Rose resisters to
the Nazi regime. In 1943, after she and other White Rose members were caught by the Nazis, her fellow students at Munich

University assembled to demonstrate against White Rose, agreeing with the Nazi regime's promulgation that White Rose members were "traitors and defeatists." In 1943, German newspapers
called White Rose "degenerate rogues," and Sophie Scholl was
guillotined. The German government, 18 years later, honored
Sophie with a stamp.

In his 2015 article "To the Memory of Malcolm X: Fifty
Years After His Assassination," labor union and socialist activist Ike Nahem wrote how Malcolm X had been "transformed
by 'mainstream' forces into a *harmless* icon, with his sharp revolutionary anti-imperialist and anti-capitalist political program
diluted and softened." For Nahem, this transformation of the
genuinely revolutionary Malcolm X into "someone who can be
folded into the traditional spectrum of bourgeois Democratic
and Republican party U.S. politics . . . is a travesty of the actual
Malcolm X and his actual political and moral trajectory."

The life of Malcolm X is replete with valuable lessons. One
lesson is that when we have experienced enormous pain from
an illegitimate authority, we may be drawn toward any other
authority that validates our pain, and it can become difficult to
think critically about that validating authority, especially if we
are stressed and vulnerable.

Malcolm X's attraction to the Nation of Islam was similar
to people whom I've known who have been assaulted by psychiatry and become attracted to the Church of Scientology, and then
become embarrassed when they realize they've joined an authoritarian organization. People damaged by one authoritarian religious
organization are vulnerable to joining another one simply because
it is critical of what has damaged them. This is also the case with
authoritarian political organizations. Many people oppressed by
authoritarian company owners became anti-capitalists who were
uncritical of authoritarian Bolsheviks. The greatness of Malcolm
X lay not simply in his courage to challenge and resist illegitimate
authority but in his courage to reassess his views.

As traumatizing as Malcolm X's young life was, he was lucky
in one sense. Nowadays, a teenager with a history of stealing

would get a psychiatric diagnosis of "conduct disorder," a severe "disruptive disorder," and such kids are increasingly prescribed psychiatric drugs. After the breakup of his family, Malcolm lived in foster homes, and foster kids today in the United States are even more likely to be medicated on antipsychotic drugs than other children. And so it is quite likely that in today's world, the young Malcolm would have been prescribed antipsychotic drugs, and the arc of his life would have been a very different one.

Criminalization of Anti-Authoritarians

Emma Goldman, Eugene Debs, and Edward Snowden

Anti-authoritarians are often punished through criminalization, both to marginalize them and to send an intimidating message to others who may consider challenging or resisting illegitimate authority. Among the many criminalized U.S. anti-authoritarians, I profile three people who differ in personality and in ideology: the anarchist Emma Goldman, the socialist Eugene Debs, and the libertarian Edward Snowden.

Emma Goldman, as a girl and young woman, would today likely also be psychiatrically marginalized for her intense defiance. Eugene Debs, politically active during the same era as Goldman, provides an example of the U.S. government's wrath at one of its most beloved citizens just for speaking his mind. And Edward Snowden offers a modern example of a "patriotic" anti-authoritarian who challenged the U.S. government for its violation of the U.S. Constitution and paid a great price.

Emma Goldman

During her lifetime, Emma Goldman (1869–1940) was one of the most famous anarchists in the United States. Her notoriety resulted from her multiple arrests, trials, and imprisonments for anti-authoritarian speech; her numerous lectures to thousands of people across the United States about anarchist philosophies of freedom from coercion, anti-capitalism, anti-militarism, atheism, women's rights, birth control, sexual liberation for women and homosexuals, and other social issues; and her writings, including her two-volume autobiography, *Living My Life*.

Goldman's integrity, morality, pain, and passion compelled her to challenge a lengthy list of authorities whom she assessed to be illegitimate: her father, teachers, her first anarchist mentor, police, the U.S. government, and later, the Bolsheviks. Her list of enemies ranged from J. Edgar Hoover to Vladimir Lenin, whom she informed, "I could not co-operate with a regime that persecuted anarchists or others for the sake of mere opinion."

Throughout Goldman's life, she was unintimidated by governments, popular opinion, or peer pressure. For example, her fellow anarchists pressured her not to defend homosexuality because they worried that, as Goldman put it, "Anarchism was already enough misunderstood, and anarchists considered depraved." But for Goldman, "I minded the censors in my own ranks as little as I did those in the enemy's camp. In fact, censorship from comrades had the same effect on me as police-persecution; it made me surer of myself, more determined to plead for every victim, be it one of social wrong or of moral prejudice."

As a young child, Goldman's family lived in Kovno (now Lithuania), then moved to the German Empire, then to St. Petersburg in Russia. Her mother, Taube, had two daughters from her first marriage, and after her husband died, she remarried in an arranged loveless marriage to Abraham Goldman, Emma's father. Emma reported that her parents "were mismatched from the first." In what we would call today a highly dysfunctional family, Emma's father would regularly beat the children for disobeying him, and the rebellious Emma would get beaten the most. Goldman's biographer Richard Drinnon reported, "She was whipped, forced to stand in the corner for hours, or made to walk back and forth with an overflowing glass of water in her hands—a lash was her reward for each spilled drop." Compounding her misery with her father, Emma noted, "My mother, while less violent with the children, never showed much warmth."

Goldman recounted how her father "tried desperately to marry me off at the age of fifteen." She protested, begging to continue her studies, to which her father responded, "Girls do not have to learn much! All a Jewish daughter needs to know is how to prepare *gefüllte* fish, cut noodles fine, and give the man plenty of children." Emma's interest in boys provoked rage in her father, as she recounted, "He pounded me with his fists, shouted that he would not tolerate a loose daughter." But Emma disregarded him, "For several months my admirer and I met clandestinely." Only one family member provided Emma with warmth and love, her older sister, Helena.

School teachers, as was the case for Malcolm X, were abusive for Emma. Her geography instructor sexually molested Goldman and other girls. She fought back and got him fired. Emma also had a religious instructor who beat the palms of students' hands with a ruler. In response, Goldman later recounted, "I used to organize schemes to annoy him: stick pins in his upholstered chair . . . anything I could think of to pay him back for the pain of this ruler. He knew I was the ringleader and he beat me the more for it." A good student, Emma passed the exam for admission to gymnasium, but to be enrolled she needed a certificate of good character from her religious instructor. In front of her entire class, he refused and declared, Goldman recalled, that "I was a terrible child and would grow into a worse woman. I had no respect for my elders or for authority, and I would surely end on the gallows as a public menace."

In 1885, her sister Helena made plans to move to New York to join another sister, Lena, and Emma wanted to accompany Helena, but Emma's father refused. Desperate, Emma threatened to throw herself into the Neva River, a ploy that today could well get a teenage girl admitted to a psychiatric hospital. Instead, her strategy worked, as her father finally agreed to allow her to leave. She immigrated to the United States in 1885, staying with family in Rochester, New York.

Emma married a fellow worker in 1887, but she quickly discovered that they were emotionally and sexually incompatible. Within less than a year, they divorced. For ending this marriage, Goldman reported, "I was immediately ostracized by the whole

Jewish population of Rochester." She reported that her parents, who had by then also come to Rochester, "forbade me their house, and again it was only Helena who stood by me." Helena then financially helped Emma move to New York City in 1889.

New York City was a hub of anarchist activity, and Emma Goldman had been pulled to anarchism as a social and economic justice movement after the execution of the Haymarket martyrs in 1887. Almost immediately after arriving in Manhattan, the 20-year-old Goldman connected with two men who would become important for her. One was anarchist Alexander "Sasha" Berkman, who became her lifelong friend and, for a short period, her lover. The other was Johann Most, editor of the radical publication *Freiheit*.

Johann Most was a captivating orator who mentored Goldman in anarchist philosophy and public speaking. She later recounted, "Most became my idol. I worshipped him." However, Goldman didn't worship him for long. After receiving feedback from her worker audience, Goldman began seeing errors in Most's thinking (for example, his belief that workers shouldn't fight for small gains such as fewer hours but focus only on abolishing capitalism). She concluded that Most "cured me somewhat of my childlike faith in the infallibility of my teacher and impressed on me the need of independent thinking." For not parroting his views, Most terminated his relationship with Goldman, which deeply hurt her. Previous to their split, Goldman had been so loyal to him that she had argued for blowing up the office of a newspaper that had humiliated Most (an idea that Berkman nixed).

In 1892, Goldman, Berkman, and his cousin Modest "Modska" Aronstam (later changed to Stein) together planned the assassination of steel plant manager Henry Clay Frick during the steelworkers strike in Homestead, Pennsylvania. Berkman was arrested following his failed assassination attempt, and police raided Goldman's apartment but found no evidence to indict her. Goldman talked about bombing the Pittsburgh courthouse where Berkman was put on trial but didn't act on this.

Berkman's actions were condemned by most Americans, but Goldman was appalled by Johann Most's attack on Berkman. Most had preached "propaganda of the deed" and the use of violence to instigate change, which Goldman knew had influenced Berkman. While Most had altered his views on violence prior to Berkman's actions, when Most condemned Berkman, the loyal Goldman used a horsewhip to publicly lash Most. For Most's faithful anarchist followers, Goldman reported, "My public punishment of their adored teacher roused furious antagonism against me and made me a pariah."

The Panic of 1893 resulted in high unemployment, hunger, poverty, and unrest, and Goldman, then age 24, spoke at large protest demonstrations, including one estimated between 1,000 to 3,000 people in Union Square in New York City. At this demonstration, Goldman recalled saying: "If they do not give you work, demand bread. If they deny you both, take bread. It is your sacred right!" For this, she was arrested for inciting a riot. Goldman reported that police offered to drop charges and pay her a "substantial sum of money" if she would become an informer to which, Goldman recounted, "I gulped down some ice-water from my glass and threw what was left into the detective's face."

At her trial, the judge told her "I look upon you as a dangerous woman in your doctrines," and she was sentenced to one year in prison on Blackwell's Island. However, her arrest and imprisonment for speaking her mind gained Goldman much sympathy and popularity. She recounted, "Thanks to my imprisonment and the space given to my name in the newspapers, I also became a celebrity." When she was released from prison, 3,000 people greeted her, and she soon received many requests for interviews and lectures.

Affection for Goldman dramatically declined following Leon Czolgosz's assassination of William McKinley in 1901, which resulted in Goldman being arrested and held for two weeks. Czolgosz had claimed to have been inspired by Goldman, but he denied that she was involved in his actions. Police could not link Goldman to the assassination, and she was released from custody.

Goldman refused to condemn Czolgosz, instead expressed sympathy for him, "I feel very deeply with him as an individual who suffers. If I had the means I would help him as far as I could." She chastised other anarchists for abandoning him. Her fellow anarchists condemned Goldman, as they knew that support for a presidential assassin was politically detrimental for anarchism, making it easy for newspapers and politicians to equate anarchism with violence.

For Goldman, this attack on her by her fellow anarchists (including from Berkman in prison) pained her deeply, "Our movement has lost its appeal for me; many of its adherents filled me with loathing. . . .The struggle and disappointment of the past twelve years had taught me that consistency is only skin-deep in most people." She withdrew from the movement, adopted a pseudonym (Miss E.G. Smith) and practiced nursing, which she had learned during her time imprisoned at Blackwell's Island (in Europe, in 1896, she had been awarded diplomas in midwifery and in nursing).

Goldman's absence from the anarchist movement was a brief one. She returned in part because of the U.S. Congress passing the Anarchist Exclusion Act (also called the Immigration Act of 1903), which was signed into law by Theodore Roosevelt. The Act included barring any immigrant "who disbelieves in or who is opposed to all organized government, or who is a member of or affiliated with any organization entertaining or teaching such disbelief in or opposition to all organized government." For many freedom-loving people—not just anarchists—this criminalization of ideology violated what they believed the United States stood for. Goldman rejoined the fight.

In 1906, Goldman created the publication *Mother Earth*; and Berkman, after his release from prison in 1907, became editor. Over the next decade, Goldman traveled around the United States delivering lectures, often with large paying crowds. She raised money for *Mother Earth* and raised awareness for causes that she cared about. With Berkman involved with another woman, 39-year-old Goldman fell in love with Ben Reitman, called "the hobo doctor" (for being homeless as a youth and later provid-ing medical care to the financially impoverished). Goldman and Reitman shared a commitment to "free love." However, virtually the entire radical community had contempt for Reitman (labor union activist Elizabeth Gurley Flynn called him "an insufferable buffoon"). For almost ten years, with Reitman as her manager, Goldman was regularly on the road giving talks. Over one six-month period, she delivered 120 lectures in 37 cities to approxi-mately 40,000 people.

In 1916, Goldman again was arrested. Among her many lecture topics was birth control, which she believed was hugely important for the empowerment of women. She was charged under the Comstock Law for instructing her audience as to how to use contraceptives. She refused to pay a $100 fine and instead served a two-week jail sentence.

Also in 1916, Woodrow Wilson ran for re-election for presi-dent with the slogan "He kept us out of war," promising to keep the United States out of World War I; but Wilson reversed him-self once re-elected. He signed into law the Selective Service Act of 1917 (also called the Conscription Act), requiring all males between 21 and 30 (later lowered to 18) to register for military conscription. Goldman abhorred war in general, especially the U.S. government's involvement in this war, and she loathed con-scription. Goldman and Berkman organized the No Conscrip-tion League. In June of 1917, Wilson signed the Espionage Act, and later that year Goldman and Berkman were arrested under it for conspiring to induce men not to register for conscription. After their release from prison in 1919, they were deported to Russia, arriving in January 1920.

Goldman was an anarchist—not a Bolshevik. She opposed state power of any kind, but she and many other anarchists had been optimistic about the Russian Revolution and its aim of abol-ishing the oppressive force of capitalism. However, Goldman and Berkman soon discovered the oppressive nature of Lenin's regime and the new Bolshevik leadership, which suppressed free speech among the working class. There were horrible living conditions, unrest, and strikes in Russia, most famously in Kronstadt—a bastion of anarchist dissent where the Russian government killed over a thousand strikers and arrested many more, many of whom were later executed.

Goldman, like Malcolm X, not only had the courage to fight for her convictions but also the courage to challenge her own convictions and admit her errors, "Getting people out of jail had been among our various activities in America. But we had never dreamed that we should find the same necessity in revolutionary Russia . . . . we had not yet forgotten how to laugh at our own follies, though more often my laughter only thinly veiled my tears." Goldman and Berkman left Russia in 1921, moving to various European cities. Goldman published a book in 1923 which she had titled "My Two Years in Russia" but which her publisher retitled *My Disillusionment in Russia*. Goldman, again compelled to tell the truth about a cruel authority, enraged many communist loyalists.

Scottish anarchist James Colton offered to marry Goldman purely to provide her with British citizenship, and she agreed in 1925, and this provided her with some relief and freedom to travel. Beginning in 1928, she spent the next two years in Saint-Tropez, France, writing her autobiography, living in a cottage on money raised by her admirers (including the wealthy Peggy Guggenheim). Goldman's autobiography *Living My Life* was published in 1931. One of the book's fans was Eleanor Roosevelt, and in 1933, Goldman acquired a visa to speak in the United States, but she was not allowed to remain. Goldman went to Spain during the Spanish Civil War, and she then spent the remainder of her life in Toronto, where she died in early 1940.

We see in the life of Emma Goldman many of the traits of other anti-authoritarians: a compulsion to speak out against cruelty and illegitimate authority, no matter what the political cost; a willingness to sacrifice her own freedom for the cause of freedom; a compulsion for truth-telling, that included admitting her own errors; a fierce loyalty along with a scorn for disloyalty; and a repulsion with hypocrisy. She mocked people who were fascinated by people such as herself but had no courage and no real sense of social justice, saying about *bohemianism* that it was "a sort of narcotic to help them endure the boredom of their lives."

The wisdom to utilize good luck and opportunities is crucial for many anti-authoritarians. A major piece of luck for Emma Goldman was the enduring loving support from her sister Helena, as many anti-authoritarians lack support from even one family member. Goldman was also lucky in that the criminalization of her early anti-authoritarianism gained her great publicity—some of it even positive. She parlayed this fame into being a charismatic speaker who could acquire income from her talks, money which she used for her survival and her causes. Goldman was lucky to live in an era in which many Americans were curious about her and what she had to say.

Historians Paul Avrich and Karen Avrich note that "Goldman's list of hostile impulses was long." And so, she was also lucky to live in an era when adolescent rebellion and volatility did not result in psychopathologizing of anti-authoritarianism as is often the case today. I have talked to many anti-authoritarian women who, in their youth, for their anger and rebellious behaviors were labeled with "bipolar disorder" and "borderline personality" and heavily medicated. Several of these women have told me that the pathologizing of their anger and rebellious behaviors delayed their political consciousness. They, similar to Goldman, experienced abusive authorities; but the labeling of their anger as a symptom of mental illness made it more difficult for them to become politicized—and recognize that it was the coercions of illegitimate authorities, not a mental illness, which had fueled their behaviors, and that there are political ideologies such as anarchism that address this issue.

Emma Goldman's survival and fascinating life are certainly not solely due to good luck. She had great intelligence, courage, and made several wise choices.

Like Malcolm X, Emma used her prison time wisely. During her first stint at Blackwell's Island, Goldman expanded her knowledge by reading widely and learning nursing skills, and she quit smoking. And during her time at the Jefferson City, Missouri, prison prior to her deportation, Goldman developed strong bonds with fellow women radicals, including Kate Richards O'Hare, the prominent U.S. socialist, and the Italian anarchist Gabriella Antolini.

Though Emma Goldman was a fervent anti-capitalist, she had a passion for independence and autonomy, and she learned how to survive within a world that demands money for survival. She acquired many skills—as a seamstress, nurse, midwife, masseuse, cook, and speaker—and throughout her life would use those skills to make money.

Paul and Karen Avrich write: "Charismatic, domineering, and sexually free, Goldman was a whirl of willful determination. Unapologetically menacing in her rhetoric, remembered as abrasive and imperious by her friends, she nevertheless was a driving force within the radical community, and no one questioned her commitment to her causes."

It is important to note that Goldman was never jailed for acts of violence. She was imprisoned for speaking her mind and challenging what she considered to be illegitimate authority. For this, she was incarcerated several times and ultimately deported from the United States.

Goldman's life provides more than another famous example of the state's attempt to punish anti-authoritarian speech with criminalization. Her early life also provides an example of a girl and young woman who today in the United States, from my experience, might well be psychopathologized. Similar to Malcolm X, in not being psychiatrically marginalized, Goldman was lucky.

Eugene Debs

Eugene "Gene" Debs (1855–1926) was imprisoned twice for his anti-authoritarianism. Unlike Emma Goldman, Debs was a well-mannered, likable child and a decidedly non-radical young man who attempted to work within the system. A conservative labor union leader well into his late thirties, in 1895, he was imprisoned for becoming a reluctant strike leader. At that point, it became clear to him that the U.S. government was the property of giant corporations and the wealthy, who also owned most politicians, the judiciary system, the major newspapers, and other institutions. Radicalized by his initial incarceration, Debs became a socialist—ultimately the most influential socialist in U.S. history. He ran for president five times, the last time from a prison cell, having been convicted for speaking out against the U.S. government's entry into World War I.

"Eugene Debs had been known as one of the most likeable boys in Terre Haute," notes his biographer Ray Ginger. Growing up in Indiana, Debs did favors for his elders and was generous with younger children, providing them with candy from his father's grocery store. Ginger observed that Gene Debs's "kindliness" remained a dominant motive of his life. Gene dropped out of high school and began working in the railroad industry, first cleaning grease from the trucks of freight engines, then as a painter and railroad car cleaner, and then as a locomotive fireman.

As a young man, Debs was an advocate of self-improvement, believing in the doctrine of "lifting yourself by your own bootstraps." At age 20, Debs left railroad work, attended business college, and became a billing clerk for a large wholesale grocery house. Even though he no longer worked in the railroad industry, Debs maintained loyalty to his fellow workers, and became a member of the Brotherhood of Locomotive Firemen and the editor of their *Firemen's Magazine.* He then went into politics, and he never lost an election running as a Democrat. The voters in his home town of Terre Haute twice elected him city clerk, and he was elected to the Indiana General Assembly in 1884 at age 29.

The Brotherhood of Locomotive Firemen was quite tame, notes historian David Shannon in his article, "Eugene V. Debs: Conservative Labor Editor." Shannon points out, "In its early days the Brotherhood of Locomotive Firemen was more of a fraternal lodge and a mutual insurance company than a trade union." Debs, as *Firemen's Magazine* editor, scolded the bad habits of his fellow workers, as he knew that alcohol abuse combined with the lack of occupational safety resulted in job fatalities and serious injuries.

Even into his mid-thirties, Debs was anti-strike. He saw the differences that arise between labor and capital as ones that arise between "friendly brothers." Debs believed that differences could be settled by reasonable and peaceful means, rather than by strikes or violence. Debs preached peace and co-operation between labor and capital, and he preached mutual respect, accusing radical labor union leaders of being cranks and demagogues.

Only gradually did Debs begin to recognize the naivety of this "brotherly" view. Reluctantly, he began to accept that a more confrontational approach was necessary. He adopted a unifying strategy of organizing an entire industry, creating an "industrial union" rather than organizing trades (such as exclusively the firemen) separately. This resulted in his founding of the American Railway Union (ARU), which struck Great Northern Railway in early 1894 and won most its demands.

Later in 1894, as leader of the ARU, Debs became involved in the now famous Pullman Strike. The strike was precipitated by the Pullman Company cutting wages (a Federal commission estimated a 25% cut, but others estimated the cut to be from 33% to 40%). Again, Debs was relatively conservative and reluctant to strike. He reminded workers that the federal government might intercede militarily as it had previously done in the strike by silver miners at Coeur d'Alene, Idaho. However, workers rejected his warnings and voted to strike, and Debs joined in.

As Debs had predicted, President Grover Cleveland and Attorney General Richard Olney got an injunction against the Pullman Strike. The injunction was enforced by the U.S. Army, and this broke the strike. Debs scrupulously made all efforts to prevent violence. Nonetheless, Debs was found guilty of contempt of court for violating the injunction and was sentenced to prison.

Debs was not a socialist when he began his prison term. He recalled in 1902 in his article "How I Became a Socialist" that at the time of the 1894 Pullman Strike, "I had heard but little of Socialism, knew practically nothing about the movement, and what little I did know was not calculated to impress me in its favor." But then, Debs recounted, "a swift succession of blows that blinded me for an instant and then opened wide my eyes— and in the gleam of every bayonet and the flash of every rifle *the class struggle was revealed.*" It became clear to Debs that the ownership class has at its disposal "an army of detectives, thugs and murderers . . . equipped with badge." It was also clear to him that this ownership class owned most of the press and politicians. Debs was first incarcerated in Cook County Jail in Chicago and then imprisoned for six months in Woodstock, Illinois. Here, between books and visitors, he came to conclude that capitalism had to be abolished so as to create social and economic justice.

"Eugene Debs, a lifelong Democrat who three times campaigned for Grover Cleveland," notes Ginger, "was deprived of faith in the major political parties by the actions of Cleveland and Olney. He could no longer advocate labor's adherence to parties which were firmly controlled by the large corporations." Beginning in 1900, Debs ran as the Socialist candidate for president of the United States, and would ultimately run five times. In the 1912 presidential election, Debs obtained 6% of the vote, and running from a prison cell in 1920, he garnered 3.4% of the vote.

Debs received his most severe punishment from the U.S. government for speaking out against its entry into World War I. Democrat Woodrow Wilson had been re-elected president on his pledge of neutrality; but, pressured by Wall Street, which had engineered large war loans to the English and French, Wilson reversed himself and venomously attacked those who did not follow suit.

In 1918, Debs gave a speech in Canton, Ohio, stating: "Wars throughout history have been waged for conquest and plunder. . . . And that is war, in a nutshell. The master class has always declared the wars; the subject class has always fought the battles."

Debs told the thousands of people in the Canton audience, "They tell us that we live in a great free republic; that our institutions are democratic; that we are a free and self-governing people," and the crowd responded in loud laughter. Debs responded to their laughter, "This is too much even for a joke."

Under Wilson in the United States, there was no free speech when it came to war opposition. Debs, in his own defense at his trial, pointed out, "The Mexican war was bitterly condemned by Abraham Lincoln, by Charles Sumner, by Daniel Webster and by Henry Clay." But anti-war speech during World War I in the United States was not tolerated. Debs was convicted of the willful obstruction of the Conscription Act, though Debs had actually been careful to avoid the subject of conscription in his talk, noting later, "I never mentioned the draft in my speech, nor made any reference to it."

At his sentencing speech, Debs again affirmed his commitment against violence: "Your honor, I have stated in this court that I am opposed to the form of our present government; that I am opposed to the social system in which we live; that I believe in the change of both but by perfectly peaceable and orderly means." It did not matter. Debs was sentenced to ten years in a federal penitentiary.

Thousands of Americans who knew nothing about socialism knew that Debs was sent to prison for opposing the war. Unlike the arrest and imprisonment of less famous or less liked anti-authoritarians such as Emma Goldman, the imprisonment of Eugene Debs had a chilling effect. During this time period, twelve anti-war publications were deprived of their second-class mailing permit, and some formerly anti-war publications moderated their views to become more patriotic (this including the once radical *New York Forward*, the *Liberator*, and the *Appeal to Reason*). Many radicals who had once called themselves socialists became pro-war, patriotic Americans. U.S. government intimidation had worked to suppress opposition. Ginger observed, "America had become a strange land, in which Eugene Debs was a bewildered and unnoticed vagabond."

Wilson's venom for Debs was such that even after the end of the war, Wilson announced, "This man was a traitor to his country and he will never be pardoned during my administration." Wilson even denied a pardon for Debs when such a pardon was recommended because of Debs's poor health by Attorney General A. Mitchell Palmer (notorious for his "Palmer Raids," incarcerating and deporting dissenters). Ironically, it was the Republican president Warren Harding, following Wilson, who commuted Debs's sentence in 1921, and he was released from the federal penitentiary in Atlanta.

Previous to prison, Debs had suffered from recurrent headaches, severe rheumatism, and debilitating low back pain; and Ginger notes, "Prison food had completely wrecked his stomach and his kidneys." Prison time for Debs exacerbated his health issues, and he died in 1926, shortly before he would have turned 71 years old.

Eugene Debs was a beloved figure, and his treatment by the U.S. government was shocking for many Americans. Ginger notes, "To most American Socialists, Debs had a status near to divinity," and Debs was loved not only by radicals but by almost everyone he encountered. During his incarceration in Atlanta, Debs "won the hearts of his fellow prisoners," notes historian Howard Zinn, as owing to his presence, guards were "less free with their nightsticks." When Debs had been in the prison less than a month, Ginger notes, "The other inmates began calling him Little Jesus." Debs did many favors for prisoners and refused any special privileges for himself. On the day of his release, more than 2,000 inmates gathered to say good-bye to him.

Debs was so likable that after he was interviewed in 1921 by Attorney General Harry Daugherty regarding amnesty and release, Daugherty recounted: "He spent a large part of the day in my office, and I never met a man I liked better." Even anarchist Emma Goldman who had little patience for socialists, said of her meeting him, "We parted good friends. Debs was so genial and charming as a human being that one did not mind the lack of political clarity."

After Debs was released from the Atlanta prison, estimates of the crowd that welcomed his return to his hometown Terre Haute ranged from 25,000 to 50,000, and Debs was hoisted above the crowd and carried. Sheriff George Eckert, his 1895 Woodstock jailer who had become friends with Gene and his wife Kate during Debs stay in his jail, visited Debs in 1922. Clarence Darrow, Debs's former defense attorney, said after Debs's death, "I never knew a man whom I loved more than I did him. No better, kindlier man ever lived than Gene. I shall miss him as I have missed few others."

When Debs died, there was a huge outpouring of national sorrow. Ginger notes, "So it became fashionable to minimize his radical beliefs in favor of his purity of character. On this count he was deemed above reproach." In this regard, the journalist Heywood Broun sarcastically commented: "Eugene V. Debs is dead and everybody says he was a good man. He was no better and no worse when he served a sentence at Atlanta."

Debs was revered by the oppressed for the same reason that Malcolm X was revered. The oppressed knew that the integrity of those men would never allow them to exploit their popularity for selfish reasons. Both Malcolm X and Eugene Debs concluded, at approximately the same age, that capitalism was an illegitimate authority that oppressed the majority of people, a realization for both of them that was based on direct personal experiences.

The life of Eugene "Gene" Debs offers another validation for anti-authoritarians as to just how violent the U.S. government can be if one creates tension for it—no matter how nonviolent one's actions. Debs, similar to Ralph Nader, personifies those anti-authoritarians who initially believe that economic and social justice are possible to achieve within the system; but through experience, come to realize that the only option is to refuse to comply with an illegitimate authority. Both Nader and Debs came to see the Democratic Party to be no different than the Republican Party in terms of being corporatist lackeys.

The 1979 documentary *Eugene V. Debs: Trade Unionist, Socialist, Revolutionary* was written and produced by a

38-year-old Bernie Sanders about his hero. It begins: "It is very probable, especially if you are a young person that you have never heard of Eugene Victor Debs. . . . Why? Why haven't they told you about Gene Debs and the ideas he fought for? The answer is simple. More than a half century after his death, the handful of people who own and control this country—including the mass media and the educational system—still regard Debs and his ideas as dangerous, as a threat to their stability and class rule, and as someone best forgotten about."

Ironically, the arc of Bernie Sanders's political career moved in the opposite direction from the arc of his hero. Sanders began as an anti-war socialist member of the Liberty Union Party which rejected the corporatism of both the Democratic and Republican Parties. Then Sanders got elected to various offices in Vermont and supported popular military expenditures and military actions; and he ultimately supported the Democratic Party's pro-militarist presidential candidate Hillary Clinton. In contrast, Debs began as a successful Democratic politician, became radicalized by his experiences as a labor union leader, became a socialist who was hated by the ruling class, and was imprisoned by its U.S. government.

Sanders began with dissent but moved to obedience, obeying even the Democratic Party. Debs began conciliatory, moved on to dissent, and then to disobedience—not only disobeying the Democratic Party but the U.S. government. Sanders's initial dissent propelled his political career, and his ultimate obedience kept his career intact. Debs, in contrast, paid a severe price for his ultimate disobedience.

Edward Snowden

Edward Snowden (born in 1983) was charged in 2013 for violating the U.S. government's Espionage Act of 1917. Unlike Emma Goldman and Eugene Debs, Snowden was not charged for speaking out against a war or military conscription. Snowden was charged for leaking classified information from the U.S. government's National Security Agency (NSA) that revealed mass warrantless surveillance on U.S. citizens. The NSA's warrantless surveillance is in violation of the Bill of Rights of the U.S. Constitution. For his disobedience and resistance, Snowden has been criminalized by the U.S. government.

The Fourth Amendment reads: "The right of the people to be secure in their persons, houses, papers, and effects, against unreasonable searches and seizures, shall not be violated, and no Warrants shall issue, but upon probable cause, supported by Oath or affirmation, and particularly describing the place to be searched, and the persons or things to be seized."

Attorney and journalist Glenn Greenwald points out that the Fourth Amendment "was intended, above all, to abolish forever in America the power of the government to subject its citizens to generalized, suspicionless surveillance." When Snowden saw the Fourth Amendment being violated by both Republican and Democratic administrations, he challenged and resisted their intelligence agencies.

Snowden's path to resisting illegitimate authority could not have been more different than the anarchist Goldman or the socialist Debs—though Snowden's "patriotic path" is not unique among U.S. anti-authoritarians.

Snowden's father was an officer in the U.S. Coast Guard, and his mother was a chief deputy for the U.S. District Court of Maryland. Snowden grew up as a patriotic American, even more so after the events of September 11, 2001. In 2004, Snowden enlisted in the U.S. Army, recounting later, "I wanted to fight in the Iraq war because I felt like I had an obligation as a human being to help free people from oppression."

Snowden was discharged from the army after breaking both his legs in a training accident. Though having dropped out of high school, Snowden had high-level computer skills. He began working for the Central Intelligence Agency (CIA) in 2007, but he became alarmed by the George W. Bush administration's violations of Americans' constitutional rights. Snowden recounted, "I began to understand that what my government really does in the world is very different from what I'd always been taught. That recognition in turn leads you to start reevaluating how you look at things, to question things more." Journalist Ewen MacAskill reported that at that time Snowden identified himself as a libertarian, believing in a strong adherence to the U.S. Constitution.

By 2009, the 26-year-old Snowden had become so disillusioned by the CIA's violation of Americans' rights that he decided to leave that agency and began contemplating becoming a whistleblower. He waited to see if the new president, Barack Obama, who had pledged reform, would make good his promises. However, not only did U.S. intelligence agencies' unlawful policies continue, the Obama administration would ultimately prosecute more government leakers under the Espionage Act than all previous administrations combined.

Among intelligence agencies, Snowden focused on the NSA because he reasoned that people might get hurt if he revealed CIA secrets, "But when you leak the NSA's secrets, you only harm abusive systems." So Snowden began working for Dell, an NSA contractor. He then got a position in early 2013 for the U.S. government defense contractor Booz Allen Hamilton, where he took a pay cut to be in a better position to gather data on the NSA's surveillance activities.

In March of 2013, Snowden became even more appalled by the Obama administration after its Director of National Intelligence, James Clapper, was asked by Senator Ron Wyden: "Does the NSA collect any type of data at all on millions or hundreds of millions of Americans?" Clapper's reply was, "No, sir." Snowden knew this was a boldfaced lie.

It became increasingly clear to Snowden that leaking to the press was the only way the American people would hear about U.S. government lawbreaking. Many members of the U.S. Congress had previously been briefed by the NSA on warrantless wiretapping, and they had not told the American public.

Thus, in early June 2013, Snowden provided NSA documents that revealed its lawbreaking to journalists Glenn

Greenwald, Laura Poitras, and Ewen MacAskill. Snowden's revelations were subsequently published in the *Guardian* and the *Washington Post*; and the U.S. government then charged Snowden with violating the Espionage Act. Snowden, who had just turned 30, knew that if he gave himself up, he would have no chance to make his case—in public or in court. He knew that he would not be allowed out on bail and that his testimony on the stand would be gagged by government objections. Thus, having been granted asylum in Russia, Snowden did not return to the United States.

Snowden's thinking reveals the mind of an anti-authoritarian. He recalled, "I felt it would be wrong to, in effect, help conceal all of this from the public." When Greenwald probed Snowden about his motives, Snowden replied, "The true measurement of a person's worth isn't what they say they believe in, but what they do in defense of those beliefs. If you're not acting on your beliefs, then they probably aren't real. . . . I don't want to be a person who remains afraid to act in defense of my principles." Snowden explained to Greenwald, "What keeps a person passive and compliant is fear of repercussions, but once you let go of your attachment to things that don't ultimately matter—money, career, physical safety—you can overcome that fear."

Snowden stated that he wanted to spark a worldwide debate about privacy, Internet freedom, and the dangers of state surveillance. He told Greenwald, "I want to identify myself as the person behind these disclosures. I believe I have an obligation to explain why I'm doing this and what I hope to achieve."

Greenwald, in *No Place to Hide: Edward Snowden, the NSA, and the U.S. Surveillance State* (2014), reported mainstream media's reaction to Snowden's actions. When the story broke in June of 2013, *CBS News* host Bob Schieffer called Snowden a "narcissistic young man" who thinks "he is smarter than the rest of us." The *New Yorker's* Jeffrey Toobin also diagnosed Snowden as a narcissist, specifically "a grandiose narcissist who deserves to be in prison," and the *Washington Post's* Richard Cohen joined the choir, asserting that Snowden "is merely narcissistic."

Politico's Roger Simon called Snowden a "loser" because he had "dropped out of high school," and *New York Times* columnist David Brooks mocked Snowden as someone who "could not successfully work his way through community college."

Some of the mainstream media did begin to shift their views. A *New York Times* editorial in January 2014 stated: "The shrill brigade of his critics say Mr. Snowden has done profound damage to intelligence operations of the United States, but none has presented the slightest proof that his disclosures really hurt the nation's security . . . . When someone reveals that government officials have routinely and deliberately broken the law, that person should not face life in prison at the hands of the same government."

Snowden has received more support internationally than he has received from Americans; and he has received more support from younger Americans than older ones. A 2015 KRC Research poll, commissioned by the American Civil Liberties Union, showed that only 36% of Americans had a positive opinion of him (56% among younger Americans, aged 18 to 34). However, in Germany and Italy, 84% viewed Snowden positively; 80% viewed him positively in France, the Netherlands, and Spain; and 64% viewed him favorably in Australia.

U.S. politicians have responded as expected. Politicians such as Bernie Sanders, with support from young people, have supported clemency for Sanders; while Barack Obama, Hillary Clinton, and Donald Trump all have advocated punishing Snowden.

The Milgram study, as previously detailed, revealed that the majority of Americans believe in complying with authority even when they feel the authority is a cruel one. Similarly, the majority of Americans believe "lawbreakers" such as Snowden should be punished, regardless of the fact that the consequences of these lawbreakers violating a law are highly beneficial for society.

While the majority of Americans support the criminalization of Edward Snowden, many Americans are also upset about his revelations of their having their Fourth Amendment rights violated—and many politicians recognize this distinction. In July

2013, a bill to defund NSA's bulk metadata collection program came up for a vote. The bill, the Amash-Conyers Amendment, aimed at ending "NSA's blanket collection of Americans' telephone records," was narrowly defeated 217–205 (supported by 111 Democrats and 94 Republicans), as apparently many politicians believe that their constituents care, as Snowden does, about their Fourth Amendment rights.

Snowden is in the tradition of U.S. government whistleblowers that includes Chelsea Manning. Manning was in the U.S. Army at the time she witnessed the U.S. government's war atrocities and deceit, and in 2010 she provided supporting documents to WikiLeaks. Both Snowden and Manning are in the tradition of Daniel Ellsberg, an ex-marine employed at the Defense Department and the RAND Corporation. In 1971, Ellsberg leaked government lies about the Vietnam War in what came to be known as the Pentagon Papers. In 1973, during a more anti-authoritarian cultural climate, U.S. government charges against Daniel Ellsberg were dismissed because of governmental misconduct and illegal evidence gathering. Sadly, no such anti-authoritarian climate exists today.

***

Many other U.S. anti-authoritarians, forgotten in history, have been criminalized for speaking their minds. Politically radical women such as Kate Richards O'Hare, Mollie Steimer, and many other Americans were imprisoned for speaking out against World War I. Also during that era, William Buwalda, a military veteran decorated for his service in the Philippines, was court-martialed and sentenced to three years at Alcatraz merely for, while in military uniform, attending a talk by Emma Goldman, applauding her, and shaking her hand.

There have been many anti-authoritarians for whom criminalization resulted not in prison but by life ruination and self-inflicted death. Julius Wayland was a good friend of Eugene

Debs and was the founder and publisher of *Appeal to Reason*, the largest socialist publication in U.S. history, with a circulation of approximately 500,000 at its height. But in 1912, the 58-year-old Wayland, grieving over his wife's death, was falsely smeared for sexual improprieties; and with the Federal District Attorney about to indict him under the Mann Act, he committed suicide, leaving a note indicating that he was a beaten man. And anti-authoritarian entertainer Lenny Bruce (profiled later) was hounded by local government authorities for his speech, and he was arrested on obscenity charges but died via drug overdose during the appeal process.

Some U.S. anti-authoritarians, with luck, have survived U.S. governmental assault. Frederick Douglass and Harriet Tubman (both profiled later) escaped slavery and outwitted the U.S. Fugitive Slave Act of 1850. Scott Nearing (profiled later), during the same era that Emma Goldman and Eugene Debs were imprisoned under the Espionage Act, was also indicted under the Espionage Act but found not guilty. Helen Keller (profiled later), who also publicly opposed military conscription and the U.S. government's entry into World War I, was not prosecuted by the U.S. government, most likely because Woodrow Wilson knew how ridiculous it would have been to jail the most famous deaf-blind woman in the world.

Other U.S. anti-authoritarians have simply been murdered by government agencies. One famous example was Fred Hampton. In 1969 at age 21, Hampton was assassinated in his sleep by Cook County, Illinois, law enforcement in conjunction with the Federal Bureau of Investigation (FBI). Hampton's "offense" was being a Black Panther Party member and an effective organizer. As will be discussed in the following chapter, throughout U.S. history, murder and genocide by the U.S. government has been routine with respect to Native Americans.

5

Genocide of an Anti-Authoritarian People: Native Americans

For the compliant, the U.S. government appears to be a force of good that occasionally errs, but what anti-authoritarians sense—and some directly experience—is that the U.S. government and ruling elite are powerful forces of violence when their policies are resisted. This is no revelation for Native Americans.

Tecumseh (1768–1813), Crazy Horse (1840–1877), Sitting Bull (1831–1890), as well as many other famous and non-famous Native Americans challenged and resisted the authority of the U.S. government to defraud Native Americans from their land and to destroy their communities and their way of life. For their resistance, many Native Americans have suffered violent deaths. Tecumseh was killed in battle; Crazy Horse was killed trying to escape incarceration; and Sitting Bull was killed resisting arrest.

The assault against Native Americans constitutes racism, genocide, and land theft on a massive scale. It is also an attempt to eliminate a cultural tradition that—with its relative absence of coercion and greater freedoms—undermines U.S. authoritarians.

At the time Europeans began to colonize North America, Native American societies were highly diverse with many different political systems and various religious beliefs. However, they did share certain common characteristics. Native societies in what now constitutes the United States did not have the hierarchical and authoritarian organization of the Aztec and Inca societies south of them. In what now constitutes the United States, historian Eric Foner notes, "Many Europeans saw Indians as embodying freedom." He reported that a European religious missionary during that time said about Native Americans: "They are born, live, and die in a liberty without restraint." Foner also quotes an early trader who observed that Indians had no words to express "despotic power, arbitrary kings, oppressed or obedient subjects."

European colonizers came from extremely hierarchical societies, ruled by kings and aristocracies; and within families, husbands ruled their wives. Upon marriage, a European woman surrendered her legal identity, which meant she could not own property or sign contracts, or, except in rare circumstances, get a divorce. By contrast, in most Native societies, women could divorce their husbands and choose premarital partners. And while tribal leaders were mostly men, female elders would help select male leaders and take part in tribal meetings. Thus, for European colonizing men, their absolute power within their marriage was threatened to the extent that their wives were aware of Native American life. In general, the relative attractiveness of Native American societies was threatening for authoritarians.

A common characteristic of Native American societies is an absence of impersonal authority and coercion. Ensuring civility is seen as a collective responsibility. When interpersonal conflicts arise, the emphasis is on negotiations among parties and kin groups to settle conflicts. A common characteristic of Native societies is to make all efforts toward members not experiencing coercion and resulting resentments. If consensus could not be achieved, bands would splinter off.

The Iroquois (who call themselves the Haudenosaunee) are a confederation of northeastern tribes in North America, and Foner notes that one colonial official stated that the Iroquois held "such absolute notions of liberty that they allow of no kind of superiority of one over another, and banish all servitude from their territories." Historian Gary Nash documents the anti-authoritarian nature of Iroquoian culture, including their child-rearing. Iroquois youngsters, Nash reports, "were being prepared to enter an adult society which was not hierarchical, as in the European case, but where individuals lived on a more equalitarian basis, with power more evenly distributed among men and women or old and young than in European society. . . . One aspect of child-rearing on which Europeans and Iroquoian cultures differed was in the attitude toward authority. In Iroquois society the autonomous individual, loyal to the group but independent and aloof rather than submissive, was the ideal."

Native American societies are not leaderless societies but leadership is based on consensus about a leader's wisdom. Thus, if a hunter leader, medicine leader, or warrior leader makes repeated errors that threaten their people's well-being, this likely would result in a new consensus and new leadership. The flight of the Nez Perce from U.S. government troops illustrates this.

In 1877, after a series of land concessions followed by broken promises by the U.S. government, a group among the Nez Perce were not willing to again trust the U.S. government's latest and even smaller land promises. This group of Nez Perce refused to submit and surrender, and they outmaneuvered a U.S. military force for more than three months, over approximately 1,800 miles from their homeland in what is now eastern Oregon through Montana. While standard history textbooks routinely credit Chief Joseph as the chief of the Nez Perce and recount his final painful surrender, historian Kent Nerburn documents that there were other leaders who actually directed the flight. Looking Glass initially led the group but was challenged for moving too slowly; and when the U.S. Army surprised the Nez Perce at the Battle of the Big Hole, tribal consensus replaced Looking Glass with Poker Joe (though later Looking Glass regained his leadership position). And when Joseph believed that surrender was necessary to save Nez Perce lives, several Nez Perce chose to follow another leader, White Bird, and continue to head to Canada; and the consensus was not only to accept that group's decision but to aid White Bird and his group's escape.

The enormity of the assault on Native Americans can only partially be captured by statistics. Conservative estimates of the 1492 indigenous population within what are now the borders of the United States are, according to Foner, between two and five million people; but historian Ward Churchill estimates the number closer to twelve million. There is little controversy among historians that by 1900, the Native American population in what now forms the United States had declined to approximately 250,000.

This decimation of Native Americans occurred through a variety of methods. These methods included army campaigns and massacres (famously, but not limited to, Sand Creek, Washita River, and Wounded Knee). Native American decimation also occurred because of forced removals, including most famously the "Trail of Tears," in which approximately 55% of all Cherokees died during or as an immediate result of their forced removal by the U.S. government. Also in Texas, Churchill points out, "an official bounty on native scalps—*any* native scalps—was maintained until well into the 1870s. The result was that the indigenous population of this state, once the densest in all of North America, had been reduced to near zero by 1880."

Another extremely effective genocidal method was starvation. In "Genocide by Other Means: U.S. Army Slaughtered Buffalo in Plains Indian Wars," journalist Adrian Jawort documents U.S. government policy to destroy indigenous food supply to drive them off their land. "During the Plains Indian Wars," Jawort reports, "as the U.S. Army attempted to drive Indians off the Plains and into reservations, the Army had little success because the warriors could live off the land and elude them— wherever the buffalo flourished, the Indians flourished." Jawort describes how William Tecumseh Sherman, who had found success with a "scorched earth" policy against the Confederacy during the Civil War, repeated the same strategy with Native Americans and their buffalo. Jawort also quotes anthropologist S. Neyooxet Greymorning and historian Andrew Isenberg in this regard. Greymorning points out, "The government realized that as long as this food source was there, as long as this key cultural element was there, it would have difficulty getting Indians onto reservations." Isenberg notes, "Some Army officers in the Great Plains in the late 1860s and 1870s, including William Sherman and Richard Dodge, as well as the Secretary of the Interior in the

1870s, Columbus Delano, foresaw that if the bison were extinct, the Indians in the Great Plains would have to surrender to the reservation system."

The 1948 United Nations Convention on Genocide states: "Genocide means any of the following acts committed with intent to destroy, in whole or in part, a national, ethnical, racial or religious group, as such: (a) Killing members of the group; (b) Causing serious bodily or mental harm to members of the group; (c) Deliberately inflicting on the group conditions of life calculated to bring about its physical destruction in whole or in part; (d) Imposing measures intended to prevent births within the group; (e) Forcibly transferring children of the group to another group." While a single component suffices for the UN definition of genocide, the U.S. government's genocide of Native Americans includes all of these components.

The Native American population has also been reduced by forced sterilization—and recently so. Physician Gregory Rutecki, in "Forced Sterilization of Native Americans: Late Twentieth Century Physician Cooperation with National Eugenic Policies," documents, "Independent research estimated that as many as 25–50% of Native American women were sterilized between 1970 and 1976." Psychologist David Walker details American psychologists' use of pseudoscientific psychometrics, including IQ testing, to attempt to establish the inferiority of indigenous Americans so as to justify sterilization.

Churchill also notes that "the massive compulsory transfer of American Indian children from their families, communities, and societies to Euro-American families and institutions." This compulsory transfer has occurred through, Churchill points out, "such mechanisms as the U.S. Bureau of Indian Affairs (BIA) boarding school system, and a pervasive policy of placing Indian children for adoption . . . with non-Indians. . . such circumstances have been visited upon more than three-quarters of indigenous youth in some generations after 1900." The stated goal of such policies, Churchill notes, has been "assimilation" of Native people into U.S. values and belief systems, and "the

objective has been to bring about the disappearance of indigenous societies as such."

Though Native resistance has continued, when resistance
feels impossible, as it does for many indigenous Americans
today, this results in a high rate of suicide, especially among
young Native Americans. Psychologist Roland Chrisjohn and
co-author Shaunessy McKay, in *Dying to Please You*, point out
that just as with the extraordinarily high suicide rate by Jews in
Nazi concentration camps, a high rate of self-inflicted deaths by
any overwhelmingly oppressed national, ethnical, racial, or religious group is essentially another form of genocide.

Attorney Peter d'Errico in "Native American Genocide or
Holocaust?" (2017) describes how U.S. government and society
avoid the reality that genocide has occurred in part because of
"the tenderness of American egos" and the "fallacious notion
of 'American exceptionalism.'" The U.S. government's 2009
"Apology to Native Peoples of the United States," unsurpris-
ingly, excludes any mention of *genocide*, and it includes the following: "DISCLAIMER—Nothing in this section authorizes or
supports any claim against the United States." Moreover, this
"apology" was buried in a Department of Defense Appropria-
tions Act H.R. 3326-2 and signed by then-president Obama in
a ceremony closed to the press. Thus, d'Errico concludes, "The
result was more an effort to bury the past, than to confront it."

6

Psychiatric Assault and Marginalization: Not Just Frances Farmer

"For guardians of the status quo, there is nothing genuinely or fundamentally wrong with the prevailing order and its dominant institutions, which are viewed as just. Therefore, anyone claiming otherwise—especially someone sufficiently motivated by that belief to take radical action—must, by definition, be emotionally unstable and psychologically disabled. Put another way, there are, broadly speaking, two choices: obedience to institutional authority or radical dissent from it. The first is a sane and valid choice only if the second is crazy and illegitimate. . . . Radical dissent is evidence, even proof, of a severe personality disorder."

—GLENN GREENWALD, *NO PLACE TO HIDE: EDWARD SNOWDEN, THE NSA, AND THE U.S. SURVEILLANCE STATE*, 2014

The use of psychiatric diagnoses to discredit, dismiss, and marginalize famous and non-famous anti-authoritarians is common.

Earlier I discussed how several mainstream media journalists, attempting to discredit whistleblower Edward Snowden, psychopathologized him with labels such as "grandiose narcissist." Attorney and journalist Glenn Greenwald also documents the mainstream media's psychopathologizing of other recent whistleblowers, including WikiLeaks founder Julian Assange and Chelsea Manning. The mainstream media has depicted Assange as bizarre and paranoid, the *New York Times* labeling him with "erratic and imperious behavior" and "delusional grandeur." The mainstream media also promoted a view that Manning was motivated not by her moral convictions but gender struggles, anti-gay bullying, and conflict with her father resulting in personality disorders.

Ralph Nader, as noted, for challenging the corporatism of both the Democratic and Republican parties and running for president, was described by a columnist for the *Nation* as "a very deluded man . . . . a psychologically troubled man." Malcolm X, for his distrust of authorities, was diagnosed by FBI profilers with "pre-psychotic paranoid schizophrenia."

The anti-authoritarian actions of both Thomas Paine and Eugene Debs were attributed to "dipsomania" and other terms for alcoholism. Debs biographer Ray Ginger notes that during the 1894 Pullman Strike, the *New York Times* published a smearing by the physician Thomas Robertson, who falsely claimed to have treated Debs for dipsomania; with the *Times* quoting Robertson as saying, "Those who knew Debs well . . . believe that his present conduct is in large measure, if not wholly, due to the disordered condition of his mind and body, brought about by the liquor habit."

The practice of psychopatholozing anti-authoritarians so as to discredit and marginalize them is certainly not exclusive to the United States. In the Soviet Union, political dissidents were routinely psychiatrically hospitalized and drugged; and today, Chinese dissidents continue to be diagnosed with mental illness and forcibly treated.

In the United States, the practice of psychopathologizing anti-authoritarians began at the very beginning of the nation. Benjamin Rush, as noted, was a friend of Thomas Paine in pre-Revolutionary War Philadelphia, but then shunned Paine after *The Age of Reason*. Today, Benjamin Rush is well-known among psychiatrists as "the father of American psychiatry," as his image adorns the seal of the American Psychiatric Association. In addition to Rush's abandonment of Thomas Paine, he also attempted to gain favor with the new ruling class in the United States another way. In 1805, Rush diagnosed those rebelling against the newly centralized federal authority as having an "excess of the passion for liberty" that "constituted a form of insanity," which he labeled as the disease of *anarchia*.

In 1851, Louisiana physician Dr. Samuel Cartwright reported his discovery of *drapetomania*, the disease that caused slaves to flee captivity. Cartwright believed that absent of this illness slaves were "like children . . . constrained by unalterable physiological laws to love those in authority over them." Cartwright also reported his discovery of *dysesthesia*, a disease that caused slaves to pay insufficient attention to their jobs, "breaking the tools he works with, and spoiling everything he touches," as well as being resistant to punishment and not feeling the "pain of any consequences."

In 1958, when civil rights activist Clennon W. King Jr. attempted to enroll at the all-white University of Mississippi, the Mississippi police arrested him on the grounds that "any nigger who tried to enter Ole Miss *must* be crazy." Following his arrest, historian David Oshinsky reports, he was then taken to the county courthouse where a "lunacy warrant" was issued on him, and he was confined to a mental hospital for twelve days, and only declared "competent" when he promised to leave Mississippi. In *The Protest Psychosis: How Schizophrenia Became a Black Disease* (2010), psychiatrist and sociologist Jonathan Metzl details systemic racism that labels "threats to authority as mental illness," and how this process increases the likelihood that black men will get diagnosed with schizophrenia.

A belief that one is being surveilled has sometimes been enough "evidence" for anti-authoritarians to be assessed as delusionally paranoid. Recall how when Ralph Nader was being followed by General Motors detectives, he sensed it and told others, and sounded like he was delusional. Nader, however, was lucky that detectives were incompetent and got caught. However, Ernest Hemingway was not so lucky.

By 1960, Hemingway was labeled delusionally paranoid about FBI surveillance. His friend and biographer A. E. Hotchner recounted Hemingway saying: "The feds . . . It's the worst hell. The goddamnedest hell. They've bugged everything. . . . Everything's bugged. Can't use the phone. Mail intercepted."

Long after Hemingway's death, the FBI released his file in response to a Freedom of Information petition, and Hotchner reported: "It revealed that beginning in the 1940s J. Edgar Hoover had placed Ernest under surveillance because he was suspicious of Ernest's activities in Cuba. Over the following years, agents filed reports on him and tapped his phones. The surveillance continued all through his confinement at St. Mary's Hospital. It is likely that the phone outside his room was tapped after all. In the years since, I have tried to reconcile Ernest's fear of the FBI, which I regretfully misjudged, with the reality of the FBI file. I now believe he truly sensed the surveillance, and that it substantially contributed to his anguish and his suicide."

Hemingway was treated with electroshock (ECT) as many as 15 times in December 1960, then in January 1961, he was "released in ruins," according to another Hemingway biographer, Jeffrey Meyers. Hotchner reported that Hemingway's loss of memory caused by the ECT made him even more depressed and hopeless, as Hemingway had stated, "Well, what is the sense of ruining my head and erasing my memory, which is my capital, and putting me out of business?" In July 1961, shortly before his 62nd birthday and soon after Hemingway had been given still another series of shock treatments, he committed suicide.

Anti-authoritarians' intense reactions to insults and injustices can provide justification for authorities to psychopathologize them. A young Emma Goldman was lucky to live in an era in which she was not pathologized after she threw a pitcher of water at the face of a woman who was happy with the 1887 execution of the Haymarket martyrs, but other anti-authoritarians have not been so lucky and their strong reactions to insults and injustices have often been psychopathologized. This is especially true for intense reactions by women, one of the more well-known examples being actress Frances Farmer (1913–1970), brought to public attention in the 1982 movie *Frances*, starring Jessica Lange.

Farmer revealed her anti-authoritarian streak as a senior in high school when she won a writing contest with a controversial essay, "God Dies," and then again as a young woman when, in 1935, she accepted a newspaper prize for a trip to the Soviet Union over her mother's strong objections. Farmer was stunningly beautiful but rebelled against studio casting based solely on her looks. She also resisted the studio's attempt to control her private life, and she refused to attend Hollywood parties. Farmer aspired to be a serious actress, and she took time off from movie work to appear in a Clifford Odets stage production of one of his plays.

Farmer, feeling oppressed by Hollywood authorities and betrayed by men she had trusted, began abusing alcohol. In 1942, she was stopped by the police for driving with her headlights on bright in the wartime blackout zone. She was jailed and fined; and after she hadn't paid her entire fine, the police tracked her down and entered her hotel room without permission. Then, as journalist Matt Evans recounts, "Frances, who'd been sleeping in the nude, face down on the bed, under the influence of alcohol and somnifacient—at noon!—reacted as anyone would have." She became belligerent with the police when they arrested her. And then, after she was sentenced to 180 days in Los Angeles County jail, she became physically aggressive in the courtroom and was forced into a straitjacket.

"If Frances had been left alone to serve her 180 days in jail," Evans concluded, "it's quite likely that, eventually, she would have sorted herself out." Instead, family members and others from the movie industry successfully lobbied the judge to send her to the Kimball Sanitarium, her first institutionalization. Then in 1944, Frances's mother committed Frances to Western State Mental Hospital, where she was recommitted two additional times.

"Frances was institutionalized," Evans concludes, "not because she was insane but because she'd been legally vulnerable. Because her dad, Ernest, was a lawyer. Because her mother, Lillian, despite whatever unconscious animus may have lain in her heart, may have thought in her desperation and exasperation that institutionalization was the last viable recourse to help her daughter heal. Heal? And become submissive and obedient."

In recent decades, children and adolescents in the United States who are not submissive and are disobedient have been increasingly psychopathologized. Several of the famous anti-authoritarians profiled in this book, if children today, would likely have been labeled with at least one psychiatric disorder.

Malcolm X's childhood, as noted, was replete with trauma including his family breakup and then foster homes, resulting in his rebelling and engaging in theft. Today, a teenage Malcolm X would likely be labeled with the "disruptive disorder" diagnosis called "conduct disorder" (CD) for criminally disruptive behaviors. And owing especially to the fact of being in foster care, he would very likely be prescribed psychiatric drugs, including antipsychotic drugs.

Several other anti-authoritarians profiled in this book, including Eugene Debs, Lenny Bruce, George Carlin, and Jane Jacobs quit school or didn't take it seriously. Today, for such obviously intelligent kids, this contempt for school would make them highly vulnerable to a psychiatric diagnosis.

Beginning in 1980, for noncompliant children who are *not* engaged in any illegal practices, the APA (in its *DSM-III* diagnostic manual) created the disruptive disorder diagnosis "oppositional defiant disorder" (ODD). For an ODD diagnosis, a youngster needs only *four* of the following eight symptoms for six months: often loses temper; often touchy or easily annoyed; often angry and resentful; often argues with authority figures; often actively defies or refuses to comply with requests from authority figures or with rules; often deliberately annoys others; often blames others for his or her mistakes or misbehavior; spitefulness or vindictiveness at least twice within the past six months.

In 2012, the *Archives of General Psychiatry* reported that between 1993 through 2009, there was a sevenfold increase of children 13 years and younger being prescribed antipsychotic drugs, and that disruptive behavior disorders such as ODD and CD were the most common diagnoses in children medicated with antipsychotics, accounting for 63% of those medicated.

"Attention deficit hyperactivity disorder" (ADHD) is another common diagnosis for children labeled with "behavior problems." The "symptoms" of ADHD are inattention, hyperactivity, and impulsivity. While CD and ODD behaviors are overt rebellions, ADHD behaviors can in some instances be passive-aggressive rebellions. ADHD parallels Samuel Cartwright's *dysesthesia*; while ODD and CD parallels Cartwright's *drapetomania*.

Alienated anti-authoritarian adults are often diagnosed with anxiety and depression. Often a major pain of their lives that fuels their anxiety and/or depression is fear that noncompliance with illegitimate authorities will cause them to be financially and socially marginalized; but they fear that compliance with such illegitimate authorities will result in humiliation and loss of integrity. All this can result in anxiety and depression—created not by biochemical defects but by existential realities.

While only a small number of people diagnosed with bipolar disorder, schizophrenia, and other psychoses identify themselves as anarchists, my experience is that a far higher percentage of this population as compared to the general population have anarchist politics and values (such as resenting coercion; distrusting impersonal authorities; believing people should organize among themselves rather than submit to authorities; and a willingness to risk punishments to gain freedom from coercions).

Among the people I have talked with who have been previously diagnosed with psychiatric illnesses, I am struck by how many of them, compared to the general population, are essentially anti-authoritarians. Unluckily for them, the professionals who have diagnosed them are not.

Historically, doctors have embraced authoritarianism at a higher percentage than the general population. In 2012, physician Alessandra Colaianni reported in *Journal of Medical Ethics*, "More than 7% of all German physicians became members of the Nazi SS during World War II, compared with less than 1% of the general population. . . . Physicians joined the Nazi party and the killing operations not at gunpoint, not by force, but of their own volition." Colaianni offers several reasons for this, one being doctors' socialization to hierarchy and authoritarianism: "Medical culture is, in many ways, a rigid hierarchy. . . . Those at the lower end of the hierarchy are used to doing what their superiors ask of them, often without understanding exactly why. . . . Questioning superiors is often uncomfortable, for fear both of negative consequences (retaliation, losing the superior's respect) and of being wrong."

MDs and PhDs have received extensive schooling and thus have lived for many years in a world where one routinely complies with the demands of authorities. Thus, people who reject this compliance appear to be "abnormal" for many MDs and PhDs. My experience is that most psychologists, psychiatrists, and other mental health professionals are unaware of the magnitude of their obedience, and so the anti-authoritarianism of their patients can create enormous anxiety for them—and this anxiety fuels diagnoses and treatments.

A handful of mental health professionals have challenged the legitimacy of mental health authorities—and have paid a price for so doing. In 1968, psychiatrist Loren Mosher (1933–2004) became the National Institute of Mental Health's chief of the Center for Schizophrenia Research. In 1971, Mosher launched an alternative approach for people diagnosed with schizophrenia, opening the first Soteria House in Santa Clara, California. Soteria House was an egalitarian and non-coercive psychosocial milieu employing nonprofessional caregivers. The results showed that people do far better with this Soteria approach than with standard psychiatric treatment, and that people can in fact recover with little or no use of antipsychotic drugs. Mosher's success embarrassed establishment psychiatry and displeased the pharmaceutical industry. Not surprisingly, the National Institute of Mental Health choked off Soteria House funding, and Mosher was fired from his NIMH position in 1980.

There continues to be a movement of dissident mental health professionals and ex-patient activists. This movement attempts to get the word out on the lack of science behind the *DSM* diagnostic bible, and to expose the illegitimacy of biochemical disease explanations such as the "chemical-imbalance" theory. Recently, even some members of mainstream psychiatry have been forced to admit failure in these areas.

In response to the *DSM-5*, published in 2013, the NIMH director, citing the lack of scientific validity of the *DSM*, stated that the "NIMH will be re-orienting its research away from *DSM* categories." Also harshly critical of the *DSM-5* was the politically astute former chair of the *DSM-IV* task force, psychiatrist Allen Frances, who published *Saving Normal* (2014), which mocked several new *DSM-5* mental illness inventions, especially the pathologizing of normal human grief. Frances's repudiation of *DSM-5* is noteworthy, as it is as if the guy who wrote Leviticus realized that his "abominating" and "sinning" had gotten out of hand.

Similar to their abandonment of the *DSM*, establishment psychiatrists have also recently fled psychiatry's long promulgated "chemical imbalance theory of mental illness." In the late 1980s, psychiatry authorities and giant pharmaceutical companies began telling the general public—despite lacking scientific evidence— that depression is caused by a "chemical imbalance" of low-levels of serotonin that could be treated with "chemically balancing" antidepressants, such as Prozac, Zoloft, Paxil, and other selective serotonin reuptake inhibitors (SSRIs). The idea that depression is caused by a chemical imbalance that could be corrected with SSRI antidepressants was made to sound like taking insulin for diabetes, and so the use of these SSRIs skyrocketed. Today, the falseness of this chemical-imbalance theory of mental illness is not controversial.

In 2011, leading establishment psychiatrist Ronald Pies, editor-in-chief emeritus of *Psychiatric Times,* stated, "In truth, the 'chemical imbalance' notion was always a kind of urban legend—never a theory seriously propounded by well-informed psychiatrists." After National Public Radio correspondent Alix Spiegel learned that the chemical imbalance theory was untrue, she then discovered establishment authorities' justifications for promulgating it. One such rationalization was that by framing depression as a chemical deficiency, patients felt more comfortable taking antidepressant drugs. While some psychiatrists view the chemical imbalance theory as a well-meaning "white lie," my experience is that many physicians continue to be ignorant of the truth. The bottom line is that no matter what the reason, mainstream psychiatrists who have promulgated untruths have broken their patients' trust.

Does psychiatry retain any legitimate authority? In a 2014 *Truthout* interview, Robert Whitaker, medical reporter and author of *Anatomy of an Epidemic: Magic Bullets, Psychiatric Drugs, and the Astonishing Rise of Mental Illness in America* (2010), stated about psychiatry, "We see that its diagnostics are being dismissed as invalid; its research has failed to identify the biology of mental disorders to validate its diagnostics; and its drug treatments are increasingly being seen as not very effective or even harmful. That is the story of a profession that has reason to feel insecure about its place in the marketplace."

Despite its scientific failure, psychiatry has retained societal authority. Its authority rests on three pillars.

First, by pushing drug treatments, it meets the financial needs of drug companies, and so it has large financial backing from Big Pharma. In 2008, congressional investigations of psychiatry revealed that the APA and several "thought leader" psychiatrists received significant amounts of money from drug companies. Big Pharma heavily funds university psychiatry departments, sponsors conferences and continuing education for psychiatrists, and pays well-known clinicians and researchers to be speakers and consultants. In 2012, *PLOS Medicine* reported, "69% of the *DSM*-5 task force members report having ties to the pharmaceutical industry."

Second, by pathologizing and thus depoliticizing malaise, psychiatry helps maintain the status quo, meeting the needs of the ruling power structure. Historically, professionals such as police and clergy have been utilized to control populations. More recently, mental health professionals have also been used.

One example of this is mainstream mental health professional's explanation for high rates of suicide among indigenous peoples, detailed by psychologist Roland Chrisjohn and Shaunessy McKay in *Dying to Please You*: "Existing explanations blame the victim, finding that they suffer from personal adjustment problems or emotional deficiencies like 'low self-esteem' and 'depression.' None of the existing explanations alleviate the situation by acting or suggesting action against the forces of oppression; they don't even recognize them."

Meeting the needs of the power structure ensures an institution's existence. And so the professions of psychiatry and psychology have had reason to want to be utilized to subvert resistance by U.S. soldiers via psychiatric drug "treatments" and behavioral manipulations. According to the *Military Times* in 2013, one in six U.S. armed service members were taking at least one psychiatric drug, many of these medicated soldiers in combat zones. And in 2009, the *New York Times* reported how Martin Seligman, a former president of the American Psychological Association, consulted with the U.S. Army's Comprehensive Soldier Fitness positive psychology program. In this program, in one role-play, a sergeant is asked to take his exhausted men on one more difficult mission, and the sergeant is initially angry and complains that "it's not fair"; but in the role-play, his "rehabilitation" involves reinterpreting the order as a compliment.

A third pillar of psychiatry's societal authority is its coercions to control people who create societal tension but who have done nothing illegal. Mental health professionals meet the control needs of authoritarians in charge of society but also meet the control needs of authoritarian subordinates. "This coercive function is what society and most people actually appreciate most about psychiatry," concludes David Cohen, professor of social welfare, in his 2014 article, "It's the Coercion, Stupid!" Cohen explains the societal need for psychiatry's "extra-legal police function" compels society to be blind to psychiatry's complete lack of scientific validity, "Because of psychiatric coercion, society gives psychiatric theories a free pass. These theories never need to pass any rigorously devised tests (as we expect other important scientific theories to pass), they only need to be asserted."

In the history of American psychiatry, there have been several adult populations lacking political power—including Native Americans, women, and homosexuals—who have been psychopathologized and marginalized for the "offense" of asserting their humanity. In the 1970s, homosexuals were able to gain some political power and fought so as to no longer be at the mercy of the APA. In 1970, the Gay Liberation Front (GLF) infiltrated a conference of the APA where a film was demonstrating the use of electroshock treatment to decrease same-sex attraction. GLF members shouted "Torture!" and seized the microphone to rebuke psychiatrists. Using multiple political strategies and tactics, gay activists effectively forced the APA to stop pathologizing homosexuality as a mental illness in 1973. While organized adults have successfully liberated themselves from being psychopathologized and marginalized, mental health authorities have increasingly zeroed in on a politically powerless population: anti-authoritarian youth.

Many young people labeled with psychiatric diagnoses are essentially anti-authoritarians who are pained and angered by coercion, unnecessary rules, and illegitimate authority. When young anti-authoritarians are labeled with a psychiatric diagnosis, they get ensnared in an authoritarian trap. Resistance to diagnosis and treatment often results in professionals labeling young rebels as "noncompliant with treatment," increasing the severity of the diagnosis, and increasing the dosage of tranquilizing medications. All this can be enraging for young people, sometimes so much so it makes them appear not just angry but crazy.

Today, a potentially huge army of young anti-authoritarians are being depoliticized by mental illness diagnoses and by attributions that their inattention, anxiety, depression, and disruptiveness are caused by defective biochemistry—and not by their alienation from a dehumanizing society and their resistance to illegitimate authorities.

Schooling's Assault on
Young Anti-Authoritarians

"The institutional role of the schools for the most part is just to train people for obedience and conformity, and to make them controllable and indoctrinated—and as long as the schools fulfill that role, they'll be supported."

—NOAM CHOMSKY, *UNDERSTANDING POWER:*
THE INDISPENSABLE CHOMSKY, 2002

"There's a reason education sucks, and it's the same reason it will never, ever, ever be fixed. . . . Because the owners, the owners of this country don't want that. . . . They don't want well-informed, well-educated people capable of critical thinking. . . .You know what they want? They want obedient workers. . . . People who are just smart enough to run the machines and do the paperwork. And just dumb enough to passively accept all these increasingly shitty jobs."

—GEORGE CARLIN, "THE AMERICAN DREAM" FROM
LIFE IS WORTH LOSING, 2006

"When I think back on all the crap I learned in high school, it's a wonder I can think at all."

—PAUL SIMON, "KODACHROME," 1973

As a young child in school, before I understood the words *authoritarian* or *dehumanizing*, I thought there was something terribly wrong with a place where I had to raise my hand to go the bathroom. I recall thinking that I was lucky that I wasn't shy, because if I had been too shy to ask for permission, then I might wet my pants. Having to ask permission to go the bathroom was bad enough, but there were teachers who made us either say— or show with our fingers—whether we needed to urinate (one finger) or defecate (two fingers). I remember thinking this must be especially horrific for prim-and-proper girls, and I thought that these teachers must be perverts to demand that.

Nowadays, many kids tell me that they still must get permission from a teacher to leave their classroom to relieve themselves. Recently, a high school student told me that, in his school, students get a limited number of restroom passes per semester. I asked him what happens if a student runs out of passes and has to take a shit—do they expect students to just shit in their pants? He laughed. Then I told him that I was serious—what do they expect you to do? Then he got serious and said, "So much of school is fucked up, we never really think about *each* fucked up thing."

Social psychologist Stanley Milgram in *Obedience to Authority*, after reporting on his studies showing a frightening compliance to abusive illegitimate authority, attempted to understand the reasons: "As soon as the child emerges from the cocoon of family, he is transferred to an *institutional system of authority*, the school," where the student learns that "deference is the only appropriate and comfortable response to authority." Standard schools not only demand our compliance to authority regardless of our assessment of its legitimacy, they require our compliance with impersonal authorities. Milgram notes that "the modern industrial world forces individuals to submit to impersonal authorities, so that responses are made to abstract rank, indicated by an insignia, uniform or title." In other words, *badges*.

In their 1962 book *Cradles of Eminence*, psychologist Victor Goertzel and educator Mildred Goertzel examined the childhood of 400 eminent people, and they reported that the majority of them disliked school immensely.

The Goertzels detailed the pain that the anti-authoritarian Albert Einstein had with his schooling. When Einstein was a teenager, he found school so intolerable, he asked the school doctor to give him a certificate saying that he had a nervous breakdown so that he did not have to attend (a tactic that worked). Einstein later concluded about schooling: "It is, in fact, nothing short of a miracle that the modern methods of instruction have not yet entirely strangled the holy curiosity of inquiry. . . . It is a very grave mistake to think that the enjoyment of seeing and searching can be promoted by means of coercion and a sense of duty."

One of Einstein's biographers, Ronald Clark, tells us that young Albert didn't pay attention to his teachers and failed his college entrance examination twice. Einstein recalls hating authoritarian discipline in his schools: "The teachers in the elementary school appeared to me like sergeants and in the Gymnasium the teachers were like lieutenants." After Einstein finally did enter college, one professor told him, "You have one fault; one can't tell you anything." Today, a young Albert Einstein would very likely receive an ADHD diagnosis and maybe an ODD one as well. The very characteristics of Einstein that upset authorities—questioning and challenging illegitimate authority—are the characteristics most required to be a great scientist.

The primary method of "motivation" in standard schools is coercion through grades. Students focus on what they need to memorize for a good grade, and they stop asking their own questions and pursuing answers to them. As dissident educator John Holt noted, "To a very great degree, school is a place where children learn to be stupid. . . Children come to school curious; within a few years most of that curiosity is dead, or at least silent." The motivational method of coercion not only subverts curiosity, it prevents students from even retaining facts. "You did your homework," Noam Chomsky reminds us, "you passed the exam, maybe you even got an 'A'—and a week later you couldn't even remember what the course was about."

Standard school coercions subvert a love of reading. A report released by Common Sense Media in 2014 stated: "The proportion of children who are daily readers drops markedly from childhood to the tween and teenage years. One study (Scholastic,

2013) documents a drop from 48% of six- to eight-year-olds down to 24% of 15- to 17-year-olds who are daily readers, and another (National Center for Educational Statistics, 2013) shows a drop from 53% of nine-year-olds to 19% of 17-year-olds."

What turns most teenagers off from reading for pleasure is compulsory reading of books that they have no intrinsic interest in. I recall one teenager who had loved to read as a kid but became turned off to reading because of required reading. I joked with him that if schools one day made kids have compulsory sex with people they weren't interested in that this would turn kids off from sex in general. He thought about this for a few seconds, then told me that adults would probably do just that if they realized how making something compulsory turns kids off from it.

What are the origins of the U.S. mass educational system? Chomsky points out, "In the late 19th century it was largely designed to turn independent farmers into disciplined factory workers, and a good deal of education maintains that form." Chomsky also concluded that those at the top of the societal hierarchy support the educational system because they believe: "People are supposed to be passive and apathetic and doing what they're told by the responsible people who are in control. That's elite ideology across the political spectrum—from liberals to Leninists, it's essentially the same ideology: people are too stupid and ignorant to do things by themselves so for their own benefit we have to control them."

As Americans have received increasingly more schooling, they have become less capable of effectively challenging the ruling class. In 1900, only 6% of Americans graduated high school, and a college education was rare for ordinary Americans; today, approximately 85% of Americans graduate high school, and college is increasingly expected for all. However, in the 1880s and 1890s, American farmers with little or no schooling created a Populist movement; organized America's largest-scale working people's cooperative; formed a People's Party that received 8% of the vote in 1892 presidential election; designed a "subtreasury" plan (that had it been implemented would have allowed easier credit for farmers and broken the power of large banks) and sent 40,000 lecturers across the United States to articulate this plan; and evidenced all kinds of sophisticated political ideas, strategies, and tactics absent today from America's well-schooled population.

There are anti-authoritarian educators who have the courage to publicly assert the authoritarian nature of standard schools. John Taylor Gatto, accepting the New York City Teacher of the Year Award, January 31, 1990, stated: "The truth is that schools don't really teach anything except how to obey orders. This is a great mystery to me because thousands of humane, caring people work in schools as teachers and aides and administrators, but the abstract logic of the institution overwhelms their individual contributions."

Standard school teaches compliance with hierarchy; obedience to authorities for whom one does not necessarily respect; and regurgitation of meaningless material for a high grade. The standard classroom socializes students to be passive; to be directed by others; to take seriously the rewards and punishments of authorities; to pretend to care about things that they don't care about; and that one is impotent to change one's dissatisfying situation.

In a hierarchical society, prestigious schools confer prestigious badges. Dissident educator Jonathan Kozol was a student at an elite prep school and then at Harvard. Kozol concluded, "Children come to realize, early in their school careers, the terrible danger to their own success in statements that give voice to strong intensities." Kozol recounted how he was taught to obey orders and "to channel our dissent into innocuous patterns of polite 'discussion and investigation.'" Kozol explains how schools, especially elitist institutions, teach what he called an *inert concern*—that "caring" in and of itself is "ethical" but that disobedience is immature.

Recall Ralph Nader's contempt for Harvard Law School, which he saw as narrowing minds and producing lawyers to serve corporations. And with respect to all his standard school-ing, Nader observed, "With the exceptions of some marvelous teachers, our many hours in class teach us to believe, not to think, to obey, not to challenge."

Noam Chomsky was named to the Society of Fellows at Harvard in 1951, and later he reflected on the difference between Harvard and Oxford, "We only had a phony superficiality, while they had a genuine superficiality." In looking back at his student years, Chomsky recounted that "most of the people who make it through the educational system and get into the elite univer-sities are able to do it because they've been willing to obey a lot of stupid orders for years and years—that's the way I did it, for example. Like you're told by some stupid teacher, 'Do this,' which you know makes no sense whatsoever, but you do it, and if you do it you get to the next rung, and then you obey the next order, and finally you work your way through and they give you your letters: an awful lot of education is like that. . . . Some people go along with it because they figure, 'Okay, I'll do any stupid thing that asshole says because I want to get ahead'; others do it because they've just internalized the values. . . . But you do it, or else you're out: you ask too many questions and you're going to get in trouble. Now, there are also people who *don't* go along—and they're called 'behavior problems,' or 'unmotivated,' or things like that."

Elitist schools and their conferred badges can provide liars and bullshit artists with great confidence in their ability to get away with lies and bullshit throughout their entire lives, and such projected confidence provides them greater influence. Susan Cain in *Quiet* quotes the Harvard Business School (HBS) infor-mation session on how to be a good class participant: "Speak with conviction. Even if you believe something only fifty-five percent, say it as if you believe it a hundred percent." Cain dis-covered that at HBS, "If a student talks often and forcefully, then he's a player; if he doesn't, he's on the margins." She observed that the men at HBS "look like people who expect to be in charge . . . . I have the feeling that if you asked one of them for driving directions, he'd greet you with a can-do smile and throw himself into the task of helping you to your destination—whether or not he knew the way."

For authoritarians, a degree from Harvard Business School is a prestigious badge of authority. For anti-authoritarians, an HBS degree is especially suspect, as they know that HBS alumni include George W. Bush, 1975 graduate, in charge at the advent of the 2008 financial meltdown, and Jeffrey Skilling, 1979 graduate, former CEO of Enron and convicted of securities fraud and insider trading. Business journalist Duff McDonald's 2017 book about HBS, *The Golden Passport*, concludes that HBS teaches greed and socializes students to the idea that "if everybody assumes you're a whore, you might as well grab as much money as possible while you're still in demand."

The more absolute the power of institutional authorities—be they in parochial schools, Native American residential boarding schools, or public schools—the more likely their physical and emotional abuse. Recall the excellent student Malcolm X being told by his public school teacher that being a lawyer was "no realistic goal for a nigger" and the teacher-inflicted physical and emotional abuse on Emma Goldman. I remember in junior high school, one kid raising his hand desiring to contribute to the class discussion but told by the teacher, "I'm not calling on you, you are in the crud group." While certainly many teachers try to be civil and kind, I can recall more than one teacher thinking themselves funny when they were being cruel. That's why, for several decades now, young people continue to resonate to Pink Floyd's "Another Brick in the Wall" and its lyrics about "dark sarcasm in the classroom."

While teachers today might well be fired for certain kinds of emotional and physical abuse, standard schools are replete with acceptable psychological violence. These schools force kids to compete against one another. The better some students do on an exam, the worse this is for others. School not only punishes most academic cooperation—it's called *cheating*—school encourages resentment for others' success.

Today, we hear much about peer bullying but little about what fuels that cruelty. Human beings in institutions replete with coercions and humiliations—whether these institutions are penitentiaries or schools—are often going to take their pain out on others they perceive as weaker than they are. Similarly, the fuel for abusive parenting is also often a lifetime of coercions and humiliations, including job and schooling ones.

Working with teenagers for over three decades, my experience is that the source of their suicidal thoughts is actually more often located in the school than the family. And while occasionally the source of overwhelming pain is a single abusive teacher or a bullying peer, often suicidality is fueled by the anxiety of being overwhelmed by bureaucratic coercions; for example, having failed classes in subjects they have no interest in and being forced to go to summer school or not graduate.

With young people increasingly expected to attend college, a relatively new abuse is student-loan debt. Large debt—and the fear it creates—is a pacifying force. There was no tuition at Queens College, City University of New York, when I attended in the 1970s, a time when tuition at many U.S. public universities was so affordable that it was easy to get an undergraduate and even a graduate degree without accruing any student-loan debt. The Project on Student Debt reported, "Seven in 10 seniors (68%) who graduated from public and nonprofit colleges in 2015 had student loan debt, with an average of $30,100 per borrower." While that's the average debt, I routinely talk to college graduates and dropouts with far higher debt. During the time in one's life when it should be easiest to resist authority because one does not yet have family responsibilities, many young adults worry about the cost of bucking authority, losing their job, and being unable to pay an ever-increasing debt.

Among the famous anti-authoritarians who I profile as well as among non-famous anti-authoritarians who I have known, schools and psychiatric hospitalization—sometimes even more than prison—can result in great anger. Few anti-authoritarians report gaining anything of value in their coercive schooling or psychiatric treatment, while some anti-authoritarians report gains from their prison time (Malcolm X, Emma Goldman, Eugene Debs, and Alexander Berkman used their prison time to educate themselves in a wide array of areas).

When I began researching this book, I certainly was aware of the ill effects of schooling on anti-authoritarians, but I underestimated their level of anger toward their schooling. Emma Goldman and Malcolm X, for example, recounted greater anger with some of their teachers than with any prison officials. One pattern I noticed—among this small sample of famous anti-authoritarians who I profile as well as among the far larger sample of non-famous anti-authoritarians who I have known—is that the more extensive their schooling, often the greater their anger. Among those with advanced degrees, there is anger about having had to fight off schooling's ill effects so as to acquire their degree-badges, and there is anger about their employment in academia.

PART THREE

TRAGEDY
OR
TRIUMPH

8

Lessons From Anti-Authoritarians Who Have Hurt Themselves, Others, or the Cause

Self-Destructive Anti-Authoritarians:
Phil Ochs, Lenny Bruce, and Ida Lupino;
Violent Anti-Authoritarians: Alexander Berkman,
Leon Czolgosz, and Ted Kaczynski

Anti-authoritarians often cannot stop authoritarians from assaulting them, but some anti-authoritarians compound this assault with a self-inflicted one. Overwhelmed by pain, there are many anti-authoritarians—famous and non-famous—who have hurt themselves, hurt others, or hurt the cause of resisting illegitimate authority.

Self-Destructive Anti-Authoritarians: Phil Ochs, Lenny Bruce, and Ida Lupino

Among anti-authoritarians who move into self-destructive behaviors, substance abuse (with alcohol, illegal drugs, and psychiatric drugs) often plays a large role. Anti-authoritarians, by their nature, do not take seriously authorities' admonitions, as they often see through hypocrisy; and U.S. authorities have historically manifested a great deal of hypocrisy around drugs (for example, the revolving door of psychiatric drugs becoming illegal ones, and vice versa). Anti-authoritarians' disregard for alcohol and drug consequences may not, early on, be costly for them, and this can further diminish their caution and result in a tragic irony: self-created dependency on a nonhuman illegitimate authority—specifically, a chemical substance.

Another common theme among self-destructive anti-authoritarians is a deterioration toward self-absorption. An obsession with one's moods can result in feeling even more overwhelmed by pain, which fuels compulsive unwise actions. A sense of humor is vital for anti-authoritarian survival and joy, and, when self-absorption displaces their sense of humor, anti-authoritarians find it painful to be with themselves—and so too do others, which, in a vicious cycle, makes anti-authoritarians even more self-loathing.

A lack of self-care creates more pain and makes anti-authoritarians more vulnerable to unwise actions. This lack of self-care can include a lack of attention to physical health and personal finances, along with unwise relationships with abusive and exploitative people. Relationships are critical. If an anti-authoritarian lacks anyone they trust, they are highly vulnerable to unwise actions fueled by their pain. And if they trust untrust-worthy people, that too can result in self-destructive behaviors.

Phil Ochs

In the 1960s, singer-songwriter Phil Ochs (1940–1976) was some-times described as "Tom Paine with a guitar." Without regard for political correctness, both Paine and Ochs challenged illegitimate authorities and hypocrisy. Both achieved fame during eras when anti-authoritarianism was fashionable, and both were marginal-ized at the end of their lives when anti-authoritarianism fell out of fashion. In 1976, at age 35, Ochs committed suicide, which came as no surprise to his friends and family. In Ochs's last years, he often talked about suicide, and it had been preceded by an array of self-destructive behaviors. However, triumph preceded tragedy for Phil Ochs, as it had for Thomas Paine.

In the 1770s, Paine's *Common Sense* helped spark the Amer-ican Revolution and his *American Crisis* helped keep George Washington's troops from quitting on him. In the 1960s, no one could be counted on more than Phil Ochs to perform at an anti-war rally and supply energy for the anti-war movement. Ochs's performance of his song "I Ain't Marching Anymore" during a protest concert outside the 1968 Democratic National Convention inspired many young men to burn their draft cards.

As a teenager, what I loved most about Ochs was how he confronted the liars and hypocrites who had created misery for my generation. Ochs's humor was far more energizing for me than the tired rants of his anti-war contemporaries. Even though liberals were a large part of his audience, Ochs also made fun of hypocrites on the Left, most famously in his song "Love Me, I'm a Liberal."

What made Phil especially endearing was that he reserved some of his most pointed barbs for himself. In his songs and his quips, Phil Ochs modeled a hugely important trait for anti-authoritarians—maintaining a sense of humor and not taking oneself too seriously. However, at the end of his life, Ochs modeled the opposite trait—an anti-authoritarian who loses his sense of humor, becomes self-absorbed, and ends up in a dark place.

Because his rise and fall came during my most impressionable years, Phil Ochs's life served as both an inspiring model and a cautionary tale for me. I remember as a teenager listening repeatedly to "When I'm Gone," his song about the value of staying alive despite the pain of life. As beautiful and life-affirming as that song is, I recall wondering whether he might commit suicide. It was clear to me that he was a fragile guy trying his best not to be defeated by life's pains. Ochs's songs were therapy for many of us fragile teenagers, inspiring us to have the courage to face life. However, Ochs himself ultimately succumbed to his overwhelming pains.

Throughout Phil Ochs's life, there were very real pains, beginning in his household growing up. Phil's mother was disappointed in her marriage and her life, and she took out her frustrations on her husband, "berating him as a failure and criticizing his every move around the house," notes Ochs biographer Michael Schumacher. Phil's father, Jack Ochs, was a physician but a financially unsuccessful one. In the U.S. military during World War II, Jack had treated soldiers injured in the Battle of the Bulge. The carnage was traumatizing for Jack, and he became a war casualty, receiving an honorable medical discharge. When Jack came home, he was psychiatrically hospitalized for two years, disconnecting Phil from his father.

Phil was a shy child and tended to be withdrawn even in his own family; and throughout his career, he used and abused alcohol and drugs to reduce his performance anxiety. There is, of course, a long and ever-growing list of anti-authoritarian musicians who have engaged in self-destructive behaviors, especially substance abuse, though not all abused substances for the same reason.

As a performer, Ochs was known for his playful bravado, however, he was sensitive to criticism, and music critics were rough on him. Some critics focused on the range of his voice and guitar-playing skills rather than what we Phil Ochs fans cared about—which was what he was saying and how powerfully he said it. An *Esquire* music critic in 1968 mocked Ochs's album *Pleasures of the Harbor*: "Too bad his voice shows an effective range of about half an octave . . . too bad his guitar playing would not suffer much if his right hand were webbed." Around that time, Ochs also began experiencing a more general career pain, as the mainstream popularity of folk music began disappearing, and there was especially a decreasing market for his niche of topical-political folk music.

Political impotency in effecting change was also painful for Ochs. After the police violence at the 1968 Chicago Democratic National Convention and the nomination of Vietnam War supporter Hubert Humphrey, Ochs said, "I don't think fairness wins anymore." Phil's friend Lucian Truscott observed: "There were so many awful things that happened in the 60s, the war in Vietnam, both the Kennedy brothers getting killed, and Martin Luther King. It just seemed like one hammer blow after another. And I think Phil was a big enough egomaniac to take it all personally."

In 1973, Ochs was devastated by the torture and assassination of his friend and hero Victor Jara, the Chilean protest singer who was murdered during the U.S.-backed military coup d'état that overthrew the democratically elected Salvador

Allende government in Chile. Compounding these pains, a blow to Ochs's physical health had occurred earlier. On a trip to Africa in 1973, in Dar es Salaam, Tanzania, walking alone on the beach, Phil was attacked and robbed. During the assault he was choked, which ruptured his vocal chords and damaged his vocal range.

While Ochs was assaulted by others—physically and psychologically—he also assaulted himself. There is a lengthy list of anti-authoritarian artists who, overwhelmed by the pains of their lives, move down the path from casual alcohol and drug use to its abuse, with eventually this abuse being a major factor in their demise. Phil Ochs is on that list.

"As a casual drinker," Schumacher notes, "Phil was fun to be around, but when he was drinking heavily, especially if he was in a depressed state, he could be unreasonable and contentious and, on rare occasions, violent." Earlier in Phil's life, Schumacher notes, "he looked at Valium the same way he regarded other drugs—as substances that could hinder, rather than open, the mind." However, when he moved to California in 1967, Schumacher reported, "Phil stepped up his intake of Valium, and his dependency became more apparent," at one point flying into a rage when a drug store refused to sell him any. He increasingly drank alcohol and this coupled with his Valium dependency made him no fun to be around.

After 1968, friends reported that he drank day and night, and that his house was a wreck. Fellow musicians reported that he increasingly took drugs to get through performances. Pianist Lincoln Mayorga reported that Phil was abusing himself very badly on a 1970 tour, "He was drinking a lot of wine and taking uppers. . . . The wine was pulling him one way and the uppers were pulling him another way, and he was kind of a mess. There were so many pharmaceuticals around—so many pills. I'd never seen anything like that."

In 1971, after an evening of excessive drinking, Ochs had an argument with his girlfriend and got into his car and began racing down Sunset Boulevard in Los Angeles. He crossed over the center line and crashed into a car coming from the opposite direction. The collision slammed Ochs's face into the steering wheel and knocked out several of his teeth. Police arrested Phil for felonious drunken driving and he was taken in handcuffs to the hospital. Luckily, he did not kill the other driver, and because the other driver was also drunk, Phil faced no lawsuit, and criminal charges against him were dropped.

Phil's brother, Michael Ochs, who managed Phil's later career said, "He never should have followed me to L.A. Whenever I don't want to get into a lengthy conversation with people who ask me, 'What killed your brother,' I'll say 'L.A.'"

Beyond physically assaulting himself with alcohol and drugs, Ochs psychologically beat himself up for his lack of success. Even among artists who don't aspire to great wealth, it's difficult to have the energy to persevere without the ambition of reaching a larger audience, and that was certainly the case with Phil Ochs. Larry Marks, producer of Phil's album *Pleasures of the Harbor*, recalled that everybody else involved in it was realistic that it wasn't going to have wide appeal but that Phil saw no reason why this album would not top the charts. Ochs greatly admired Víctor Jara but also envied Jara's achievement of being a protest singer with popular appeal throughout Chile. Ochs fantasized about having that kind of massive appeal in the United States, but his fantasies were unrealistic given the far less politicized U.S. general public. And because Ochs couldn't dial back expectations around success, he felt like a failure, and he punished himself for it.

Ochs also gave the wrong people too much psychological power over him. His desire for Bob Dylan's respect and friendship made him vulnerable to Dylan's cruelty. Dylan would taunt and mock his fellow folk singers' desire for fame, saying, "Nobody's gonna make it. Maybe you think you're gonna do what I did. Nobody's gonna do it.'" Dylan was brutal with Ochs, "You ought to find a new line of work, Ochs. . . . Why don't you just become a stand-up comic?" Perhaps one of Dylan's most psychologically lethal communications to Ochs was: "The stuff you're writing is bullshit because politics is bullshit. It's all unreal. The only thing that's real is inside you. Your feelings. Just look at the world you're writing about and you'll see that you're wasting your time." This Dylan comment was especially psychologically lethal for someone with Phil's temperament, the dark side of which was wallowing in his feelings.

Sadly, Ochs did turn more inward. Singer-song writer Judy Henske, Ochs's friend, recounted Ochs's deterioration, "He had stopped looking outward. See, that's the scary thing. Before it had been all outward . . . . What do I think about this politician? What do I think about this action? What do I think about this person? That's what he did before. But then he got sick, and it was all: What do I think about me? What do I think about me?"

Many people who cared about Phil Ochs saw his friend-ships with Abbie Hoffman and Jerry Rubin as hurtful. They saw Hoffman's and Rubin's narcissism as hurting Ochs's career and hurting the anti-war movement—and both those failures pained Phil. At a Carnegie Hall concert that was important for Ochs's career, Hoffman took the microphone and started yelling, "Fuck Lyndon Johnson! Fuck Robert Kennedy! And fuck you if you don't like it!" The crowd demanded Rubin and Hoffman leave, which they did but not before they had destroyed the concert. After the 1968 Democratic convention, Ochs concluded that the outrageous theatrics of Rubin and Hoffman might have gained them attention but had served to alienate America's working class from the anti-war movement, and Phil beat himself up for being a part of those negative theatrics.

"When Phil was depressed, he wallowed in it," Michael Ochs observed. A year before his suicide, Phil became bizarre, taking on the identity of John Train. Phil announced, "On the first day of summer 1975, Phil Ochs was murdered in the Chelsea Hotel by John Train, who is now speaking. I killed Phil Ochs. The reason I killed him was he was some kind of genius but he drank too much and was becoming a boring old fart. For the good of societies, public and secret, he needed to be gotten rid of." Ochs's John Train creation drank heavily, picked fights in bars, and was unkempt and homeless. Eventually John Train disappeared, and

Phil Ochs returned, but many friends wanted him to admit himself to a psychiatric hospital, which he resisted.

In 1976, Phil moved in with his sister, Sonny, living in Rockaway, New York. He was quiet and passive, doing little but watching television and occasionally playing cards with his nephews. Sonny finally convinced Phil to consult with a psychiatrist, and she was happy when he told her that he received a psychiatric drug prescription. Sonny was also happy when she was able to talk Phil into playing a few songs for a gathering of her friends, and she was hopeful when two days later they went shopping for a new guitar. But four days after that, Phil committed suicide, hanging himself in Sonny's home. Later, Sonny found Phil's container of psychiatric drugs and discovered that he had taken none of them.

From my experience, it is not uncommon for anti-authoritarians such as Phil Ochs to readily admit that they are in bad mental shape but to reject psychiatric diagnoses and treatment. This is especially true when psychiatric treatment has not been of great benefit to either themselves or to a family member—in Phil's case, his father. Later, I will discuss ways to approach destructive and self-destructive behaviors that differ from standard psychiatric treatments, approaches that anti-authoritarians are more receptive to.

Lenny Bruce

Lenny Bruce (1925–1966) is revered by many modern comedians for sacrificing his career for free speech. The essence of being both a stand-up comedian and social critic is to be anti-authoritarian—to question and make fun of illegitimate authority. *Rolling Stone's* top three stand-up comics in U.S. history—Richard Pryor, George Carlin, and Lenny Bruce—were all talented anti-authoritarians who engaged in dangerous substance abuse. Bruce was assaulted by the criminal justice system, but he also assaulted himself, primarily with drugs—lethally so.

Born Leonard Schneider in Long Island, New York, Lenny Bruce had a very different temperament than the shy Phil Ochs. "As a child," Bruce recounted, "I loved confusion: a freezing blizzard that would stop all traffic and mail; toilets that would get stopped up and overflow and run down the halls; electrical failures—anything that would stop the flow and make it back up and find a new direction. Confusion was entertainment for me."

At age 16, Lenny ran away from home and boarded with the Dengler family, working on their Long Island farm. He would give Mr. Dengler big hugs, and Mrs. Dengler called him the "kissing bug," and both the Denglers told Lenny that he would probably end up being a politician. For many people today, it's difficult to imagine a young Lenny—who would later be labeled the "sick comedian"—living and working on a farm for two years.

From early on, Bruce was attracted to a fun scam, especially one with family involvement. When Bruce worked for the Denglers in the 1940s, they had a roadside stand, and city and suburban folks loved the idea of fresh farm eggs, but the Denglers didn't have enough chickens to meet the demand. So the Denglers would buy eggs wholesale, and a teenage Lenny repackaged them in Dengler cartons. Bruce would later recount, "With my philanthropic sense of humor, I would add a little mud and straw and chicken droppings to give them an authentic pastoral touch."

Bruce's rebellions against authority, on stage and off, remain legendary among comics. Fed up with the navy in 1945, Bruce told medical officers he was overwhelmed with homosexual urges, and this tactic worked to get him discharged. He then fell in love with Honey, a stripper at the time, and they married in 1951. To raise money so that Honey could leave her profession, Lenny engineered the Brother Mathias Foundation scam, in which he impersonated a priest and solicited donations. Bruce was arrested for that scam but was lucky and found not guilty.

On stage, Bruce was fearless. He worked as an MC at strip clubs, and following one performer, he himself came on stage completely naked and said, "Let's give the little girl a big hand." In Bruce's time, it was still common for some Christians to accuse

Jews of killing Jesus Christ, and this would put most Jews on the defensive—but not Lenny. In his act, Lenny would "fess up" that not only did the Jews kill Jesus but that it was his Uncle Morty who did it. In one variation of this bit, he said that what in fact Jews really had covered up was that his Uncle Morty had killed Jesus with an electric chair but that Jews thought that Christian women wouldn't be as attractive wearing necklaces with Jesus in an electric chair dangling over their chests, so Jews made up the crucifixion story.

However, as Bruce became more famous for his risk-taking humor that fearlessly mocked authorities, his luck eventually ran out. He was arrested multiple times for obscenity during his stand-up act as well as for drug possession. Bruce believed that authorities went after him mostly because he made fun of organized religion. His friend George Carlin (profiled later) agreed, "Lenny wasn't being arrested for obscenity. He was being arrested for being funny about religion and in particular Catholicism. A lot of big city cops . . . tend to be Irish Catholic," and as the Irish Catholic Carlin pointed out, so too were many prosecutors and judges.

In the years before his death, Bruce became increasingly pre-occupied by how to prevent arrest for drug use. In his autobiography, Bruce wrote, "For self-protection, I now carry with me at all times a small bound booklet consisting of photostats of statements made by physicians, and prescriptions and bottle labels." Bruce displayed one of those statements from Dr. Norman Rotenberg who wrote about Lenny: "His response to oral amphetamine has not been particularly satisfactory, so he has been instructed in the proper use of intravenous injections of Methedrine."

In 1964, Bruce was arrested on obscenity charges in New York and, despite petitions and protests from many renowned people, he was convicted and sentenced in December 1964 to four months in a workhouse. Free on bail during the lengthy appeals process, he continued to appear on stage in 1965.

In July 1966, with Bruce still free on bail, Carlin and his wife visited him, and Carlin recalled, "He was completely immersed in his legal battles. . . . He didn't appear in clubs anymore—the Irish cops and judges had indeed shut him the fuck up. He was just about bankrupt, having spent all his income and intellect trying to vindicate himself. We visited for a while and he was as affectionate and lovable as ever. That was the last time we saw him alive." Twelve days after their visit, on August 3, 1966, Lenny Bruce, at age 40, died of a drug overdose.

At the time of his death, Bruce was blacklisted by almost every venue in the United States, as owners feared that they too would be arrested for obscenity. One of the district attorneys who prosecuted Bruce's last 1964 obscenity case, Vincent Cuccia, later admitted, "We drove him into poverty and bankruptcy and then murdered him. . . . We all knew what we were doing. We used the law to kill him." In 2003, the governor of New York gave Bruce a posthumous pardon.

Bruce famously said, "I'm not a comedian. And I'm not sick. The world is sick and I'm the doctor. I'm a surgeon with a scalpel for false values. I don't have an act. I just talk. I'm just Lenny Bruce." At the end of his career, Bruce became dominated by his legal proceedings. When he was still able to get gigs, audiences who came to see him to laugh would hear Bruce read courtroom transcripts onstage, which were funny to him but not for most of his audience. In Bruce's situation of being deprived of First Amendment rights to free speech necessary for his craft and thus deprived of the ability to make a living, it is understandable that he became increasingly self-absorbed and lost some of his sense of humor.

The legal assault on Bruce accelerated his self-destructive substance abuse. And substance abuse—especially with opiates— along with increased self-absorption is a lethal combination for many anti-authoritarians, both famous and non-famous.

Ida Lupino

Among the long list of anti-authoritarian actors and others involved in the film industry who have moved to self-destructive behaviors, I am most drawn to Ida Lupino (1918–1995). It is a sad commentary on modern U.S. society that perhaps the most talented and accomplished anti-authoritarian woman in the history of U.S. cinema has received so little attention, even from many self-identified feminists.

To the extent that Lupino is remembered at all, it is often only as a beautiful actress who played femme fatale characters, but she was far more accomplished. Ida Lupino exhibited raw honest emotionality before "method acting" became fashionable; she rebelled against the control of major studios and created an independent production company; and she wrote screenplays and directed films in a time when female directors were virtually unheard of.

Born in England, Ida's parents were well-known English entertainers. Young Ida, even after her father's death, cared about fulfilling the Lupino family legacy in a way that her father would be proud of. As a teenager, while working in the film industry in England, she was spotted by Hollywood, and she signed with Paramount and moved to the United States. Similar to Frances Farmer, the studio attempted to exploit her sex appeal, and Lupino also rebelled.

Even though only a teenager, Lupino made clear to Paramount executives that she wanted roles that she could "get [her] teeth into." So when she was given just a few lines in the 1934 film *Cleopatra* and ordered to stand behind its star (Claudette Colbert) and wave a palm frond, Lupino refused the role. Paramount placed her on suspension. Finally getting a substantive acting role, she won critical acclaim for her performance in *The Light That Failed* (1939). Eventually she got fed up with Paramount authorities and signed with Warner Brothers, and in her early twenties, she again won acclaim in *They Drive by Night* (1940) and *High Sierra* (1941). But increasingly disgusted with the studio system, Lupino got suspended from Warner Brothers. Unfazed by her studio suspensions, she used that time to go on movie sets and acquire directing skills.

Dreaming of bucking the Hollywood studio system, Lupino partnered with producer Collier Young (whom she married in

1948), and they created an independent production company, Filmmakers (originally called Emerald Productions). They produced movies about social issues that major Hollywood studios were afraid to touch. Lupino wrote *Not Wanted* about an unmarried pregnant woman, and when the film's director suffered a heart attack early in production, Lupino took over directing. She became the second woman ever to belong to the Screen Directors Guild, and at the time of her induction, the only working female director in the guild. Lupino went on to co-write and direct *Outrage,* which focused on rape, and Filmmakers made other films on social issues that the big Hollywood studios avoided. Unlike major Hollywood studio executives, Lupino and Young were unintimidated by the witch hunts of the U.S. Congressional House Un-American Activities Committee.

Lupino's marriage with Young dissolved in part because of the strains of their working relationship, but they remained friends. In 1951, Lupino married actor Howard Duff, a marriage which she would later view as a major mistake, as Duff had made clear to all that he was not fit to be a husband. Lupino remained loyal to Duff, who was a casualty of redbaiting, listed in the smear publication *Red Channels.* This smearing cost Duff acting offers, and Lupino financially kept him and their marriage afloat. Lupino's production company employed Duff, and when Filmmakers was forced to close down because of lack of funds, Lupino compromised herself and took on film roles solely to make a buck.

Duff was a heavy drinker, and when he refused to stop, Lupino angrily reacted by abusing alcohol herself. Between her career difficulties and financial pains, the death of her mother, with whom she had a close relationship, and a tumultuous on-and-off-again relationship with Duff (whom she finally divorced in 1983), Ida Lupino was propelled into heavier drinking and psychiatric drug use. With Hollywood gossip about her substance abuse, her career was hurt even more and this increased her self-destructive behavior. By age 66, the once fiercely independent Lupino had become incapable of self-care. Her friend

Mary Ann Anderson, who would ultimately run Lupino's estate reported, "She had become like a grand bag lady. . . . Everything was a disaster." At age 77, Lupino died while undergoing treatment for cancer.

According to her daughter, Ida Lupino was full of doubts about her talents, as is the case with many self-destructive performers. Ida Lupino had overwhelming pain in her life and resorted to substance abuse to deal with that pain.

The general public is repeatedly told that these life-ending tragedies could be avoided if substance abusers were not resistant to treatment early on. But there is a long list of famous performers who have taken the standard professional treatment route to no avail. In the end, anti-authoritarians need to find a wise way to reduce pain and increase joy, while also finding the morale and energy to change bad habits.

By coincidence, Phil Ochs, Lenny Bruce, and Ida Lupino each had one child, a daughter. A sweet aspect of the bittersweet legacies of these talented anti-authoritarians is that each of their daughters—Meegan Ochs, Kitty Bruce, and Bridget Duff— today make known their great affection for their deceased anti-authoritarian parent.

Violent Anti-Authoritarians:
Alexander Berkman, Leon Czolgosz, Ted Kaczynski

Overwhelming pain is also common among those anti-authoritarians whose violent actions have hurt others and the cause of anti-authoritarianism. Overwhelmed by the pain of societal injustices and their own personal humiliations and powerlessness, they can act compulsively and reactively rather than wisely choosing actions that can best liberate themselves and others. Violent actions fueled by rage are usually not well thought out actions, especially with regard to the ultimate consequences for others.

Anti-authoritarians who move to violence are often quite willing to die. While they may sincerely believe that they are willing to die for their cause, they are often unaware of their need to be perceived as courageous by others. This lack of awareness skews their judgment as to the likely consequences of their violence.

For many violent anti-authoritarians, a need for life's pleasures signifies weakness and an inadequate loyalty to the cause. However, the absence of pleasure in their lives can make their pains even more excruciating, driving them to compulsive actions.

Among this group of violent anti-authoritarians, anger over societal and personal injustice is often quite justifiable, and their experience of powerlessness to produce justice for society and themselves is often quite painful. This combination of rage and impotency can act like a disinhibiting drug that allows for the sort of moral and strategic justifications for violent actions that would not seem moral or strategic at all without this disinhibiting emotional state.

Violence by anti-authoritarians is often welcomed by authoritarians. Such violence provides authoritarians with ammunition to persuade the public of the danger of anti-authoritarians and the need for strong rulers.

Alexander Berkman

Alexander Berkman (1870–1936) was one of the most famous anarchists in U.S. history. He is most remembered for his failed attempt to assassinate Carnegie Steel Company manager Henry Clay Frick during the Homestead, Pennsylvania, steelworkers' strike in 1892. Among anti-authoritarians who have violently reacted to oppressive authority, I will focus most on Berkman because his *Prison Memoirs of an Anarchist* provides us with his justifications and motivations. Unlike others who have turned to violence, Berkman cannot so easily be dismissed as unstable or "mentally ill," as he was admired for his integrity even by those outside the anarchist movement.

The famously cynical journalist H. L. Mencken, criticizing the U.S. government's deportation of Berkman, described

Berkman as a "transparently honest man," but said that "we hunt him as if he were a mad dog—and finally kick him out of the country. And with him goes a shrewder head and a braver spirit than has been seen in public among us since the Civil War." For historian Paul Avrich, Berkman was "a man of uncompromising integrity." And while Berkman gained fame for one act of violence, he also undertook life-saving actions.

Known to his friends and family as Sasha, Alexander Berkman was born in the Russian Empire in present-day Lithuania. His father was a successful merchant, and his mother came from an affluent family. At age twelve, his father died, the family business was sold, and his mother moved the family so as to be close to her brother.

At a young age, Sasha admired Nikolay Chernyshevsky, a Russian revolutionary, and he was attracted to the Russian nihilist movement which rejected societal authorities and embraced individual freedom. Berkman had initially done very well at school but then began blowing off his school work to read revolutionary political works. He turned in a paper titled "There Is No God," resulting in a one-year demotion as punishment. This punishment forced him to be with younger children, and Berkman recounted, "My senior class looks down upon [me] with undisguised contempt. I feel disgraced, humiliated."

Berkman's mother died when he was 18, and his uncle became responsible for him, but young Sasha had contempt for his uncle, who Sasha viewed as cowardly and materialistic. Sasha was caught stealing copies of the annual school exam, and he was expelled and labeled a "nihilist conspirator." Soon after, in 1888, Berkman immigrated to the United States, where he joined a group of anarchists in New York City who admired Johann Most. And soon after that, he became Emma Goldman's lover and ultimately her lifelong friend.

In 1892, Alexander Berkman, at age 21, became a household name in the United States for his failed assassination attempt of Henry Clay Frick. Berkman later recounted the arousing of his passion and his justification for attempting to kill Frick. He tells us how Emma Goldman (protecting her identity, he refers to her as "the Girl"), a year older than him, waves a newspaper and cries out, "Have you read it? . . . Homestead. Strikers shot. Pinkertons have killed women and children." Berkman tells us that Goldman's "words ring like the cry of a wounded animal, the melodious voice tinged with the harshness of bitterness—the bitterness of helpless agony."

Berkman recounts his contempt for the hypocrisy of the "philanthropist" Andrew Carnegie, who had chosen Frick to manage his company for the purpose of crushing the labor union. For Berkman, Frick is not simply an illegitimate authority, but evil in "his secret military preparations . . . the fortification of the Homestead steelworks; the erection of a high board fence, capped by barbed wire and provided with loopholes for sharpshooters; the hiring of an army of Pinkerton thugs."

Recounting his justification for killing Frick, Berkman concludes: "The removal of a tyrant is not merely justifiable; it is the highest duty of every true revolutionist. Human life is, indeed, sacred and inviolate. But the killing of a tyrant, of an enemy of the People, is in no way to be considered as the taking of a life. A revolutionist would rather perish a thousand times than be guilty of what is ordinarily called murder. In truth, murder and Attentat [a political deed of violence to awaken the consciousness of the people against their oppressors] are to me opposite terms. To remove a tyrant is an act of liberation, the giving of life and opportunity to an oppressed people."

Berkman felt that he had thought through the consequences of his action, believing his act would help his cause of anarchism. He believed that the value of his action "very much depends upon my explanation" which "offers me a rare opportunity for a broader agitation of our ideas." For Berkman, "the People" misunderstood the cause of anarchism because they had been prejudiced by the capitalist press. "They must be enlightened; that is our glorious task." In the end, Berkman tragically failed to think through the consequences of his actions. His attempt at explaining his actions to the public was a pathetic failure, and the consequences of his actions were tragic for the Homestead strikers, for other workers, and for the cause of anarchism.

At his trial, Berkman refused a lawyer and instead wrote a speech in German because his English was then still poor. He read it to the court, which used a German translator who was incompetent, and the judge cut Berkman off before he was done. And so Berkman's statement thus failed to enlighten the public.

Prior to Berkman's assassination attempt, a majority of U.S. newspapers had been supportive of the Homestead strikers, but Berkman's violence undermined public sympathy for the strikers, and thus Berkman's action was one reason for the strike failure. Especially humiliating for Berkman was that his failed assassination attempt garnered public admiration for Frick, who became seen less as a villain and more a survivor. Moreover, throughout the United States, this defeat at Homestead demoralized workers and emboldened owners to successfully de-unionize other workers.

Berkman's act of violence also hurt his cause of anarchism in immediate and long-term ways. After Berkman's assassination attempt, a mob destroyed a utopian anarchist community near Homestead. Moreover, because of Berkman's violent actions (coupled later with the self-identified anarchist Leon Czolgosz's assassination of McKinley), anarchism was now more easily marginalized as nothing but a violent philosophy. This must have been especially painful for the mature Berkman, who took great lengths in his 1929 book *Now and After: The ABC of Communist Anarchism* to describe how the essence of anarchism is the antithesis of violence, especially compared to the violence inherent in capitalism.

Following his failed assassination attempt, Berkman beat himself up, "My failure to accomplish the desired result is grievously exasperating, and I feel deeply humiliated." To make matters worse, Berkman's assassination attempt was condemned by many of those whom he had thought would praise it. Berkman was hurt when he was criticized by the strikers, and he was angered by the attack on him from his former mentor Johann

Most. Before Berkman's actions, Most had reversed himself on the value of violent "propaganda by the deed," saying that it was doomed to be misunderstood in the United States and thus would have negative consequences for the cause of anarchism.

Later in his life, Berkman himself disapproved of the assassination of McKinley. He concluded that in Russia, political oppression is popularly felt, however, "the scheme of political subjection is more subtle in America. . . .The real despotism of republican institutions is far deeper, more insidious, because it rests on the popular delusion of self-government and independence. That is the subtle source of democratic tyranny, and, as such, it cannot be reached with a bullet."

Historian John William Ward in his 1970 article "Violence, Anarchy, and Alexander Berkman" concluded that acts of violence against U.S. authorities fail because most Americans accept the idea that the United States is a uniquely free society. Ward noted, "Violence has been used again and again to support the structure of authority in American society. We are only puzzled when violence is used to attack that structure."

To attempt to kill Frick, Berkman stripped Frick of his humanity. As Ward noted, "Berkman has turned him into an object, a symbol of the repressive forces of capitalism. It is not Frick, the man, but Frick, the symbol, there before Berkman. Berkman must do the same to himself. He must deny his own humanity, his own feeling, and turn himself into an instrument of a cause, a symbol of a revolutionary ideology." Early in prison, Berkman's sentimental glorification of the People, noted Ward, "provides no room in his affections for ordinary, flawed human beings. He shrinks from familiarity with other prisoners."

However, Berkman's humanity and attitude toward his fellow prisoners evolved. Berkman recounted that at first, "I would aid them, as in duty bound to the victims of social injustice. But I cannot be friends with them. . . . I must give them my intellectual sympathy; they touch no chord in my heart." But Berkman, in prison, recognized how conditions can damage people, and he more fully accepted humanity's flaws and his own flaws, recounting, "I recall with sadness the first years of my imprisonment, and my coldly impersonal valuation of social victims."

Ward believed, "The remarkable thing is that he learns what it means to be human, that to love humanity means to love the least of men. As he moves from a cold and abstract idealism to a warm and sympathetic identification, even to an unembarrassed and untroubled acceptance of the reality of homosexual love."

Shortly after being imprisoned, Berkman planned his suicide; and in prison, he unsuccessfully attempted to hang himself. In 1906, after serving 14 years of his sentence, Berkman was released at age 35. Tormented by nightmares and having difficulty adjusting to life outside prison, he again considered suicide but agreed to go on a speaking tour with Goldman. On the tour, he purchased a gun to commit suicide but did not use it.

Berkman and Goldman, not long after reconnecting, discovered that they had lost sexual passion for one another, and Berkman became attracted to another woman. In 1907, Goldman, who would remain a loyal friend to Berkman for his entire life, invited him to become the editor of her journal *Mother Earth*. Berkman served as editor of *Mother Earth* from 1907 to 1915, and it became the leading anarchist publication in the United States.

In 1916, Berkman moved to San Francisco and started a new anarchist newspaper, the *Blast*. Not long after his move, a San Francisco bomb explosion was initially attributed to him, but blame then shifted to two local labor activists, Thomas Mooney and Warren Billings. Although neither were anarchists, Berkman came to their aid, raising a defense fund, hiring lawyers, and organizing a national campaign on their behalf. After Mooney was sentenced to death and Billings to life imprisonment, Berkman organized protests outside the U.S. embassy in Russia, resulting in international political pressure; this ultimately led to the commuting of Mooney's death sentence. Billings and Mooney both were pardoned and freed in 1939. So Berkman, who had tried to kill one man, helped save another's life.

With the U.S. government's entry into World War I and its creation of a military draft, Goldman and Berkman formed the

No Conscription League; and they were prosecuted and imprisoned for this and ultimately deported to Russia. Berkman, similar to Goldman, became disillusioned with Lenin and Bolshevik tyranny, and he published *The Bolshevik Myth* in 1925. Around that time, we again see Berkman's altruism. He organized a fund for aging anarchists and drew international attention to the plight of anarchist prisoners in the Soviet Union.

Having moved to France, Berkman spent a good part of the remainder his life struggling with money and health issues. His cousin Modska Aronstam (changing his last name to Stein)—who had been a co-conspirator in the Frick assassination but had left the anarchist movement and had become a successful artist—sent Berkman money for his expenses. However, by the 1930s, Berkman's health had deteriorated. He had two unsuccessful operations on his prostate, the second surgery leaving him bedridden for several months. In constant pain and completely dependent on others financially and for his physical care, a 65-year-old Berkman committed suicide.

Alexander Berkman's life offers many lessons for anti-authoritarians who are politically passionate and who pride themselves on uncompromising ideological integrity. Berkman, like many other violent anti-authoritarians, viewed a need for material pleasures as weakness and a betrayal of the cause. Berkman denied himself even small consumer pleasures—and he expected the same from his fellow anarchists, which created friction with his comrades. He lectured them, "Every penny spent for ourselves was so much taken from the Cause. . . . [L]uxury is a crime, worse, a weakness." Berkman was, Goldman tells us, "fanatic to the highest degree."

However, Berkman's insufficient attention to money created humiliating financial dependency for him, compounding his pain. Throughout their lives, Berkman was at odds with Goldman and her view of money. After being deported with Emma Goldman to Russia, Berkman was robbed while carrying their entire travel fund. Goldman became upset, "Our independence! . . . [I]t's gone." For Goldman, that money was crucial to their independence, "We did not have to beg or cringe like so many others. . . . We had been able to keep our self-respect and to refuse any truck with the dictatorship." But Berkman mocked her for thinking of money and not appreciating the fact that he wasn't killed. For Goldman, "I simply could not face the possibility of eating out of the hand of the Bolshevik State." Throughout Berkman's life and especially late in life, his financial dependency on others was humiliating, one of several painful reasons for his suicide.

In *Sasha and Emma*, Paul Avrich and Karen Avrich report that while Berkman was "admired by his friends for his brains and his nerve, he also could be self-centered and dogmatic. . . . Yet he possessed a gentle demeanor, a disarming humor. Within him mingled the visionary and the subversive, the humane and the harsh, the passionate and the pitiless." His cousin Modska's daughter recalled that when she was a child, Berkman "often came to our apartment in New York, a sweet and charming man." The Avriches note, "Sasha had a way with children; they were drawn instinctively to him, and he was indulgent and affectionate in return, treating them with patience, kindness, and respect."

Among anti-authoritarians who have acted violently, Alexander Berkman is not dismissed by most historians as "mentally ill" or a "nut." Unfortunately, other violent anti-authoritarians are so dismissed, and so the lessons from their life are ignored, which compounds the tragedy of their lives.

Leon Czolgosz

The man who assassinated President William McKinley was Leon Czolgosz (1873–1901). The socially awkward Czolgosz is routinely dismissed by historians as "mentally ill" or a "nut," but Czolgosz's tragic life has lessons worth considering.

Leon was born in Michigan, and his mother died when he was ten years old. The 1893 financial crash put him out of work, and he became interested first in socialism and then in anarchism. At age 25, he moved back with his father on his father's farm but did not get along with his stepmother, and Leon did little to help out.

Forensic psychiatrist L. Vernon Briggs in his 1921 book *The Manner of Man That Kills* reported family and friends' observations of Czolgosz. Leon's sister, Victoria, described him as a nice boy who would read and sleep a good deal of the time and preferred being alone. His brother said that Leon got called names. Their father said that Leon was quiet and did not play with other children, but in most other ways he was an ordinary child. Leon's sister-in-law said that he "did not like it if you talked to him too much" and that he liked being alone. All agreed he was fond of reading and was the best educated member of the family. A neighbor said it was strange that Czolgosz could ever have assassinated McKinley, as Leon would never kill a fly, instead brushing them off or perhaps catching them and letting them go.

Czolgosz became a recluse, and when he finally found people he desired to connect with—other anarchists—and reached out to them, he was tragically rebuffed. Czolgosz had been inspired after hearing Emma Goldman speak; and in a brief encounter with her, he remarked to Goldman that he would like to meet other anarchists. Goldman tried to help him make connections. However, when Czolgosz did meet other anarchists, owing to his extreme social awkwardness, they were made anxious by him. Much of the anarchist community believed Czolgosz might be a police spy, and they issued a warning about him in their *Free Society* newspaper.

After gunning down McKinley, Czolgosz was coherent and offered a clear rationale for his action: "I know other men who believe what I do, that it would be a good thing to kill the President and to have no rulers. I have heard that at the meetings in public halls. . . . Emma Goldman was the last one I heard. She said she did not believe in government nor in rulers. . . . I don't believe in voting, it is against my principles. I am an anarchist. I don't believe in marriage. I believe in free love. I fully understood what I was doing when I shot the President. I realized that I was sacrificing my life. I am willing to take the consequences."

While Czolgosz had an ideological motive to assassinate McKinley, he also was overwhelmed by his life's painfulness and appears to have had a desperate desire to connect with like-minded people. He was willing to sacrifice his life, perhaps to have at least a short time of comradeship, or perhaps he envisioned the anarchist community's affection for him after he was put to death. After assassinating McKinley, Czolgosz legally protected Goldman, making it clear that, "She did not tell me to kill McKinley." Without this statement, public opinion and authorities were ready to convict Goldman as an accomplice in the assassination.

Czolgosz's jury deliberated for only an hour to convict him, and a month later in 1901, he was electrocuted. Among his last words were, "I killed the President because he was the enemy of the good people—the good working people."

Most anarchists were upset with Czolgosz's actions and angry with Emma Goldman for her support of him, but Goldman's compassion makes sense. Not only had she inspired Czolgosz to act and perhaps felt some guilt about that, she also likely felt sorry for this bashful lonely guy who had reached out to her anarchist comrades and had gotten rebuffed—but who then nobly protected her from being prosecuted.

When I have been in anti-authoritarian communities, there has often been a socially awkward person who reminds me of Leon Czolgosz, and I think about the anarchists who rebuffed him and who then later felt great guilt about having done so.

Ted Kaczynski

While Czolgosz, to the extent he is written about at all, is dismissed as a pathetic nut with nothing to teach us, Ted Kaczynski (born in 1942) is well known, but few see his life as having anything to teach, viewing him only as terrifyingly insane.

Kaczynski, who came to be known as the Unabomber, is one of the most violent anti-authoritarians in U.S. history. Of all the public figures I profile in this book, Ted Kaczynski's story is, for me, the most tragic—tragic, of course, for his murder victims; tragically traumatizing for his injury victims and near-miss victims; tragic for the position that he put his family members in; tragic for enabling authoritarians to marginalize causes that many nonviolent anti-authoritarians care about; and tragic for him.

Between 1978 and 1995, Kaczynski's bombs killed three people and injured 23 others. While some of his victims had positions of power in his hated "industrial society," others did not (for example, a murdered computer store owner and an injured secretary and graduate student). And in an early failed attempt to blow up an airplane by placing a bomb in its cargo hold, anti-authoritarians who held his same views could well have been killed if the bomb had worked.

Ted Kaczynski placed his own family, especially his brother David, in a nightmarishly tragic position. Once David read what came to be called the "Unabomber Manifesto" (*Industrial Society and Its Future*), David realized that it was Ted's work, and David had to decide between informing on his brother or complicity in further deaths. So David reported his brother to authorities. Once Ted Kaczynski was brought to trial, in order to save him from the death penalty, David and their mother Wanda helped portray Ted as being seriously mentally ill, which enraged Ted against them; as he knew that his political reasons for the bombings would now not be taken seriously.

Ted Kaczynski's biographer Alston Chase reported that much of what the world heard about Kaczynski's mental status was not true. Chase documents how Kaczynski was psychopathologized for two reasons: the concerns of his family, who wanted to spare him the death penalty; and to meet the needs of societal authorities who wanted to dismiss his societal critiques. Chase came to discover that "Kaczynski is neither the extreme loner he has been made out to be nor in any clinical sense mentally ill."

Intelligence testing conducted on Ted in the fifth grade determined that he had a "genius" 167 IQ. As a result, he skipped the sixth grade, which made it difficult for him to socialize. Chase reported, "He would never be accepted by his new classmates, who were at least a year older. The bigger boys bullied and teased him." But it is a myth that he was a complete social outcast. Robert McFadden reported in 1996 in the *New York Times* that in high school, Ted's fellow math club member and his closest friend, Russell Mosny, played chess with him, and they talked about equations and physics in Ted's attic bedroom. Mosny recalled, "He was just quiet and shy until you got to know him. Once he knew you, he could talk and talk." Ted was accepted at Harvard, and at age 16 he began his freshman year.

Early on at Harvard, Kaczynski joined the Harvard band, played pickup basketball, and made a few friends. His housemate Gerald Burns recalled hanging out with Kaczynski at an all-night cafeteria and arguing about the philosophy of Kant. The Harvard health-services doctor who interviewed Kaczynski, as required for all freshmen, observed: "Good impression created. Attractive, mature for age, relaxed. . . . Talks easily, fluently and pleasantly . . . likes people and gets on well with them. . . . Exceedingly stable, well integrated and feels secure within himself."

However, in Kaczynski's sophomore year at Harvard, he fell victim to a disturbingly abusive experiment by one of the most renowned figures in the history of U.S. psychology, Henry Murray. Experimental subjects were told they would be debating personal philosophy with a fellow student; but instead, they were subjected to abusive personal attacks that were purposely brutalizing. Kaczynski and other subjects were instructed to write an essay detailing their personal beliefs and aspirations, and the essay was given to an attorney who would belittle them based on the disclosures they had made. This humiliation was filmed, and played back to the subjects. Thus, Kaczynski had personal reasons for rage and for distrust of the elites who managed society.

Kaczynski began his 1995 manifesto this way: "The Industrial Revolution and its consequences have been a disaster for the human race." He then discussed how the increasing growth and worship of technological and industrial systems have subverted individual freedom and destroyed our natural environment. The manifesto is approximately 35,000 words and covers many extraneous areas, and with respect to the tyranny of giant industrial-technological systems, for readers familiar with public intellectuals Kirkpatrick Sale and John Zerzan, Kaczynski's work may be simplistic, unoriginal, and unenjoyable to read but not insane.

However, politics—not science—dictated that Ted Kaczynski be labeled insane. Against Kaczynski's wishes, his defense attorneys launched a "mental illness" defense for him. Defense expert psychologist Karen Bronk Froming concluded that Kaczynski exhibited a "predisposition to schizophrenia," citing his anti-technology views as having cemented her conclusion. Sally Johnson, a forensic psychiatrist with the U.S. Bureau of Prisons, provisionally diagnosed Kaczynski with "Paranoid Type" schizophrenia, largely based on her view that he harbored "delusional beliefs" about the threats posed by technology.

In addition to Kaczynski's views on technology, other so-called "evidence" for his mental illness included his personal habits and unkempt appearance living alone in a cabin in Montana. But as Chase—a former Harvard student, former professor, and Montana resident—points out, "His cabin was no messier than the offices of many college professors. The Montana wilds are filled with escapists like Kaczynski (and me). Celibacy and misanthropy are not diseases. Nor was Kaczynski really so much of a recluse."

In the end, Kaczynski's violent behaviors gave authoritarians ammunition to not only marginalize him as mentally ill, but to discredit as "Kaczynski-like" other critics of the authoritarian use of technology. Kaczynski's violence may have gotten him attention but ultimately hurt his cause.

Berkman, Czolgosz, and Kaczynski are certainly not the only anti-authoritarians in U.S. history to gain attention for themselves with violence at the expense of the cause of anti-authoritarianism.

In 1969, the violent Weatherman (later called the Weather Underground) splintered off from the nonviolent Students for a Democratic Society. The 2002 film documentary *The Weather Underground* portrays how these anti-authoritarians' rage over the injustice of the Vietnam War, along with powerlessness in stopping the war through peaceful means, resulted in their resorting to violence, including multiple bombings. This combination of rage over injustice and impotency in effecting change made them, a former Weather Underground member later acknowledged, "crazy." Here we can clearly see how that rage-impotency combination acted like a disinhibiting drug enabling moral and strategic justifications for violent actions that, as some former Weather Underground members acknowledged, did not later seem moral or strategic at all. The greatest beneficiaries of the Weather Underground violence were U.S. authoritarians, particularly Richard Nixon, as it provided him with ammunition for his "law-and-order" presidential re-election campaign and aided his 1972 landslide victory.

Some U.S. anti-authoritarians have convinced themselves of the possibility of the effectiveness of violence by pointing to John Brown (1800–1859), but Brown's violence was effective only because of extraordinary and exceptional circumstances. By the time of his death, Brown was viewed as a terrorist by many white Americans, beginning with his role in the Pottawatomie, Kansas revenge massacre that killed five people. More famously, Brown led the raid on the federal armory at Harpers Ferry, designed to foment a slave rebellion. At Harpers Ferry, several people were killed and wounded. Brown became an abolitionist martyr when he was captured, placed on trial, and hanged. The Harpers Ferry raid failed to foment a slave rebellion but successfully further polarized slavery proponents and abolitionists, escalated tensions, and helped provoke secession resulting in the Civil War.

While Brown was in fact successful in becoming an abolitionist martyr, U.S. history has repeatedly shown that individual political violence is ineffective in gaining desired results without at least some degree of support among the U.S. ruling class. Brown's Harpers Ferry assault came at a time when there were U.S. senators who were slave abolitionists and when some in the ruling elite had financial reasons to invade the South, profit from war, and further centralize authority. Thus, Brown's inflaming the South and creating another provocation to attack a federal fort and secede from the union wasn't just good news for many abolitionists. It was also good news for at least some of the elite, which was not the case at all for the actions of Berkman, Czolgosz, or Kaczynski.

In general in U.S. history, while state violence routinely succeeds at putting down dissent, citizen violence directed at authoritarianism usually subverts the cause of anti-authoritarianism.

9

Political, Spiritual, Philosophical, and Psychological Lenses for Anti-Authoritarians:
Anarchism, Buddhism, the God of Spinoza and Einstein, and the Enneagram

Anti-authoritarians tend to resist the dogmas of both secular and religious authorities. There are, however, lenses to view the world that can be attractive for anti-authoritarians. Rather than offering an encyclopedia of such lenses, I will present those that I have been drawn to and have found most useful for anti-authoritarians whom I've known.

Anarchism, Buddhism, the God of Spinoza and Einstein, and the Enneagram are each book-length topics, but I have tried to provide a sense of them. With each of these lenses, an anti-authoritarian can feel at home questioning, challenging, and resisting illegitimate authority. With each, there are no hierarchies and no coercions, and compassion is valued while badges are not. Within each of these lenses, there are different schools of thought, interpretations, and emphases; thus, there are choices within these choices.

Anarchism

In one sense, anarchism is a political philosophy, but in another sense, it is a belief about human nature, a faith in the goodness of human beings.

Anarchism rejects not only state control but also the hierarchical organization of human beings in which people have unequal power. Anarchism believes that people can best achieve autonomy, freedom, and cooperation within egalitarian organizations. Anarchism is positively impassioned by a thirst for freedom in all spheres of life, and it is negatively impassioned by a resentment with coercion. For critics of anarchism, those passions make anarchism immature and dangerous. But for advocates of anarchism, those passions make it highly mature and benevolent.

What's most radical about anarchism, for me, is its faith that human beings can organize themselves without *fear*. This is a radical notion, because people are so accustomed to being controlled by fear that they don't even notice it The state, whatever ideology it claims, keeps people in line using policing authorities and prisons. Orthodox religions keep congregants in line using the fear of God, clergy, and hell. Standard schools keep students in line using grades, suspensions, expulsions, and threats to withhold diplomas. And employees are kept in line by their fear of being fired and falling into poverty.

Authoritarians routinely smear anarchism as advocating chaos and violence. Some of these authoritarians are ignorant of anarchism, while others are not. It is true some anarchists have used violence to achieve their aims, but anarchists don't seek a violent and chaotic society. Informed authoritarians who spread falsehoods about anarchism fear that should people actually grasp the truth of anarchism, many would be attracted to it.

"Anarchism," according to Alexander Berkman, "means that you should be free; that no one should enslave you, boss you, rob you, or impose upon you. It means that you should be free to do the things you want to do; and that you should not be compelled to do what you don't want to do. It means that you should have a chance to choose the kind of a life you want to live, and live it without anybody interfering. It means that the next fellow should have the same freedom as you, that everyone should have the same rights and liberties. It means that all men are brothers, and that they should live like brothers, in peace and harmony. That is to say, that there should be no war, no violence used by one set of men against another, no monopoly and no poverty, no oppression, no taking advantage of your fellow-man." Of course, Berkman clearly meant to include all genders here—or else he would not have had Emma Goldman's lifelong loyalty.

Free association is paramount in anarchism, which is optimistic about humanity and its capacity to cooperate. In Emma Goldman's essay "Anarchism: What It Really Stands For," she wrote: "Anarchism stands for a social order based on the free grouping of individuals for the purpose of producing real social wealth; an order that will guarantee to every human being free access to the earth and full enjoyment of the necessities of life, according to individual desires, tastes, and inclinations."

The vision of a society without coercion is attractive to many people—intoxicatingly attractive to some people. And anarchism's attractiveness makes it so threatening for various authoritarians that anarchism is their common enemy. For example, in the 1930s, Nazi Germany, fascist Italy, Stalinist Soviet Union, Western capitalist nations, and the Catholic Church all played a role in destroying a successful anarchist society in Spain.

Authoritarians are horrified by anarchism because they believe that without coercions, people would run amok and life would be fraught with chaos and violence. The reality is that coercions do "work" to keep certain populations in line. Social critic Alfie Kohn, in his book *Punished by Rewards*, documents that coercions such as rewards and punishments can be effective in shaping behaviors of laboratory animals, children, institutionalized adults such as prisoners, and others who are dependent on authorities for the necessities of their survival. In order to most effectively control people's behavior, research shows that people have to be needy enough of the rewards and terrified enough of the negative reinforcements and punishments. And so there is actually an incentive for authoritarians to keep people alienated and infantilized, as such people are easier to control. Coercions can effectively control behavior in certain populations, but not without humiliation, resentment, and rage. Not coincidentally,

U.S. society is replete with people feeling humiliated, resentful, and enraged.

In anarchism, people perform activities that they desire to perform, and so coercion is unnecessary. However, in U.S. society, people are mostly performing activities they dislike. In 2013, the *Los Angeles Times* reported, "Seven out of 10 workers have 'checked out' at work or are 'actively disengaged,' according to a recent Gallup survey." The more one is disengaged from an activity and dependent on authorities for survival, the more coercion is necessary to maintain order.

Anarchism's opposition to coercion is not an advocacy of chaos but rather a faith that human beings can be organized with love. A key belief of anarchism is *mutual aid* (discussed later) and cooperation. This requires altruism. Concern for others is not created by coercive rewards and punishments. Kohn's review of the research confirms that children whose parents use rewards to motivate them are less cooperative and generous children than their peers who are not so coerced. Instead of coercions, it is the experience of love and the modeling of love that best creates caring and cooperative people.

In U.S. society, anarchism is not only a radical political idea but also a radical psychological one. Anarchism asserts that human beings can have community without being dominated by fear. Most of us, consciously or unconsciously, live with great fear and anxiety. Given our ordinary fear-based existence, when people experience fearlessness through an extraordinary experience, that fearlessness can feel so exhilaratingly different that it can be intoxicating, sometimes so intoxicating that we can become manic. The more fear pervades a culture, the more extraordinary is the experience of fearlessness, and the more likely it will be so intoxicating that it can cause us to behave irrationally. Fearlessness does not intoxicate people who are accustomed to it.

There are anarchists who are rigid ideologues. For them, attempting to survive in an economic system based on the coercion of money is so shameful that they either deny their hypocrisies or self-flagellate for their failure to live up to their ideals.

In either case, the rigid ideologue is not going to be much fun to be around. In current society, if we have no money, we cannot pay the bills that most of us have. Without money, we are likely to become either a financial burden on friends or family, at the mercy of some of the most oppressive authorities in society, or dead. The reality is that while all aspects of the anarchist ideal cannot be implemented in non-anarchist society, some aspects can be implemented, even within the workplace. For example, the publisher of this book, AK Press, is an egalitarian organization without hierarchical control but accepts the present reality of money. There are many other such non-hierarchical workplaces in the United States.

Among anarchists, there are several different schools of thought that emphasize different aspects of anarchism. *Anarcho-syndicalism*, Noam Chomsky explains, is a particular variety of anarchism which is concerned primarily, though not solely, with control over the workplace. "It took for granted that working people ought to control their own work, its conditions . . . control the enterprises in which they work, along with communities, so they should be associated with one another in free associations, and . . . democracy of that kind should be the foundational elements of a more general free society." Another anarchist school of thought is *anarcho-primitivism*, a major concern of which is gaining freedom from the tyranny of large-scale authoritarian technology. Among different schools, there are also different views as to how to achieve an anarchist society.

Anti-authoritarian perspectives like anarchism don't simply provide an individual with an ideology. Discovering a belief system that rings true can also serve as a vehicle for connecting with like-minded people. In the 1880s and 1890s in the United States, if you were an alienated anti-authoritarian, you could go to the Lower East Side in New York City and hang out at places such as Sach's Café on Suffolk Street or Justus Schwab's basement tavern on First Street which called itself a "gathering place for all bold, joyful, freedom-loving spirits." Here you would meet and connect with all kinds of anti-authoritarians. Your belief system would be a vehicle for a support group and provide an opportunity to connect with friends and lovers. That's what happened to Alexander Berkman, Emma Goldman, and many others who created a rich social network for themselves that mitigated some of the pain of being an anarchist in the United States. In 1900 when Schwab died, 2,000 mourners followed the hearse down Second Avenue.

Buddhism

In *The Religions of Man*, religious studies scholar Huston Smith states, "Buddha preached a religion devoid of authority," and so, not surprisingly, Buddhism appeals to many anti-authoritarians. Buddhism is a rebellion against what is normally considered religion.

Smith detailed how Buddhism is "a religion almost entirely dissociated from each of the six corollaries of religion": (1) authority; (2) ritual; (3) speculation; (4) tradition; (5) God's supreme power to confer grace; and (6) mystery. In Buddhism, authority is confronted in several manners. Born into the top of India's Hindu caste system, the Buddha challenged that hierarchy's legitimacy. Rituals, rites, and prayers were frowned upon by the Buddha who considered it a waste of time speculating on that which one can never know for certain, and he told his followers to reject traditions if they had no value in reducing suffering. Rather than depending on God's grace and resigning oneself to fatalism, the Buddha preached intense self-effort to a path that can lead one out of suffering in one's own lifetime. And finally, unlike figureheads of other religions, Smith noted, "Buddha preached a religion devoid of the supernatural."

Buddhism is in direct contrast to what we normally view as a religion. Buddhism is empirical, as one's direct personal experience is the final test for truth. Buddhism is scientific, aimed at uncovering the cause and effect. Buddhism is pragmatic, concerned with problem solving. Buddhism is psychological, in its study of human nature. Buddhism is therapeutic, aimed at alleviating suffering. And Buddhism is democratic, in its attack on the hierarchy of the caste system.

Siddhartha Gautama of the Sakyas (approximately 560–480 BCE) was born in northern India into wealth and royalty. At age 29, deeply discontented, he rejected his society and took the next six years to discover the root of his despair and the solution to it. He probed the minds of Hindu masters, then joined a band of ascetics but ultimately rejected the path of asceticism. Finally, he sat under a fig tree, which has since become known as the Bo tree (short for *Bodhi* or enlightenment), and with a combination of meditation, rigorous thought, and mystic concentration, he remained in a rapture of sorts for 49 days. When he opened himself to the world again, he had become the Buddha, meaning the Enlightened One or the Awakened One.

The Buddha would spend the next 45 years teaching what he had discovered about the roots of suffering and solutions for it. "Perhaps the most striking thing about him," philosopher James Pratt noted in *The Pilgrimage of Buddhism and a Buddhist Pilgrimage*, "is his almost unique combination of a cool scientific head with the devoted sympathy of a warm and loving heart."

We in the West commonly learn that the essence of Buddhism is the "Four Noble Truths": that life is suffering; the cause of suffering is desire; the cure for suffering is the cessation of craving; and that this can be done through the Eightfold Path (of the right knowledge, aspiration, speech, behavior, livelihood, effort, mindfulness, and absorption). This is not wrong, but it does not truly capture the essence of Buddhism.

In Buddhism, it is certainly true that craving ephemeral pleasures is a bad idea—not because it is shamefully sinful but because we become enslaved by it, as these pleasures will be transient and interfere with peace, freedom, and equanimity. In Buddhism, it is not a good idea to desire things that in the long run will bring us more pain than pleasure. However, for the Buddha, not *all* desires are evil.

"It is perfectly plain that the Buddha desired a number of things," Pratt noted. The Buddha was filled with pity for human suffering, and he desired alleviation of that suffering. He dedicated his life to disseminating truths that would liberate people from misery, and he trained others to spread these truths. The Buddha actually taught that there are "bad" and "good" desires. It is a good desire to want less ignorance and more compassion. "The two cardinal virtues of Buddhism," Pratt tells us are "wisdom and love."

The Buddha saw great ignorance about suffering and attempted to simplify the major cause of self-inflicted human despair. While suffering is caused by societal oppressions, suffering can also be a result of our own self-oppression, specifically through self-preoccupation. Pratt summarizes: "The great bulk of our woe, thinks the Buddha, most of us bring upon ourselves quite needlessly by viewing everything from its bearing upon our little selves."

In Buddhism, compassion and generosity are not—as they are viewed in most other religions—righteous good deeds, but instead are pragmatic vehicles for pulling us out of our self-absorption. If one is attached to getting recognition, praise, or other rewards from God or fellow congregants for one's generosity, one is self-focused and will not receive the psychological benefits of moving out of one's self-preoccupation.

The path away from self-induced suffering is moving out of self-absorption, yet, in a tragic comedy, virtually the entirety of the modern mental health profession promotes self-focus. Psychiatrists' most common treatment consists of "medication management" in which patients are directed to self-focus, as they are asked questions solely about their symptoms so as to tweak their drug prescription. Even doctors who conduct "talk therapy" may direct emotionally suffering people to become even more self-focused. For Buddhist teachers, a focus solely on our symptoms and our feelings will only give them greater power over us.

Buddhist "therapy," in contrast, consists of dialoguing with a person in a way that pulls them out of self-absorption. This is most apparent in Zen Buddhism, which Smith tells us, "is a world of bewildering dialogues, obscure conundrums, stunning paradoxes, flagrant contradictions, and abrupt non-sequiturs." He offers some examples: "An ancient master, whenever he was asked the meaning of Zen, lifted one of his fingers. That was his entire answer. Another kicked a ball. Still another slapped the inquirer in the face." The Zen therapist knows that without provoking us out of our ordinary consciousness, we will not be able to see life differently.

As is the case for anarchism, there are different schools of thought in Buddhism with different emphases and differing ideas about therapeutic methods and techniques. Chögyam Trungpa (1939–1987), Buddhist scholar, teacher and founder of the Naropa Institute, was a controversial figure for his personal drug and alcohol use, his sexual choices, and his provocative style. But Trungpa was sought after by the famous and non-famous for instructions on meditation. In his *The Myth of Freedom and the Way of Meditation*, Trungpa tells us, "Meditation is not a matter of trying to achieve ecstasy, spiritual bliss or tranquility, nor is it attempting to become a better person"; instead the goal is "to expose and undo our neurotic games, our self-deceptions, our hidden fears and hopes." The purpose of mediation is greater enlightenment, including becoming "aware of our awareness," especially of those mental events that result in suffering.

From the perspective of Buddhism, most mental health professionals are trained to be out of touch with reality—to be *psychotic* and *delusional*—to the extent that they are trained to view the causes of human suffering as chemical imbalances and defective genes. To assert the true cause of human suffering would put professionals in conflict with oppressive hierarchies and a consumer economy based on self-focus and attachments. And mental health professionals tend to comply with societal norms rather than rebel against them.

The God of Spinoza and Einstein

When it came to religion in the 1950s and 1960s, Lenny Bruce was perhaps the most outrageously courageous Jew around, as he was unintimidated by authorities and paid a legal and career price for his words. In the 1650s and 1660s, the most outrageously courageous Jew was Baruch Spinoza (1632–1677), who so infuriated Jewish religious authorities that they excommunicated him, and who so enraged a religious fanatic that he attacked Spinoza with a knife in an unsuccessful assassination attempt.

The anti-authoritarian God of Spinoza can be more threatening to religious authoritarians than an atheist rejection of God. Religious authoritarians know that "Godless atheists" will have no influence over people who sense a force that is greater than they are; however, the anti-authoritarian God of Spinoza offers a real alternative for them.

The God of Spinoza is in no way the Biblical fatherly God who personally punishes individuals and populations for disobedience and who rewards for compliance. Spinoza's God doesn't have a "personality" and is in no way a "top-dog" in the hierarchy of life. Spinoza does not anthropomorphize God.

The God of Spinoza, instead, includes *all* aspects of nature and the universe, including its finite and infinite aspects and all of its laws—physical, psychological, and otherwise. Human beings are part of nature but limited in their capacity to understand all of nature. And thus Spinoza's idea of God compels a humility in the sense that we may connect to some of God but that it is rationally impossible to connect with all of God. So for Spinoza, someone who self-certainly claims to have God's truth is arrogant and delusional.

Philosophers debate whether Spinoza was a *pantheist* (God is all, and God and the universe are identical) or a *panetheist* (God is the soul of the universe, transcending the universe). However, there is no debate that the God of Spinoza has absolutely nothing to do with the God of Cecil B. DeMille's *The Ten Commandments*, whose God speaks with a deep powerful voice, gets pissed off, and cruelly punishes transgressors. Spinoza's God is just way too cool to do that kind of thing.

Spinoza wrote, "The greatest good is the knowledge of the union which the mind has with the whole of nature. . . .The more it understands the order of nature, the more easily it will be able to liberate itself from useless things." To know Spinoza's God is to know the truth of nature, to know its laws, and how the universe functions. That's why the anti-authoritarian scientist and humanitarian Albert Einstein (1879–1955) believed in the God of Spinoza.

"Einstein Believes in 'Spinoza's God'" was a 1929 headline in the *New York Times*. In response to a public criticism by a Boston cardinal that Einstein was a Godless atheist, Rabbi Herbert Goldstein sent Einstein a telegram asking him, "Do you believe in God?" Goldstein requested that he respond in 50 words but Einstein needed only 32: "I believe in Spinoza's God, who reveals himself in the lawful harmony of all that exists, but not in a God who concerns himself with the fate and the doings of mankind."

Just as religious authorities had accused Spinoza of being an atheist, Einstein also was similarly accused. In response to this atheist accusation, Einstein responded, "From the viewpoint of a Jesuit priest I am, of course, and have always been an atheist." Einstein called the idea of a personal God "a childlike one." However, Einstein rejected the "crusading spirit of the professional atheist whose fervor is mostly due to a painful act of liberation from the fetters of religious indoctrination received in youth." Instead, Einstein asserted, "I prefer an attitude of humility corresponding to the weakness of our intellectual understanding of nature and of our being."

"Einstein's God," concludes Einstein biographer Ronald Clark, "thus stood for an orderly system obeying rules which could be discovered by those who had the courage, the imagination, and the persistence to go on searching for them." Michael Gilmore, writing in *Skeptic*, concludes, "Einstein continued to search, even to the last days of his 76 years, but his search was not for the God of Abraham or Moses. His search was for the order and harmony of the world."

Einstein's view of God had pragmatic psychological value for him. Einstein biographer Walter Isaacson points out that for Einstein, a belief in something larger than himself produced a mixture of confidence and humility. "Given his proclivity toward being self-centered," Isaacson concludes, "these were welcome graces. Along with his humor and self-awareness, they helped him to avoid the pretense and pomposity that could have afflicted the most famous mind in the world."

Spinoza studied optics and made lenses for telescopes and microscopes, and, like Einstein, had an interest in all the laws of the universe. While Einstein focused mostly on the laws of physics, Spinoza was more of a psychologist, focusing more on the "mental laws" of human beings. Spinoza cared very much about what he called our "passions" and our emotions, which are part of our humanity and thus part of nature. For Spinoza, to sin, shame, or pathologize our emotions and our passions would sin, shame, or pathologize an aspect of God. However, what was clear to Spinoza was that our passions and our emotions can become tyrannical forces, destructive to ourselves and others.

Like Spinoza, Lenny Bruce realized that organized religion was in many ways an oppressive force, but had Bruce absorbed Spinoza's great work, *Ethics,* he might have realized that so too could his own passions and emotions be freedom-depriving tyrants. To be controlled solely by one's passions and emotions is to be incapable of wise judgments about ultimate consequences of behaviors. Like Bruce, Spinoza championed freedom and tolerance and opposed the tyranny and intolerance of political and religious authorities. But Spinoza also knew that we could tyrannize ourselves, making ourselves less tolerable to ourselves and others.

For Spinoza, one cannot be truly free if one is in bondage to one's emotions. As Spinoza scholar Joseph Ratner put it, the wise human being "does not madly satisfy or repress one passion at the expense of the rest of his nature." If only one aspect of our humanity takes over, then the remainder of our humanity—including our intellect and our need for justice, community, wisdom, beauty, autonomy, and freedom—will suffer.

Sinning, shaming, or pathologizing our emotions and passions actually gives them the power to tyrannize us; while simply acknowledging them gives them the influence they merit, which is not the power to dominate and control but merely the capacity to partially inform.

Spinoza was not an ascetic. He simply had few material needs. He had a view of happiness in which fame or material goods would not provide him with joy. For Spinoza, the incremental understanding of the universe, of nature, of life, and thus of God is the supreme source of happiness.

Both Spinoza and the Buddha are very much psychologists who came to similar conclusions. Both taught how to gain freedom from self-induced tyrannical attachments. And both practiced what they preached. There are other anti-authoritarian views of God, or at least less authoritarian views than the God of the Bible and the God of Cecil B. DeMille.

Thomas Paine, like Spinoza and Einstein, was condemned as an atheist for his attack on Christianity. However, Paine was not an atheist. After reflecting on religion a good part of his life, he came to believe in deism, the belief in a God that was the Cause or the Creator of the universe, not a God who interferes with the universe. For deists, a universe created by God does not require an intervening God. Deism was actually the belief system of many Enlightenment thinkers, including Benjamin Franklin and other so-called "founding fathers" but most of them, more politically astute than Paine, did not widely publicize these views.

Other anti-authoritarians are attracted to the God of Martin Buber (1878–1965). Buber's God or *Eternal Thou* is found not by looking high up in the sky but within an *I-Thou* encounter. An I-Thou relationship may be between lovers, friends, strangers, or even between a person and a pet. In this I-Thou encounter, there is no using of the other in any way. In the I-Thou, there is simply an experiencing of the other, and this results in the experience of God or the Eternal Thou. Buber recognized that life is not possible without some objectifications or what he called *I-It* (e.g., cutting down a tree and using it to fuel a fire to warm oneself), so Buber does not shame or sin the I-It. But Buber was troubled by a world that was increasingly entirely I-It and without I-Thou, and he famously said, "Without *It*, man cannot live, but he who lives with *It* alone is not a man."

Some anti-authoritarians sense a divine force that can liberate humans from social and economic injustices, and they selectively believe in only the anti-authoritarian aspects of the Bible. That would describe Harriet Tubman (profiled later), often called "Moses" for leading multiple slave escapes in the mid-nineteenth century. Tubman believed in a God that told both Moses and herself to free their people, but she scorned the part of the Bible that sanctioned slavery and promoted slave obedience. Similarly, Frederick Douglass (profiled later) espoused what today is called "liberation theology." Douglass confronted the hypocrisy of those who claim to be Christians but dishonor Jesus by their support of slavery.

The Enneagram

The Enneagram is a lens by which people can better understand themselves and others in a manner that is almost completely opposite from the way psychiatry categorizes people. Unlike psychiatry and the *DSM*, in the Enneagram there is no labeling pronouncements of "mentally healthy" and "mentally ill" people. Lenny Bruce's comedian mentor Joe Ancis was known to say, "The only normal people are the ones you don't know very well," and that is certainly the view of the Enneagram.

When I first heard about the Enneagram—composed of nine interrelated personality types—I reflexively rejected it. In my professional training, I had been exposed to not only the *DSM* but to several other classifying systems, and they all seemed unhelpful. It was ludicrous for me that mental health professionals, who themselves didn't seem all that together, were the people deciding who was normal and who was mentally ill. Psychiatrists and psychologists, more than the general public, appeared to me to get a control buzz out of classifying people; but their control was illusory, as human beings are not consistent and have a large range of potential behaviors. It seemed to me that putting people into boxes caused a great deal of harm and did very little good.

Thus, initially I had no interest in the Enneagram, and only by serendipity did I become intrigued by it. Three decades ago, a client demanded that I listen to audiotapes about the Enneagram by a Franciscan friar, Richard Rohr. This felt so ridiculous—to listen to one more personality system and this time from clergy—that the utter preposterousness of the request made me chuckle and comply. By luck, the tape was not completely rewound, and I began listening to it just as Rohr was matter-of-factly asserting that the nine "compulsions" of the nine Enneagram personality types included two compulsions that were omitted from the seven deadly sins (pride, greed, lust, envy, gluttony, wrath and sloth). I was surprised that a Catholic priest would assert this "defect" in the seven deadly sins list, and I was curious as to what were the two omitted sins/compulsions that are included in the Enneagram. These omissions, Rohr announced, were "deceit" including "self-deceit" and also "fear." Then he added, "America is capable of immense deceit . . . . . America has to own its capacity for deceit." I had never thought it possible that a Catholic priest could in any way be anti-authoritarian, and so I became curious about the Enneagram.

What I like and respect most about the Enneagram is that it is decidedly non-hierarchical. No doctor, researcher, clergy, guru, or any authority informs you of your personality type. Typing only has value if it is you who autonomously discovers it, and it only has value if you are brutally honest with yourself. It is easy to deceive others and yourself as to the true nature of your attachments and compulsions, and the Enneagram claims no scientific pretense that it can detect your deception. Typing yourself to be a personality that you'd prefer rather than who you truly are provides you with nothing—people who are ignorant of the Enneagram couldn't care less about your type, and people who understand the Enneagram know that no type has more or less status than any other.

The Enneagram is an egalitarian system. Within the continuum of each type, it is possible to bring ourselves and others both joy and suffering. In the Enneagram, every personality type has the potential to deteriorate, which, depending on the nature of one's culture may be labeled as mental illness, criminality, adjustment, or success. And similarly, each personality type can transcend its compulsions and create joy for themselves and others.

Among the Enneagram's recent well-known disseminators—Richard Rohr, Helen Palmer, and Don Richard Riso—all address the problem of how classification systems can neglect the uniqueness of the individual and disrespectfully pigeonhole people. But as Palmer notes, "The Enneagram . . . is not a fixed system," as it allows for movement within our own personality type continuum and even toward other types. To know another's personality type does not mean one can control or predict another's behavior, because typing does not tell you whether someone is transcending their compulsions or surrendering to them.

The idea that human beings have a variety of temperaments based on the domination of different ego attachments, passions, and compulsions rings true for me. Any observer of young children sees that they have different innate temperaments. I have found that the Enneagram rings true for many anti-authoritarians, including many adolescent anti-authoritarians, and it creates a more satisfying and meaningful life for them. While scientific objective validity in the area of personality may be illusory, the Enneagram is pragmatically valid for many anti-authoritarians.

The descriptions of ONE through NINE personality types vary slightly among Enneagram authors. Type ONE is called the "Reformer" or the "Perfectionist," compelled to be morally right, fearful of condemnation. Type TWO is called the

"Helper" or the "Giver," compelled to being needed, and fearful of not being loved. Type THREE is called the "Performer" or the "Motivator," compelled to be seen as successful, fearful of failure and not being admired. Type FOUR is called the "Artist" or the "Individualist," compelled to be unique, fearful of being defective. Type FIVE is called the "Thinker" or the "Observer," compelled to understanding and freedom, fearful of being overwhelmed by others. Type SIX is called the "Loyalist" and the "Doubter," compelled to have security and certainty, fearful of abandonment and insecurity. Type SEVEN is called the "Generalist" or the "Epicure," compelled to fun and pleasure, fearful of deprivation. Type EIGHT is called the "Leader" or the "Boss," compelled to self-reliance and power, fearful of submitting to others. Type NINE is called the "Peacemaker" or the "Mediator," compelled to union with people and the natural world, fearful of conflict. The number does not in any way signify any one type being superior to any other; but the numbers are significant in that, for example, the TWO is adjacent to both the THREE and ONE, and so the TWO has elements of ONE and THREE as well.

Within any Enneagram type, there is a wide continuum of behavior. Take type FIVE, the "Thinker." At their most transcendent best, the FIVE accurately observes the world, makes perceptive connections, and generates profound insights. The FIVE can also be a one-dimensional intellectual analyzer and a boring professor. And a deteriorated FIVE can become so fearful of human attachments that this leads to becoming reclusive and making intellectual connections based more on fears than on reality, resulting in becoming paranoid, delusional, impulsive, erratic, and even violent. System creators such as Baruch Spinoza, Albert Einstein, and Noam Chomsky appear to me as part of the FIVE group, but so too does Ted Kaczynski.

I say "appear to me" because we cannot be certain of the true personality type of others. We can easily mistype others based on how they appear which may not be who they really are. We should be wary of certainty when it comes to typing famous people, yet typing their public persona is one way of conveying the Enneagram and learning it. My apologies to Spinoza, Einstein, Chomsky, and Kaczynski if they are not FIVES—they just appear to me to be in my FIVE group.

The Enneagram offers a psychologically pragmatic way of transcending our ego attachments and compulsions. When we type ourselves, we are recognizing our imbalances of being too dominated or too devoid of an aspect of humanity, and so a path for balance and wholeness becomes quite clear. Returning to the FIVE who is compelled to observe, think, and analyze: the Enneagram does not shame or pathologize observing, thinking, and analyzing but instead informs the FIVE that if the FIVE has the courage to move outside one's head and engage the world, the FIVE will have more accurate observations and thus more superior insights. For all Enneagram types, if they transcend compulsive pursuits—and acquire a sense of humor about them—they will be rewarded with what they care most about.

Anti-authoritarians exist among each personality type, though, given their type, their anti-authoritarianism plays out very differently. Whether any type becomes an anti-authoritarian who challenges and resists illegitimate authority is determined by an array of many variables that includes luck and choice. Because of the subjective, unmeasurable, and indeed mysterious nature of the variables that determine one becoming an anti-authoritarian, scientific prediction is not possible. This is good news for anti-authoritarians, because if powerful authoritarians could scientifically predict anti-authoritarians through personality typing or genetic testing, they would try to eliminate them.

The Enneagram is similar to the teachings of the Buddha and Spinoza in that all these lenses are concerned with how we create suffering for ourselves and others by being enslaved by our ego attachments, passions, and compulsions. But the Enneagram is actually more satisfying for me in helping myself and others break loose from our self-enslavements because the Enneagram takes the next step. While all human beings have the general problem of being enslaved by ego attachments, passions, and compulsions, the Enneagram helps us understand how we are dominated by *different* ego attachments, passions, and compulsions.

Lessons From Anti-Authoritarians Who Have Helped Themselves and the Cause

Counterculture Beacons: Henry David Thoreau and Scott Nearing / Two-Strike Hitters: Frederick Douglass, Harriet Tubman, and Helen Keller / Modern Models: Jane Jacobs, Noam Chomsky, and George Carlin

The following anti-authoritarians who have helped themselves and the anti-authoritarian cause have experienced various degrees of assault by authoritarians but for the most part have not assaulted themselves. These anti-authoritarians would most likely admit that luck is certainly a factor in preventing a tragic life, but they also took advantage of opportunities that came their way.

These anti-authoritarians used their unique talents to the fullest. They also recognized the importance of relationships, specifically having mutually respectful and affectionate ones. None of them were broken by their standard schooling. Some of them were self-taught or educated outside of a standard school; others quit school; and others fought off the ill effects of schooling.

Overwhelming pain is the fuel for self-destructive behavior and violence, so wise reductions of pain—financially, interpersonally, and in one's physical health—are crucial for surviving and thriving. All of the following anti-authoritarians were committed to enjoying life, though some of their ideas about fun are uncommon ones.

None of the following anti-authoritarians are perfect because no person is perfect. While this group models some admirable characteristics, their lives also include hypocrisies, inconsistencies, and less admirable traits. However, it would be a mistake to dwell only on their imperfections and lose the wisdom and energy that their triumphs provide.

Counterculture Beacons: Henry David Thoreau and Scott Nearing

Henry David Thoreau and Scott Nearing are "off-the-grid" and "back-to-the-land" legends. They provide great lessons for anti-authoritarians who dream of escape from authoritarian society. While I've long shed my romanticized image of Thoreau and Nearing, I've also discovered that most who knew them had affection and respect for them despite their shortcomings.

Henry David Thoreau

During his lifetime, Henry David Thoreau (1817–1862) was not completely unknown outside of his hometown Concord, Massachusetts, but nowhere near as famous as he would become after his death. Today, Thoreau has worldwide fame for his essay "Civil Disobedience" (originally titled "Resistance to Civil Government"). In that essay, Thoreau challenged the authority of government that forces people to ignore their conscience and then to support unjust institutions.

Thoreau's refusal to pay a tax was a resistance to supporting the U.S. government's war with Mexico and the expansion of slavery; and for his tax resistance, he was briefly jailed. Unlike most Americans, including even abolitionists such as William Lloyd Garrison, Thoreau supported John Brown when he was captured and later hanged. Thoreau also disobeyed the Fugitive Slave Act of 1850 by participating in the Underground Railroad, assisting runaway slaves on their way to Canada, including providing them with money.

Thoreau is a beacon for countercultural anti-authoritarians for many reasons. To say that he was a naturalist is an understatement. He was in love with nature. He modeled simple living and self-reliance and was an early critic of consumerism. He was an advocate of preserving the wilderness and the environment, and he celebrated recreational canoeing and hiking. For what he modeled and advocated, Thoreau was seen as eccentric by much of his contemporary society.

As a young man, Thoreau (born David Henry Thoreau) went to Harvard, graduated, taught, and famously exited to the woods for two years. In contrast to Ted Kaczynski's tragic victim-victimizer existence and isolation, Thoreau's life was filled with reciprocal support from friends and family members. While Thoreau praised solitude, he nurtured relationships, showed great loyalty, and enjoyed his travel companions. Thoreau had fun—this an important but too often neglected aspect of his life.

Thoreau famously observed, "The mass of men lead lives of quiet desperation. What is called resignation is confirmed desperation." Thoreau did not romanticize rural living: "From the desperate city you go into the desperate country, and have to console yourself with the bravery of minks and muskrats." He saw despair everywhere, "concealed even under what are called the games and amusements of mankind. There is no play in them, for this comes after work." Thoreau knew the importance of having a good time. While authoritarians would rather remember Thoreau's self-denial of material luxuries and his rejection of alcohol, coffee, and almost all beverages except water, Thoreau was not essentially an ascetic any more than the Buddha or Spinoza. All desired the good life, their version of it.

Thoreau biographer Walter Harding, in *The Days of Henry Thoreau*, tells us that in 1837, there were four roads open to a college graduate such as Thoreau—the ministry, law, medicine, or teaching. Thoreau, at age 20, chose teaching, but it didn't take him long to get in trouble with authorities, as he was reprimanded for not using corporal punishment to keep his classroom quiet. Thoreau's way of dramatizing the preposterousness of this demand was to gratuitously whip several surprised students and then immediately resign. This kind of rebellion made sense for the immature Thoreau, but obviously not for his students.

After a short period of working in the Thoreau family pencil-making business (where he added useful innovations), Henry and his brother John opened up their own school in 1838. The Thoreau brothers' school was noted for its innovations, devoting a considerable part of its program to field trips, including frequent walks in the woods where Henry would excite the children's interest in botany and animals. Other field trips included farms, boat repairers, and gunsmith shops. Henry purchased surveying instruments and introduced it into the curriculum as a practical way to make math come alive. Surveying not only stimulated his students, but ultimately Henry became proficient enough to have an alternative way to make a living after John's tragic death in 1842, which ended the Thoreau brothers' school.

As a young adult, Thoreau became friends with Ralph Waldo Emerson, who was a well-known public intellectual during this era. Emerson introduced Thoreau to other unconventional and eccentric writers and thinkers in the Concord, Massachusetts, community. Some in this group struggled financially, including Bronson Alcott, the father of Louisa May Alcott, and Ellery Channing, who would become perhaps Thoreau's best friend and often travel companion. Thoreau lived in the Emerson household from 1841 to 1844, serving as a tutor for Emerson's children and also a handyman and gardener.

Thoreau had a sense of humor, though his brand of humor sometimes rattled friends. Later in Thoreau's life, when his former jailer Sam Staples bought some land adjacent to Emerson, Staples asked Thoreau to survey it. Thoreau brought Staples and Emerson together to announce that Emerson's hedge was several feet over on Staples's property, that Emerson had been stealing land for years, and that he was happy to be able to disclose Emerson's dishonesty. Then with Emerson completely embarrassed, Thoreau finally let out a laugh, making it clear that he had been pulling Emerson's leg.

A 26-year-old Thoreau's embarrassing mistake might interest anti-authoritarians who beat themselves up for imperfect fidelity to nature. Returning to Concord from a trip, Thoreau and his friend Edward Hoar accidentally set a fire that destroyed 300 acres of Walden Woods. I've known many anti-authoritarians who are so ashamed by mistakes far smaller than Thoreau's that they can move into a depression or into substance abuse and remain there for decades. Thoreau quickly moved on.

In 1845, shortly before turning 28, Thoreau began his legendary experiment on the shore of Walden Pond, living for two years in a small simple home that he built. Thoreau famously tells us in *Walden*, "I went to the woods because I wished to live deliberately, to front only the essential facts of life, and see if I could not learn what it had to teach, and not, when I came to die, discover that I had not lived." Actually, Thoreau was not all that removed from civilization, as his family home was approximately one and a half miles away.

Walden certainly celebrates the joys of solitude and connecting with nature. However, Thoreau does mention visitors, and actually had a regular stream of them. While Thoreau was an individualist and critic of conformity, he does not model social isolation. To raise the roof for his Walden cabin, Thoreau's crew included Emerson, Alcott, Channing, and other friends, as well as his favorite Concord farmer Edward Hosmer and three of Hosmer's sons. And Harding reports, "The children of Concord were always happy to go out to Walden Pond and Thoreau was equally happy to have them," as he would take them on nature walks. One child would later recount, "He could lead one to the ripest berries, the hidden nest, the rarest flowers, but no plant life could be carelessly destroyed, no mother bird lose her eggs."

While Thoreau mocked material luxuries, he clearly loved the luxury of travel, alone or with companions. In 1839, Henry and his brother John built a boat, and they took a trip on the Concord and Merrimack Rivers to the White Mountains, and Henry would return there with Edward Hoar in 1858.

In 1837, Thoreau first toured Maine. He returned there in 1846 (leaving his cabin on Walden Pond for a while), connecting with his cousin in Bangor and joined by two of his cousin's friends for a camping trip to Mount Katahdin. In 1853, he came back to the Maine woods, this time joined by a Native American guide Joe Aitteon. And in 1857, with Hoar, Thoreau again journeyed to the Maine woods, hiring Native American guide Joseph Polis. Polis showed Thoreau, who was already a skilled canoe paddler, how to be even better. Thoreau was impressed in many ways by Polis, and he would later write, "The Indian, who can find his way so wonderfully in the woods, possesses so much intelligence which the white man does not,—and it increases my own capacity, as well as faith, to observe it."

Thoreau's brief life included several other trips and excursions. In 1843, he stayed with Emerson's brother in Staten Island. In New York City, he made writing contacts and hung out with Emerson's transcendental community acquaintances. And in 1856, he returned to the New York City area, hanging out with Bronson Alcott who introduced him to Walt Whitman. Whitman had been criticized by others for publishing a private letter from Emerson praising him, but Thoreau cut slack to Whitman for his self-promotion, and later he called Whitman a "great fellow" and praised his *Leaves of Grass*. Whitman spoke of other meetings with Thoreau, and it is possible they might have reconnected again in 1858 when Thoreau briefly returned to the New York City area.

Cape Cod was a frequent destination for Thoreau. In 1849, Thoreau and Channing traveled there. Thoreau returned to Cape Cod by himself in 1850, returned with Channing in 1855, then again alone in 1857. Thoreau also traveled to Canada with Channing in 1850. And in 1861, Thoreau along with the son of educator Horace Mann, went to Minnesota. The Minnesota trip was taken in large part to help improve Thoreau's health, but it failed. Thoreau died from tuberculosis in 1862 at age 44.

For modernists who focus only on *Walden* and on selective quotes, as did Kathryn Schulz in her 2015 *New Yorker* article "Pond Scum: Henry David Thoreau's Moral Myopia," they may ask as Schulz asked, "Why, given his hypocrisy, sanctimony, and misanthropy, has Thoreau been so cherished?" Schulz calls Thoreau: "self-obsessed: narcissistic, fanatical about self-control," and depicts him as "adamant that he required nothing beyond himself to understand and thrive in the world." She describes *Walden* as the "original cabin porn: a fantasy about rustic life divorced from the reality of living in the woods, and, especially, a fantasy about escaping the entanglements and responsibilities of living among other people."

Hypocrisy is certainly there in *Walden*, as Thoreau was in no way removed from civilization, so close to his mother and sister that they routinely brought him cookies. But in response to Schulz, Jedediah Purdy's "In Defense of Thoreau" noted that while she was right that Ralph Waldo Emerson did say, "I love Henry, but I cannot like him," Schulz excluded other Emerson reflections about Thoreau that give us a fuller and kinder picture of him. Emerson also said Thoreau was a man who "threw himself heartily and childlike into the company of young people whom he loved, and whom he delighted to entertain, as only he could, with the varied and endless anecdotes of his experiences by field and river."

Schulz also accused Thoreau of having "no understanding whatsoever of poverty and consistently romanticized it," offering as evidence Thoreau's quote: "Farmers are respectable and interesting to me in proportion as they are poor." Yet I have known financially struggling farmers who have used that exact Thoreau quote for comfort, preventing them from acting on suicidal thoughts as their bills overwhelm them. Moreover, Purdy points out, "Emerson noted that farmers who hired Thoreau as a surveyor usually started out treating him as an oddity, but ended by admiring him."

Walden, for Schulz, makes Thoreau appear to be a selfish jerk, but the personal Thoreau, while eccentric, was actually generous with both his funds and time. Thoreau financially helped out his more impoverished friends and gave money to causes. And Purdy reminds us, "Thoreau took a genuine interest in the lives of Native Americans, too, seeking them out for long conversations at a time when this was unusual."

For modern anti-authoritarians, the life of Henry David Thoreau provides several lessons: making a buck with various skills; living within one's means; nurturing relationships despite social clumsiness; loyalty to friends; cutting slack to his fellow anti-authoritarians—and having fun.

Scott Nearing

In certain "sustainable-living" circles, Scott Nearing (1883–1983) is as much of a beacon as is Henry David Thoreau. Nearing lived to be 100 years old, the last 50 of those years as a prophet and model—along with his wife Helen—for back-to-land home-steaders who sought escape from Western civilization and longed for a simple and meaningful "good life."

Like Thoreau, Nearing was also socially awkward. In order to become a nationally known public speaker, Nearing recounted, "It meant conquering bashfulness, overcoming stage fright, reducing self-consciousness to a minimum." Like Thoreau, Nearing had little regard for ordinary social niceties, as Helen Nearing (1904–1995) recounted about Scott, "He abhorred gossip and small talk, avoiding commonplace trivia . . . he was not an easy or avid conversationalist." Both Thoreau and Nearing were socially quirky and clumsy and at times obnoxious, yet both elicited admiration and affection from anti-authoritarians who knew them. Like Thoreau, Nearing abstained from alcohol, coffee, and many consumer goods. And both liked to travel, with Nearing traveling even more widely than did Thoreau.

Scott Nearing grew up in a wealthy household. In 1903, at age 20, he decided to make teaching his profession, ultimately acquiring a PhD in economics. He taught at the University of Pennsylvania's Wharton School of Business but became increasingly outspoken about the cruelties of capitalism, including its child labor practices, and he was fired in 1915. His dismissal was seen by many Americans across the political spectrum as a serious breach of academic freedom; it made Scott Nearing a national public figure, a victim of academic authoritarianism. Nearing found another teaching post at the University of Toledo, but after he spoke out against the U.S. government's entry into World War I, he was fired again in 1917. At that point, his academic career "lay in ruins," he later recounted, "my experience and competence as a professional teacher were brushed aside."

A serious young man, Nearing became even more serious, "Beginning with the war of 1917–18," he recalled, "I deliberately stopped introducing any form of humor or lightness into my talks . . . . I no longer tried to ingratiate myself with audiences or with the organizations sponsoring the lectures."

Nearing joined the Socialist Party in 1917 and authored several pamphlets, including *The Great Madness: A Victory for the American Plutocracy*, for which he was indicted by the U.S. government under the Espionage Act. However, Nearing, unlike many others so prosecuted, had greater luck and was not convicted in his 1919 trial. In 1927, Nearing joined the Communist Party, but in 1930 he was expelled from it for contradicting Leninist dogma. Estranged from Left political parties, his academic career destroyed, Nearing had also separated from his first wife.

Marginalized and disillusioned, Nearing later recounted that as long as he continued to speak out, "I would be cut off from the country's major channels of publicity. No more of my articles would appear in newspapers or magazines nor would my books be reviewed in them. No more books would be published by representative publishers. I would be excluded from the lecture platform. Most important of all to me, the academic field would be closed tight."

Nearing had little choice but to cut a different path, "I decided to continue as a freelance teacher, to talk and write as opportunity offered. In the meantime, how to live? . . . Many of my friends and associates on the Left who stayed true to the cause, drove trucks for a living, served milk routes, delivered papers, worked as waiters or stevedores, or drove taxies. I chose homesteading as a way of life under United States right wing pressure in the 1930s."

In 1932, a 49-year-old Nearing, along with his new partner, 29-year-old Helen Knothe (whom he later married) purchased land in rural Vermont. In 1954, Scott and Helen Nearing published *Living the Good Life* about their then approximately two-decade experiment in homesteading. They proudly reported that they had succeeded in restoring depleted mountain land so as to grow vegetables, fruits, and flowers; had done so organically without chemical fertilizers; created a subsistence homestead; had a small-scale successful business enterprise, a maple sugar "cash crop"; maintained excellent health, with neither needing to see a doctor for two decades; simplified their lives; were able with six months a year "bread labor" to have six months a year of leisure time for research, travel, writing, and speaking; and fed and lodged many people who stayed with them for days, weeks, or longer.

When ski resorts and developers intruded on their Vermont homestead, Scott, at age 69, and Helen decided to start over. They relocated their homesteading to Cape Rosier, Maine, again calling it "Forest Farm," replacing maple sugar with blueberries as their cash crop. In addition to vegetable growing and other typical homesteading activities, Scott deepened a pond by shoveling out thousands of wheelbarrow loads of mud, built a stone wall around his large garden, and in his early nineties was mixing cement for the Nearings' new stone house.

With the Nearings' *Good Life* books (that would include *Continuing the Good Life: Half a Century of Homesteading*), they became legends. "The Nearings became counterculture celebrities in the 1970s," writes historian and philosopher John Faithful Hamer in his article "The Forest Farm Romance." The Nearing homestead became a sacred place for thousands of young people who would make their pilgrimage there—some just to gawk but others who the Nearings would feed and put to work. Scott once again had his students, and he was in his glory. Many of these young people were so inspired by the *Good Life* books and by Forest Farm that they embarked on their own homesteading attempts. They reasoned that if Scott could begin homesteading at age 49, start over again in Maine at age 69, and could be making it work for another three decades, then certainly with hard work, they too could also succeed.

However, in their popular *Good Life* books, the Nearings were not candid about their sources of income. In Scott Nearing's 1972 autobiography *The Making of a Radical*, he does tell us that he had an insurance annuity, a minimum monthly social security check, a modest trust fund left by his sister, and another trust fund left to him by a Boston friend which he used to contribute money to his favorite causes. However, many young hopeful homesteaders were ignorant of these realities, and plunged in with only their hard work and enthusiasm.

In the late 1960s and 1970s, the Nearings began to sell off—quite inexpensively—significant acreage from their large tract to young homesteaders. In *Meanwhile, Next Door to the Good Life*, Jean Hay Bright, one of the recipients (along with her then partner Keith), makes clear that she continues to have great respect for what the courageous and hardworking Nearings accomplished, and she maintained her friendship with them until their deaths. However, it troubled Hay Bright that the Nearings were not completely candid with the public about economic realities. Although the Nearings did grow much of their food, worked hard, and were frugal, it was their outside income and other people's labor that helped make their lives sustainable.

Another land recipient was Eliot Coleman; and his daughter Melissa, as an adult, wrote about her childhood with her homesteading parents living next to the Nearings. Melissa Coleman notes, "Helen was known to have a soft spot for exotics like avocados, bananas, and Florida oranges, which she had shipped to Maine, but as they didn't support the self-sufficiency stance, these were conveniently not mentioned in their books."

The Nearings' reported that they spent only four hours a day on "bread labor" survival, enabling them to spend four hours a day on intellectual pursuits and four hours a day on socializing, and that they traveled six months a year. However, as Stanley Joseph—who also acquired property from the Nearings—tragically discovered, this kind of good life is impossible without additional income. After the end of Joseph's marriage to his homesteading partner Lynn Karlin, Joseph, alone facing the hard realities of homesteading, committed suicide in 1995.

Self-promotion by anti-authoritarians, so to survive and thrive, is not rare. The Nearings' self-promotion of self-sufficiency—especially given their ages when they accomplished this—was what provided them with celebrity status. For Scott, given his banishment from his beloved teaching profession, young people's attention had to be exhilarating; he not only had students again but awe-struck ones. Self-promoting U.S. anti-authoritarians have existed in many walks of life. Not only did the poet Walt Whitman publish Emerson's personal letter for positive publicity, he anonymously published his own highly flattering review of his poetry collection *Leaves of Grass*.

Despite Scott Nearing's less admirable traits, even his greatest detractors would acknowledge that he was stubbornly persistent, hardworking, resilient, and dedicated. Despite the hypocrisies, there are many important lessons to be learned from Nearing's life, including how he dealt with his anger.

Scott Nearing clearly asserts his anger about the direction of the United States, and one also senses his anger about the ruin of his academic career and the sellout of many U.S. leftists. Nearing did not use that fuel of anger to kill enemies (as Leon Czolgosz and Ted Kaczynski had) but instead as energy to prove his enemies wrong and prove the value of his way of life, and to seize attention and respect from his detractors' children and grandchildren. However, Scott Nearing was very human, and though he mostly used anger as fuel for his worthy achievements, it leaked out elsewhere in psychologically destructive ways. People could be made to feel inferior by Scott for not living up to his moral standards. Also, there was Scott's relationship with his son John (from Scott's first marriage). Scott cut John out of his life because of John's mainstream political views and lifestyle, not returning John's letters and not attending John's funeral.

Scott did maintain his relationship with his other son and many other people, though he had no really close relationships with anyone except Helen. Scott's best decision was partnering with Helen. As a young woman, Helen had been an aspiring musician and bohemian who was charmed by charismatic older men (prior to Scott, Helen, in her late teens, had been emotionally intimate with the philosopher and self-help guru Jiddu Krishnamurti). Helen was a perfect partner for Scott because Scott needed a woman who would both compliment and complement him. Helen wrote in her memoir that "my life for more than fifty years was Scott-centered. . . . There were times . . . when he had to poke or pull me along toward his own rare intense level of dedication." It is clear that the Nearings had deep mutual affection, however, as Melissa Coleman observed, though the Nearings were progressive in their teachings, "the Nearings' marriage was rooted in an earlier era." Coleman recounts that, "Once, when Helen interrupted Scott during a particularly long ramble, he cut her off by saying, 'Quiet, woman.' The younger onlookers were scandalized, but it didn't faze Helen."

For anti-authoritarians who long to escape Western civilization, there are many lessons to be learned from Scott Nearing's life. His self-taught survival skills, self-discipline, and resilience were self-promoted virtues but were virtues that he truly possessed. Not self-promoted was his anger, and though he was far from perfect in how he channeled it, he did use it positively in many ways.

The "good life" that the Nearings promoted is mostly true and genuinely inspiring, but there is also much to be learned from the imperfections of lives. In both my research and my personal experience, I have discovered realities about those who have failed and succeeded in some kind of off-the-grid escape. Without some outside "passive income," or a spouse with some mainstream job that provides at least a modest income, or some other concession to the moneyed economy, one cannot likely make it—even with twelve hours a day of labor rather than four "bread labor hours."

Henry David Thoreau and Scott Nearing are deservedly beacons for anti-authoritarians who dream of escape from authoritarian society. And for off-the-grid anti-authoritarians who need to let go of their shame about imperfections, the realities of Thoreau and Nearing's entire lives are instructive.

Two-Strike Hitters: Frederick Douglass, Harriet Tubman, and Helen Keller

Being an anti-authoritarian in the United States means having one strike against you. Having a second strike against you—as Frederick Douglass and Harriet Tubman had being born slaves, and as Helen Keller had becoming deaf and blind at 19 months of age—makes the margin for error all the more narrow. Douglass, Tubman, and Keller knew that to have any chance at all, they had to use their talents to the fullest and take advantage of every opportunity.

Douglass, Tubman, and Keller have each achieved an almost mythical status, so much so that their flesh-and-bones humanity has been lost. Unfortunately, their lives have been used by authoritarian society to instruct Americans that anyone who perseveres can overcome any obstacle—a message that is untrue and insults their legacies.

Frederick Douglass

Frederick Douglass (approximately 1818–1895) questioned the authority of the slavery system as a young boy, asking, "Why am I a slave? Why are some people slaves and others masters?" As he grew up, he challenged and resisted this system. He first psychologically emancipated himself from a slave mentality, then escaped from slavery, then fought for the abolition of slavery, and after its abolition continued to fight for full human rights for African Americans.

Douglass (born Frederick Augustus Washington Bailey) began life as a slave on the Eastern Shore of Maryland, relatively fortunate in that he lived close to non-slave states. As a young child, Douglass was sent from a rural plantation to Baltimore, and he later recounted, "I regard my removal from Col. Lloyd's plantation as one of the most interesting and fortunate events of my life. . . . [I]t is quite probable that but for the mere circumstance of being thus removed, before the rigors of slavery had fully fastened upon me; before my young spirit had been crushed under the iron control of the slave-driver; I might have continued in slavery until emancipated by the war."

In Baltimore, the relatively kind wife of his master assisted young Frederick in learning the alphabet. He took full advantage and continued to learn to read from white children around him as well as from the writings that he came into contact with; and even when he was ultimately forbidden to read, he secretly pursued reading and writing. This would make all the difference, as he would discover writings that confirmed his instinct that slavery was wrong.

With his growing knowledge, he became increasingly resistant to his slave status, and ultimately got sent to "rehab," which consisted of being sent to a farmer who had a reputation of being a "negro-breaker." The teenage Frederick was regularly whipped and almost psychologically broken. He concluded that if he was broken, he might as well be dead, and he took a risk. He physically fought back against the farmer, and this ended his abuse. Later he recalled that fighting back "revived a sense of my own manhood. I was a changed being after that fight. I was nothing before; I was a man now. . . . I had reached the point at which I was not afraid to die. This spirit made me a freeman in fact, though I still remained a slave in form." Douglass considered himself lucky that his resistance did not result in him being handed over to authorities and hanged. Psychologically astute, he intuited that the negro-breaker was ashamed of his defeat and did not want it to be known, as such a defeat would affect his reputation as a negro-breaker.

Douglass's initial attempts at escape failed but he remained resilient. In 1838, his well-thought-out escape was a successful one with the help of Anna Murray, whose parents had been freed before her birth and so she had been born free in Maryland. Anna Murray was five to six years older than Frederick, and she was exceptionally entrepreneurial with her laundry service. The two may have first met when her laundry work took her to the Baltimore docks where Frederick was working. Using her income, Anna was able to financially aid Frederick for his escape. Frederick changed his last name to avoid capture, and Anna followed him to New York City where they wed, eventually having five children together and remaining married for 44 years until her death.

After living for a short period in New York City, Douglass moved to New Bedford, Massachusetts. He joined anti-slavery groups and made alliances with fellow former slaves and white abolitionists, connecting with perhaps the most famous U.S. abolitionist, William Lloyd Garrison, who encouraged Douglass. At age 23, Douglass began his life as an abolitionist orator, initially as a nervous novice but quickly becoming one of the most powerful speakers in U.S. history.

In 1845, at the age of 27, Douglass published the first version of his autobiography (which he twice revised), and he became something of a celebrity. This publicity made him a marked man for recapture. Not naively believing that his new fame would be an antidote to authoritarian assault, he fled the United States in 1845. In England and Ireland, Douglass was emotionally moved by the relative absence of racial discrimination. He became a popular lecturer and remained overseas for two years, impressing British philanthropists who raised funds to buy his legal freedom so he could return to the United States without fear of recapture.

Douglass was the consummate networker. He recognized the parallels of the women's rights movement with the slave abolition movement, and in 1848, Douglass attended the Seneca Falls Convention, the first women's rights convention in the United States. He connected with Elizabeth Cady Stanton, and used his newspaper, the *North Star*, to push for women's rights. Douglass would later have political disagreements with Stanton, but they remained friends.

After John Brown's Harpers Ferry raid in 1859, Douglass again evidenced his political astuteness about U.S. "justice." Even though Douglass had opposed the raid for strategic reasons, he was cynical about being exonerated from involvement in the raid and again fled the United States, first to Canada and then to England. He later recounted, "I knew that if my enemies could not prove me guilty of the offense of being with John Brown, they could prove that I was Frederick Douglass; they could prove that I was in correspondence and conspiracy with Brown against slavery; they could prove that I brought Shields Green, one of the bravest of his soldiers, all the way from Rochester to him at Chambersburg; they could prove that I brought money to aid him, and in what was then the state of the public mind I could not hope to make a jury of Virginia [which Harpers Ferry was then part of] believe I did not go the whole length he went, or that I was not one of his supporters; and I knew that all Virginia, were I once in her clutches, would say 'Let him be hanged.'" Douglass knew that he would not get a fair shake and that remaining in the United States would only serve to allow authorities to shut him up.

With the beginning of the Civil War, Douglass helped recruit for the 54th Massachusetts Infantry Black regiment, and he used his hard-earned political capital to push Abraham Lincoln for greater rights for African Americans. Following the war, Douglass, who had become politically well-connected, received several job offers. He became president of the Freedman's Saving Bank, Chargé d'Affaires for the Dominican Republic, U.S. marshall for the District of Columbia, recorder of deeds for the District of Columbia, and minister to Haiti. He continued to be widely sought as a speaker, and, with income from his writing and speaking and these job positions, Douglass not only gained financial security but could afford in 1877 to buy a large house in Washington DC (which he expanded).

After Anna Murray Douglass died in 1882, Frederick Douglass in 1884, at age 66, married Helen Pitts, a white suffragist twenty years his junior. Douglass had achieved such stature in both white and black America that despite the great controversy that his second marriage created, he continued to thrive. From 1886 to 1887, Douglass and his second wife took a year-long tour of Europe and the Middle East. At age 77, in 1895, Frederick Douglass died.

Throughout his life, Douglass recognized opportunities and took full advantage of them. As an adolescent, he was psychologically astute, and as a young man, he was resilient in the face of failure. He acquired money-making skills and financial wisdom. He valued physical and mental effort but also fully recognized the importance of relationships. He showed his appreciation for kindness, respected those who respected him, and formed relationships with people who had influence and money.

Douglass was also way ahead of his time in recognizing the power of images to promote both himself and dignity for African Americans. He became enamored by photography, writing extensively about it. And after achieving fame, in order to counter the racist images of African Americans, he became the most photographed person in the United States in the nineteenth century. He was well aware that he was the most famous black man in the United States and of the importance of conveying an image of strength and dignity.

While aggressively promoting full human rights for African Americans, Douglass was in some ways less radical than his mentor abolitionist William Lloyd Garrison. Their falling out was in part because Garrison had long declared the U.S. Constitution to be pro-slave and thus needed to be abolished, and Douglass came to oppose that view. Douglass favored the annexation of Santo Domingo by the United States and was clearly not a socialist or anarchist. However, Douglass was a triumphant anti-authoritarian who challenged and resisted white domination of himself and of all African Americans.

Harriet Tubman

Harriet Tubman (approximately 1822–1913), like Frederick Douglass, was born into slavery and eventually escaped. Even Douglass was awed by Tubman's courage. It was daring enough for a slave to attempt escape, but to return to slave territory several times to help other slaves escape was courageous in the extreme. Tubman, unlike Douglass, never had the opportunity to learn how to read and throughout her life she had to deal with the effects of a head injury (caused by a slave owner) that resulted in dizziness, pain, seizures, and sleep difficulties. Tubman's triumphs so transcend her circumstances that she appears almost as an unreal superwoman character. Thus, few Americans reflect upon the realities of her life.

Tubman (born Araminta "Minty" Ross), like Douglass, started life enslaved on the Eastern Shore of Maryland. Her severe head injury occurred in early adolescence when she was struck by a heavy metal weight thrown by her master intending to hit another slave. In her early twenties, she married John Tubman, a free black man, and soon after she also changed her first name to Harriet. Despite her husband being free, Harriet remained a slave.

Tubman went up for sale in early 1849, but luckily she had been ill, and there were no buyers. Later that year, despite her husband's attempts to dissuade her, she escaped with her brothers Ben and Henry, who then forced her to return with them. Shortly after, she escaped again without her brothers. Returning later for her husband, she discovered that he had remarried and had no desire to leave, so she used the trip to help other slaves escape. In Tubman's abolitionist fundraising, she would tell the story about her husband's refusal to leave so as to get a laugh and a donation. In 1854, she returned to rescue Ben and Henry, as well as a third brother, Robert, their wives, some of their children, and other slaves, taking them to Canada because of the Fugitive Slave Act of 1850.

The precise number of slave-rescue trips and number of slaves whom she freed is controversial. Based on the claims of Tubman's initial biographer Sarah Bradford (*Scenes in the Life of Harriet Tubman*, 1869; *Harriet Tubman, Moses of Her People*, 1886) monuments honoring Tubman routinely state that she freed more than 300 slaves in 19 trips. What recent biographer

Kate Clifford Larson discovered was that Tubman in the late 1850s told audiences that she had rescued 50 to 60 people in eight or nine trips. Larson concludes that Tubman directly helped approximately 70 to 80 slaves escape in 13 trips, and that Tubman had also given instructions to help another approximately 60 slaves escape.

Tubman was extraordinarily brave but not arrogant, as she restricted her rescue trips to the Maryland area that she knew. Larson notes, "Tubman depended on her great intellect, courage and religious faith . . . . She followed rivers that snaked northward, and used the stars and other natural phenomena to guide her. She relied on sympathetic people, black and white, who hid her, told her which way to go and connected her with other people she could trust. She wore disguises. She paid bribes."

Tubman did not create the Underground Railroad but used the network effectively. Though Tubman couldn't read, she knew what days of the week that newspapers printed runaway notices, and so she began escape trips on Saturday evening, knowing that the notice wouldn't be printed until Monday, providing her with a head start. Tubman also carried a revolver for two reasons: protection against slave catchers and their dogs, and to threaten to shoot those who she was rescuing if they wanted to turn back (as this endangered the remainder of the group).

Tubman's fame, historian Eric Foner notes, spread quickly in abolitionist circles, "By the late 1850s, she had become known as the slaves' 'Moses'. . . . Nonetheless, Tubman struggled to raise money for her undertakings. She worked in Philadelphia, New York, and Canada as a laundress, housekeeper, and cook, and solicited funds from abolitionists. On one occasion, she camped out in the anti-slavery office in New York City, asking visitors for donations."

Harriet Tubman gave direct assistance to John Brown for his 1859 raid at Harpers Ferry, as upon Brown's request, Tubman gathered former slaves who were willing to join his raid. Then in 1860, in Troy, New York, Tubman was involved in the rescue of a fugitive slave, freeing him from the custody of U.S. marshals.

With the advent of the Civil War in 1861, Tubman aided the Union army as a cook, nurse, scout, and spy for Union forces in Hilton Head, South Carolina. Then, in 1863, Tubman became the first woman to plan and lead an armed raid during the Civil War. The raid freed 700 slaves from several plantations along the Combahee River. The raiders, who included 300 black soldiers, also burned several buildings and crops and either captured or destroyed stockpiles of munitions and food. The *Wisconsin State Journal* printed a story about the raid and acknowledged Tubman's important role, "A Black She 'Moses'—Her Wonderful Daring and Sagacity," and described the raid as "striking terror to the heart of rebellion."

After the Civil War, Tubman returned to her home in upstate New York. Prior to the war, Tubman had purchased a home and land on the outskirts of Auburn, New York, from William Seward, at that time an abolitionist U.S. Senator from New York, who gave Tubman extremely favorable terms. Auburn was a significant abolitionist stronghold, and Seward and his wife were participants in the Underground Railroad. In 1869, Tubman married Nelson Davis, an African American Civil War veteran who was approximately twenty years her junior. She had difficulty getting government compensation for her war contributions, but she did receive financial assistance from the profits of Sarah Bradford's biography about her.

Tubman's survival instincts and her physical strength were astonishing, but even she did not win every encounter. In 1873, financially vulnerable, Tubman and her brother were scammed by two con artists, who beat her and robbed her of $2,000 of an investor's money that she had raised.

Continuing to farm her seven-acre property, she and Davis ran a small brick-making business in the 1880s before he died in 1888. In the 1890s, Tubman became more involved in the women's suffrage movement. In 1896, she purchased 25 acres near her property, which she ultimately transferred to the AME Zion Church. And in 1908, she opened the Harriet Tubman Home for Aged and Infirm Negroes—a dream of hers. She died in 1913.

Tubman survived and triumphed because of her intelligence, her relationships, and her almost superhuman physical courage. William Still, a fellow African American abolitionist who would chronicle the Underground Railroad, said that Tubman "seemed wholly devoid of personal fear."

That her fearlessness came from her religious beliefs is uncontroversial. Tubman spoke about "consulting with God," and she had complete confidence that God would keep her safe. The abolitionist Thomas Garrett reported that he "never met with any person, of any color, who had more confidence in the voice of God, as spoken direct to her soul. . . . and her faith in a Supreme Power truly was great." For Tubman, Larson concludes, "the root of her outbursts, visions, sleeping spells, and voices" lay in her powerful faith. Given her visions and the voices that she heard, it is a good thing that Tubman only had to watch out for slave catchers and not modern psychiatrists.

Many anti-authoritarians see religion as the "opiate of the masses," locking people into passivity and compelling them to wait for the "pie in the sky when they die." But for people such as Frederick Douglass, Harriet Tubman, and Helen Keller, their religious faith informed and inspired their anti-authoritarian spirit. For people with two strikes against them, logic may tell them to give up, but faith can empower them, energized by a belief that they are chosen by a supreme being to lead their people out of oppression. For Tubman, her faith helped fuel what modern psychiatrists would call hallucinations. Labeling visions or voices as a symptom of illness is an arrogant assumption, as there are many reasons why this phenomenon occurs. One reason is that when human beings experience extreme oppression, such visions and voices can be the only antidotes to psychological powerlessness.

Helen Keller

There is a wide gap between what most Americans are taught about Helen Keller (1880–1968) and the truth of her life. Keller was a member of the Socialist Party, an enthusiastic supporter of her hero Eugene Debs's presidential candidacy, a leading women's rights and civil rights activist, a critic of World War I, and one of the founders and board members of the American Civil Liberties Union.

"The mythological Helen Keller that we are familiar with," notes Keith Rosenthal, "is little more than an apolitical symbol for perseverance and personal triumph." Rosenthal points out in his article "The Politics of Helen Keller" that one of the most problematic moral messages that Keller's life is used for is to promote the idea "that the task of becoming a full member of society rests upon one's individual efforts to overcome a given impairment and has nothing to do with structural oppression or inequality." That frustrated and enraged the real Helen Keller.

The mythical Keller is a version of the "American Dream" of pulling oneself up by one's bootstraps, overcoming limitations, and becoming socially and economically successful. This version of Keller has created resentment with many individuals with disabilities who know full well the truth of being disabled in the United States, and Keller also grasped this truth. While Keller enjoyed the attention and influence that her fame provided, she was frustrated by how one part of her was used to advance the American Dream mythology while her life as a socialist who confronted American injustice was quieted and marginalized.

Helen Keller lost both her sight and her hearing due to illness when she was 19 months old. This resulted, as she tells us in her autobiography, in her becoming extremely frustrated and angry. She also describes herself as a domineering (with her playmate Martha) and mischievous child: "One morning I locked my mother up in the pantry. . . . She kept pounding on the door, while I sat outside on the porch steps and laughed with glee as I felt the jar of the pounding. This most naughty prank of mine convinced my parents that I must be taught as soon as possible." Fortunately, the young deaf-and-blind Helen was not viewed by her parents as also having oppositional defiant disorder or hopelessly in need of institutionalization.

Keller was lucky to have parents with some wherewithal. Helen's mother had read about the successful education of another deaf-and-blind child, Laura Bridgman, and this put the Keller family on a path to connect with Alexander Graham Bell, who worked with deaf children. Young Helen adored Bell, and Bell recommended they seek help from the Perkins Institute for the Blind in Boston, where Helen connected with Anne Sullivan, a graduate of the institute. In 1887, Sullivan went to Keller's home in Alabama and began working with Helen, and this began a 49-year relationship between them. Keller recounted in her autobiography, "The most important day I remember in all my life is the one on which my teacher, Anne Mansfield Sullivan, came to me." Throughout her life, Keller would connect with other helpful people, who "hitched their wagon" to Helen because of her intelligence, drive, and determination, which made it clear that their assistance would not be a waste of time.

The description of Anne Sullivan as "the miracle worker" was actually first coined by Mark Twain who came to know Helen in 1895 when she was 15. Keller later recounted about Twain, "He treated me not as a freak, but as a handicapped woman seeking a way to circumvent extraordinary difficulties." When Helen was ten, she began speech classes at Horace Mann School for the Deaf in Boston and then she attended the Wright-Humason School for the Deaf in New York City, improving her communication skills including her speaking ability. She then attended the Cambridge School for Young Ladies in Massachusetts, a preparatory school for women. When Twain met her, he was amazed by Helen's "quickness and intelligence" and he pushed the wealthy Henry H. Rogers to fund Helen's further education. Rogers, equally impressed, paid for her to attend Radcliffe College, where she was accompanied by Sullivan who assisted Helen with lectures and readings. Keller, at age 24, graduated with honors.

Prior to graduating Radcliffe, Keller had published her first autobiography, *The Story of My Life*. Already well known, her autobiography propelled her into becoming even a greater celebrity. In her later life, she would be known as an international ambassador for the United States. However, most Americans are unaware of Helen Keller's radical politics.

In 1909, at age 29, Keller joined the Socialist Party of America. Keller was passionate about social and economic justice. She later recounted, "Step by step my investigation of blindness led me into the industrial world." She discovered that the leading causes of disability in the United States were an economic system in which profits were prioritized over preventing diseases and workplace accidents. She concluded that "our worst foes are ignorance, poverty, and the unconscious cruelty of our commercial society. These are the causes of blindness; these are the enemies which destroy the sight of children and workmen and undermine the health of mankind."

Keller was very public about her socialism. She was an enthusiastic proponent of the revolutionary Industrial Workers of the World. In the early twentieth century, with her fame, Keller became a leading figure in the U.S. socialist movement, using her platform to publicize and support the major strikes of her era. Predictably, the same newspapers that had celebrated Keller's triumph over her disabilities then used her disabilities as a way to dismiss her politics and to persuade readers not to take her socialism seriously. Keller later recounted, "So long as I confine my activities to social service and the blind, they compliment me extravagantly . . . but when it comes to a discussion of a burning social or political issue, especially if I happen to be as I so often am, on the unpopular side, the tone changes completely."

Socialist ideals of equality and social and economic justice fit into Keller's "disability politics." While Keller fought for expanded educational and vocational opportunities for people who were deaf, blind, and with other disabilities, she was far more radical. As Rosenthal documents, "She maintained that the larger problem was the existence of a society that did not properly fit all of its members . . . that the issue was not exclusively one of people with disabilities versus people without disabilities, but rather all of the exploited and oppressed (including disabled people) versus a form of society that . . . subjugated the former as a precondition for the wealth and power enjoyed by a dominant fraction of that society." Keller wanted to build bridges between all oppressed and exploited people.

Helen Keller was human and thus imperfect, as one biographer Kim Nielsen makes clear in *The Radical Lives of Helen Keller.* Like many of us, our hypocrisies arise out of our need to financially survive, and in Keller's case, also the need to maintain some political influence. So while Keller originally rejected financial support from Andrew Carnegie, who patronizingly threatened to lay her across his knees and spank her so she would "come to her senses" about socialism, she later accepted a Carnegie pension. In her role as spokesperson and fund raiser for the American Foundation for the Blind, for which she received a salary, she allowed the AFB to control her message so as to ignore her political radicalism. Keller was imperfect elsewhere. Like many other birth control activists, including Margaret Sanger, Keller supported some eugenic ideas though she never went as far as to support forced sterilization. And like Scott Nearing and many American socialists, she remained a supporter of the Soviet Union for several years after it was clear to anarchists such as Emma Goldman and Alexander Berkman that the Soviet Union was a totalitarian society.

Harriet Tubman and Helen Keller both saw themselves as chosen by a supreme being to lead people out of oppression. In an interview she gave at age 36, Keller stated, "I feel like Joan of Arc at times. My whole [being] becomes uplifted. I, too, hear the voices that say 'Come,' and I will follow, no matter what the cost, no matter what the trials I am placed under."

Both Frederick Douglass and Helen Keller published memoirs in their twenties that made them "stars" of their respective oppressed groups. And while there were Americans who doubted that a runaway slave or a deaf-blind person could have written such intelligent books, many other Americans were awed by what Douglass and Keller had overcome. Their awesomeness gave them a platform to be spokespeople for their groups but also made it politically difficult to be full human beings; and both rebelled against not only the inferior status of their group but also against one-dimensionality ascribed to them.

To the extent that anti-authoritarians enter the political realm, they find themselves in compromising positions. Frederick Douglass knew that there was not enough political support for women's voting rights and that if women's voting rights were included in the proposed 15th Amendment to the Constitution, the amendment wouldn't pass; and that would mean that male African Americans would continue not having voting rights. And so to the dismay of his allies in the women's rights movement, Douglass opposed the inclusion of women's voting rights in this amendment. Similarly, Keller was routinely in the position of being marginalized in her human rights fight for disabled people to the extent that she included her full socialist agenda, and so she compromised herself there.

Anti-authoritarians who choose to enter the realm of political activism will eventually be put in the position of compromising some of their integrity. Of course, anti-authoritarians can refuse to compromise, but they will likely pay a price in terms of personal and political marginalization. Historically, both the compromising and uncompromising political paths have had value in different circumstances.

Modern Models: Jane Jacobs, Noam Chomsky, and George Carlin

Anti-authoritarians Jane Jacobs, Noam Chomsky, and George Carlin challenged illegitimate authority in a straightforward and accessible manner. All three expressed contempt for standard schooling and its assault on self-learning and critical thinking. All three exuded a certainty—without superiority—that communicated: "Just forget about what the authorities with their academic credentials and official badges are telling you. I see this. What do you see?" The truths that Jacobs, Chomsky, and Carlin saw and asserted have been powerful challenges to authoritarian society, but perhaps even more threatening for authoritarians is their modeling of an unbroken human being.

Jane Jacobs

Jane Jacobs (1916–2006) was an astonishingly triumphant anti-authoritarian in several respects. First, lacking any academic credentials in urban planning and without even a college degree, her book *The Death and Life of Great American Cities* became one of the most influential challenges in U.S. history to policies that were devastating U.S. cities. Second, while viewing herself as primarily a writer, Jacobs ultimately became one of the most successful activists in recent U.S. history, leading and winning fights against one of the most powerful and intimidating authorities in New York City history. And third, while elitist authorities had tried to marginalize her as "just a housewife," her marriage was a key to her success in several areas. Her partnership with her husband was critical to her professional successes, and after raising three children together, Jane and Robert Jacobs had the wherewithal to save their sons from the violence of the U.S. government.

Jane Jacobs (born Jane Butzner) started life in Scranton, Pennsylvania. Her ancestors came from "old Protestant stock" who had arrived in America before the Revolutionary War. Her father, John Butzner, was a highly respected physician who, like Ralph Nader's father, encouraged his children to think for themselves. When she was nine years old, Jane recalled a teacher telling the class that cities always grow up around waterfalls; and though Scranton had a waterfall, young Jane didn't think that waterfalls were the critical factor, "Mines were the thing in Scranton. I was very suspicious." So Jane immediately told her teacher that she was wrong.

Winning battles with teachers, biographer Alice Sparberg Alexiou concludes, "only served to increase her already-healthy self-esteem." In one incident when Jane was seven years old, a teacher told the class to raise their hands and promise to brush their teeth every day for the rest of their lives; but Jane's father just the previous day had told her never to promise to do anything for the rest of her life when she was still a child because promises are serious. So Jane not only refused to raise her hand but told her classmates not to do so as well. This enraged Jane's teacher, who threw her out of the classroom. However, the undaunted Jane exited school and enjoyed herself, wandering along some railroad tracks. Jane was a mischievous child, "a free spirit, clever, hilariously funny and fearless," recounted a Scranton newspaper columnist who knew her when they were both children.

Alexiou notes, "Jane did just enough work to pass her courses but no more. . . . By the time she got to the third grade, she discovered that she could read anything and thereafter tuned out her teachers. All her life, she would remain a voracious reader."

Her parents, notes *New Yorker* writer Adam Gopnik, "indulged their daughter's eccentricities, clearly seeing them as part of her character, her 'spunk.'" Her upbringing allowed her to believe, Gopnik concludes, "that authority could be laughed away, a powerful notion for a provocateur to take through life."

When Jacobs graduated high school, her parents told her that they had the money to send her to college but she recalled, "I was so damn glad to get out of school I couldn't even think of going to college." Jacobs aspired to be a newspaper reporter, but she took a stenography course so as to support herself and moved to New York City with her sister. With her stenography skills, she supported herself as a secretary and explored New York City, and began loving cities as much as Thoreau loved nature. She discovered Greenwich Village and moved there with her sister.

In 1938, at age 22, Jacobs gave higher education a try. She enrolled at Columbia University School of General Studies as a non-matriculating student, taking whatever course she wanted and received good grades. After two years, she was required to matriculate, but was rejected by Barnard despite her good record at Columbia because of her poor high school grades. Jacobs claimed later that this was a blessing; and she would have, as Alexiou put it, a "lifelong disdain for formal schooling."

In the 1940s, Jacobs worked as a reporter for the State Department and Overseas Information Agency magazine *Amerika*. In 1944, she met Robert Jacobs and married him shortly later. In 1947, when their peers were moving out to suburbs, Jane and her architect husband bought an old rundown three-story building in Greenwich Village, and there they had three children together between 1948 and 1955.

In 1956, shortly before turning 40, Jacobs gave a speech that changed her life. The *Architectural Forum*, for whom she was writing, asked her go to Harvard University to speak at a conference on urban design. She first refused as she hated public speaking. "It was a real ordeal for me," she later said. But her speech made complex ideas simple, especially about how people use space. She talked about how city planners and architects imposed their ideas of order that were oppressive to people's freedom to interact. Her impressed audience included influential people, such as Lewis Mumford, architectural critic for the *New Yorker*, and William Whyte (author of *The Organization Man*), who at the time was senior editor of *Fortune* and who facilitated a piece by Jacobs for *Fortune* in 1958. This ultimately connected Jacobs with Random House editor Jason Epstein, resulting in a book deal for *The Death and Life of Great American Cities*, which she published in 1961.

The Death and Life of Great American Cities would become and remain one of the most influential books about cities and urban planning in U.S. history. Jacobs began it with this sentence: "This book is an attack on current city planning and rebuilding." In her first paragraph, using the word *attack* three times, Jacobs makes clear that she opposed the "principles and aims that have shaped modern, orthodox city planning and rebuilding." "I shall mainly be writing about common, ordinary things," Jacobs proclaimed, about what kind of streets are safe and unsafe, why slums stay slums or regenerate, and "how cities work in real life." She had contempt for elitist ideologues who don't observe realities of city life such as the harmful effects of high-rise housing projects and highways that gut cities. She coined terms such as "mixed primary uses" and "eye on the street."

Jacobs would later say, "It is not easy for uncredentialed people to stand up to the credentialed, even when the so-called expertise is grounded in ignorance and folly." Many authorities tried and failed to marginalize the book and dismiss Jacobs as merely a "housewife" or an "amateur." Readers were taken by her commonsense ideas, powerful prose, and her obvious love of cities. The anti-authoritarian Jacobs told us to form our own conclusions, "I hope any reader of this book will constantly and skeptically test what I say." Her disdain for dogma and ideology coupled with her pragmatism made the book fresh and exciting. Jacobs's work emerged in an era of anti-authoritarian women writers, most famously Rachel Carson (*Silent Spring*, 1962) and Betty Friedan (*The Feminine Mystique*, 1963).

Jacobs had become a community activist even before *The Death and Life of Great American Cities*, but she became more known after that book's publication. Her primary adversary was Robert Moses, the epitome of an authoritarian. Moses, in terms of construction—roads, bridges, parks, and housing—was the most powerful figure in New York City history. Documented by Robert Caro's 1974 book *The Power Broker*, Moses had once been lauded as a reformer and city improver, but Caro notes, "To clear the land for these improvements, he evicted the city's people, not thousands of them or tens of thousands but hundreds of thousands, from their homes and tore the homes down. Neighborhoods were obliterated by his edict." Moses's political acumen and power was such that no mayor or governor dared oppose him; and even when Franklin Delano Roosevelt, at the height of his popularity as president, attempted to oppose Moses, Caro tells us that Roosevelt "found himself forced to retreat." But Jane Jacobs stood up to Robert Moses and won.

Prior to her fame as an author, Jacobs had in the late 1950s joined the fight against a Moses project to put a roadway through Washington Square Park in Greenwich Village, linking Fifth Avenue with West Broadway. Jacobs and others formed a community group, which was uncommon at the time. Instead of pleading with city bureaucrats and with Moses, they used public pressure to intimidate vulnerable politicians. When Moses realized that he had been defeated, he became livid and transparent,

"There is nobody against this—nobody, nobody, nobody, but a bunch of, a bunch of mothers!"

Another Moses project, more potentially devastating, was the Lower Manhattan Expressway (LOMEX), which if built would have wiped out SoHo, Chinatown, Little Italy, and much of Greenwich Village. Jacobs recounted, "I felt very resistant to getting into another fight. I wanted to work on my work." But with her new clout, Jacobs knew that she was invaluable to the movement and jumped in, leading another diverse community group that included artists, business owners, homemakers, reform Democrats, right-wing young Americans for Freedom, and anarcho-pacifists. They defeated LOMEX in 1962, but as Jacobs would later say, "The rule of thumb is that you have to kill expressways three times before they die." This was the case with LOMEX. In its last defeat in 1968, at a public hearing on the project, Jacobs got arrested on several charges including inciting a riot, but luckily she avoided jail.

Not long after that in 1968, Jane and Robert Jacobs took their family and moved out of the United States to Toronto, Canada. The Vietnam War was the major reason. The Jacobs family were anti-war activists. Following one anti-war demonstration at the Pentagon in which soldiers drove back protesters with rifle butts injuring many, though Jane was unhurt, she recalled thinking, "I didn't feel part of America anymore." Moreover, Jane and Robert's sons were draft age and had announced that they would go to jail rather than Vietnam. And so faced with their sons' likely imprisonment, Robert and Jane, like Frederick Douglass and Harriet Tubman before them, sought refuge in Canada. But unlike Douglass and Tubman, the Jacobs family did not return. Jane continued as an activist in Toronto and became one of Canada's most honored and influential citizens. She died in 2006, shortly before her 90th birthday.

Like Scott Nearing, one of Jane Jacobs's best decisions was her spouse choice. Throughout their lengthy marriage, Robert complimented and complemented Jane. They discussed all the ideas that went into her books, with Jane noting about *The Death and Life of Great American Cities*, "I do not know which ideas in this book are mine and which are his." They also teamed on every civic battle, with Jane relying on Robert's political savvy. Jane later said, "He usually stayed in the background, and I don't think people realized how important he was to all the fights in Greenwich Village." Robert in turn said, "I know that my wife is more eminent than I am. I'm proud of that and I am so proud of her."

Money always matters, and early on Jane was self-reliant with her stenography skills that kept her financially afloat until she could make it as a writer. But for Jane to have both professional and domestic satisfaction, Robert was invaluable. Alexiou notes, "Robert had a long and productive career as an architect, which is fortunate because Jacobs's books were not of the sort that makes their writer wealthy."

Jacobs prided herself as being opposed to dogma, and she accepted the possibility that there could be downsides to her vision. She had championed preserving older buildings, not simply because of their architectural character but because she believed that this would ensure affordable housing. However, rehabbed older buildings such as hers led to gentrification (in the 2000s, her old Greenwich Village home would sell for $3 million), and this resulted in a decline of economic diversity.

Jane Jacobs was no great diplomat, and she was lucky that this didn't hurt her political activism. For example, the influential Lewis Mumford had been an encouraging support for her, helping Jacobs following her Harvard talk. Jacobs and Mumford agreed on many urban issues—from their mutual antipathy for Robert Moses, to their agreeing on the disaster of high-rise housing projects, urban expressways, and urban renewal destruction. However, in *The Death and Life of Great American Cities*, Jacobs attacked Mumford in some areas, compelling a counterattack by Mumford in his review of her book. But when it came time to battle Moses and LOMEX at a city hearing, upon her request, Mumford wrote what Jacobs called a "wonderfully effective letter" in opposition. She later recounted, "Nobody could have exerted the influence that he did."

In addition to *The Death and Life of Great American Cities*, Jacobs would author several other books, and at age 88, the anti-authoritarian Jacobs reminded her readers, "I don't want disciples. I want people with independent minds to read my books."

Noam Chomsky

Noam Chomsky (born 1928) may well be the most famous and admired modern U.S. anti-authoritarian. Given his political stands, it is remarkable that he has survived and thrived. In the early 1960s, Chomsky challenged and resisted the U.S. government's war in Vietnam at a time when very few Americans were criticizing the Vietnam War, risking an academic career in linguistics in which he had become highly esteemed for his groundbreaking contributions. Since his entrance on the political public stage, Chomsky has used his platform to challenge illegitimate authorities, including the U.S. government and oppressive regimes around the world. He has voiced a consistent contempt for elite rule—for its atrocities as well as for its subversion of working-class autonomy. Amazingly, in a 2013 *Reader's Digest* poll of "The 100 Most Trusted People in America," Chomsky, a self-described anarchist, was voted #20 (behind #19 Michelle Obama; in front of #24 Jimmy Carter).

Chomsky grew up in Philadelphia. His father, William, fled the Ukraine to the United States, worked in sweatshops, attended Johns Hopkins University, worked as a school principal, and later became one of the world's foremost Hebrew grammarians and faculty president at Gratz College. Noam's mother Elsie was also a teacher. Chomsky describes his parents as "normal Roosevelt Democrats," although some other family members were leftist radicals.

Noam was seen as an exceptionally intelligent child in his community. Bea Tucker, who worked as William Chomsky's secretary, recalled a conversation with Noam at age seven. Tucker pointed to *Compton's Encyclopedia* and asked Noam if he had looked through any of the volumes, and Noam responded. "I've only read half of them." Between age two and twelve, Noam went to Oak Lane, a Deweyite experimental school where children were encouraged to think for themselves and where creativity was more important than grades. All schools, Chomsky believes, could be run like Oak Lane but won't because no society "based on authoritarian hierarchic institutions would tolerate such a school system for very long."

At Oak Lane, when he was ten, Noam published an article in the school newspaper about the fall of Barcelona to fascist forces during the Spanish Civil War—an influential event for Chomsky then and throughout his life. Later as a teenager, Noam read *Homage to Catalonia*, George Orwell's account of the Spanish Civil War and the briefly successful anarchist society in Spain. Chomsky's early understanding that people can rise up against oppressive systems and create cooperative organization among themselves became part of the basis for his belief in anarchism as a real possibility.

At age twelve, Noam entered Central High School in Philadelphia, a highly regarded school but one that he hated, "It was the dumbest, most ridiculous place I've ever been, it was like falling into a black hole or something. For one thing, it was extremely competitive—because that's one of the best ways of controlling people. So everybody was ranked, and you always knew exactly where you were. . . . All of this stuff is put into people's heads in various ways in the schools—that you got to beat down the person next to you, and just look out for yourself."

Noam remained in school but recalled losing all interest in it. Instead, he self-educated during his adolescence. At age 13, Noam commuted alone by train to New York City to visit relatives. He spent many hours with an uncle who ran a newsstand in Manhattan on 72nd Street, which was a lively "literary political salon" where Noam was exposed to radical politics and Jewish working-class culture.

At age 16, Chomsky began undergraduate studies at the University of Pennsylvania, but he soon became discouraged. He recalled, "When I looked at the college catalogue it was really exciting—lots of courses, great things. But it turned out that the college was like an overgrown high school. After about a year I was going to just drop out and it was just by accident that I stayed in." He recalled later, "The vague ideas I had at the time were to go to Palestine, perhaps to a kibbutz, to try to become involved in efforts at Arab-Jewish cooperation within a socialist framework" (in 1953, he did live for six weeks in a left-leaning kibbutz but was disappointed by racist attitudes there). In 1947 at age 19, he began dating Carol Schatz, whom he would marry, and they would have three children together. Also in 1947, Noam met Zellig Harris, a charismatic linguistic professor, which resulted in Noam remaining in academia—and ultimately becoming a renowned linguist.

His biographer Robert Barsky concludes, "Chomsky's early life, indeed his whole life, was and has been literally consumed by a desire for understanding and a penchant for political commitment." Chomsky's early interests were political, not linguistic. Chomsky recalled, "I had, from childhood, been deeply involved intellectually in radical and dissident politics, but intellectually." Ultimately, intellectual involvement was not enough. Chomsky tells us, "I'm really a hermit by nature, and would much prefer to be alone working than to be in public." However, some instinct told him that he needed to transcend his comfort zone and actively engage the world.

One of the earliest influential authorities Chomsky challenged was behaviorist psychologist B. F. Skinner. Skinner's 1957 book *Verbal Behavior*, with its view that language was learned through behavior modification, was for Chomsky patently absurd, denying a fundamental characteristic of human beings—creativity. And in 1971, with many other humanists, Chomsky confronted the totalitarian nature of another popular Skinner book, *Beyond Freedom and Dignity.*

While Chomsky was bothered by irrational notions in linguistics, he was enraged by illegitimate authority in the political realm, especially when it came to the Vietnam War. Chomsky recounted, "I knew that I was just too intolerably self-indulgent merely to take a passive role in the struggles that were then going on. And I knew that signing petitions, sending money, and showing up now and then at a meeting was not enough. I thought it was critically necessary to take a more active role, and I was well aware of what that would mean." For ten years, Chomsky refused paying a portion of his taxes, supported draft resisters, was arrested several times, and was on Richard Nixon's official enemies list.

Given the potential consequence of his political stand, Noam and Carol Chomsky agreed that it made sense for her to return to school and get a PhD so she could support the family if he was put in prison. He later recounted, "In fact, that is just what would have happened except for two unexpected events: (1) the utter (and rather typical) incompetence of the intelligence services. . . . [and] (2) the Tet Offensive, which convinced American business that the game wasn't worth the candle and led to the dropping of prosecutions." Carol Chomsky ultimately secured a position at Harvard's School of Education, and went on to have a successful academic career. And so with luck and wise choices, the Chomsky family had two excellent incomes and financial security.

Chomsky continued his public attack on authoritarian policies and propaganda. In 1988, Chomsky and co-author Edward Herman published *Manufacturing Consent*, which describes a "Propaganda Model" of how the media creates a distorted view of reality that maintains the status quo for the ruling class.

Given Chomsky's many hours on the road speaking about political causes, his many publications, and his extensive work on linguistics, he is mistakenly viewed as leading a life of self-denial. However, he has long realized that to deny his full humanity—his need to have security, fun, and family—and to attempt ethical perfection would be unhelpful. Chomsky is clear: "Look, you're not going to be effective as a political activist unless you have a satisfying life." Chomsky tells audiences, "None of us are saints, at least I'm not. I haven't given up my house, I haven't given up my car, I don't live in a hovel, I don't spend 24 hours a day working for the benefit of the human race, or anything like that. In fact, I don't even come close . . . . I certainly do devote an awful lot of my energy and activity to things that I just enjoy, like scientific work. I just like it, I do it out of pleasure."

In a 2003 *New Yorker* profile of Chomsky, Larissa MacFarquhar notes, "In many ways, he and his wife, Carol, lead a conventional middle-class life. They live in Lexington, Massachusetts, a Boston suburb, in a large brown clapboard house . . . . When their children were little, they went on vacations to the Caribbean; they summer on Cape Cod." MacFarquhar quotes a Chomsky friend: "He likes to be out of doors in the summer, he likes to swim in the lake and go sailing and eat junk food."

Chomsky models an activist who does not self-flagellate about financial hypocrisies that are virtually impossible to avoid. When employed by the Massachusetts Institute of Technology, Chomsky was candid about the reality that even though the U.S. government's Department of Defense was not funding him directly, because the DOD was funding other MIT departments, such funding allowed MIT to pay him. "As far as the moral issue goes," Chomsky remarked, "It's not as if there's some clean money somewhere. If you're in a university, you're on dirty money—you're on money which is coming from people who are working somewhere, and whose money is being taken away."

Chomsky also realized that valuing family meant not only financial compromises but even an occasional philosophical one. Chomsky, a non-practicing Jew and not a member of any synagogue, was faced with a dilemma when his oldest daughter wanted to get bat-mitzvahed but was unable to do so because her family did not belong to a synagogue; Chomsky relented and became a member. Carol, prior to her death in 2008, said, "Noam will always stop whatever he's doing and do something with the family. He is totally devoted. It's his outlet."

In the area of electoral politics, Chomsky has recommended voting under certain circumstances for the lesser-of-two-evil

candidates, which for some on the radical Left is seen as a violation of integrity, but which he sees as rational and politically
astute. However, in one now infamous incident—the so-called
Faurisson affair—Chomsky chose not to be politically astute.

Specifically, Robert Faurisson was a professor of French literature who had been suspended from a university in France
because of his denials of the Holocaust. Chomsky, at the request
of a friend and because of his belief in free speech, signed a petition in 1979 for Faurisson's free speech rights, and Chomsky
also wrote a longer statement about this case (that was used
without Chomsky's permission in a book by Faurisson). By
taking this position on Faurisson, Chomsky created a distrac-
tion for his views about Israel. Regarding Israel, Chomsky has
spoken of having had "a feeling of joy" about the initial creation
of Israel as "a place where Holocaust victims could be assimi-
lated"; but he has also expressed that just as the United States
should not be a Christian state and just as Pakistan should not
be an Islamic state, Israel should not be a Jewish state, and that
all its inhabitants should have equal civil rights and political say.
For Chomsky's ideological commitment to free speech in the
Faurisson affair, he provided those who wish to discredit him
as a "self-hating Jew" with material to manufacture propaganda
against him.

As we see with all anti-authoritarians, nobody has perfect
wisdom, but Noam Chomsky may come as close to Spinoza-like
rationality as possible. Chomsky's anger over illegitimate authority certainly has leaked out in debates, but for the most part he
has not self-sabotaged. Pained enough over illegitimate authorities, he has not added to that pain any self-flagellations about
unavoidable hypocrisies; and he has made sure to include joy in
his life. He was wise with his choice of a spouse, and together
they were smart with respect to money. Importantly, he has been
wise to grow out of his hermit-like comfort zone and engage the
world—so as to not simply flee the repulsive elite but to also
connect with the non-elite.

George Carlin

In ranking George Carlin (1937–2008) as the second best stand-up comic of all time, *Rolling Stone* called him: "The hippie sage, the MIT-level linguist, the First Amendment activist, the undisputed champion gadfly of stand-up." Like the actual MIT linguist Noam Chomsky, Carlin was fascinated by language. Like Jane Jacobs, Carlin prided himself on being a writer. Jacobs, Chomsky, and Carlin—all very different personalities with very different career paths—radiated a confidence about challenging and resisting the illegitimate authorities of society.

George Carlin, as *Rolling Stone*, put it, "was the ultimate thinking man's comic, demanding that his audiences fight from underneath the mountain of bullshit heaped upon them by clergymen, politicians and advertisers." Carlin's career arc was a radical transformation, beginning as a "people pleaser" in the 1960s, then a counterculture hero in the 1970s, and finally in the last two decades of his life, an anti-authoritarian prophet.

In his autobiography *Last Words*, Carlin tells us, "I was conceived in a damp, sand-flecked room of Curley's Hotel in Rockaway Beach, New York." And so while it's difficult to disagree with *Rolling Stone's* #1 best stand-up-comic ranking of the anti-authoritarian Richard Pryor, I'm a little more drawn to Carlin, in part because he was conceived in Rockaway Park, a couple of miles west of where I grew up (a happier Rockaway connection for me than Phil Ochs hanging himself in Far Rockaway, a couple of miles to the east).

Born in Manhattan, George's parents separated when he was still an infant because, as Carlin put it, his father "drank, he got drunk, he hit people." Carlin never met his father, who was for a time a successful salesman and after-dinner speaker. George grew up in the ethnically diverse Manhattan neighborhood of Morningside Heights, raised by a single mother who was an executive secretary in the advertising business.

Growing up, George had a great deal of freedom and autonomy. At age seven, he snuck on the subway to visit his mother at work, and went downtown to Central Park, Times Square, Rockefeller Center, Wall Street, Chinatown, and the waterfront. By age eleven, he knew he wanted to be an entertainer as he loved the laughter and attention, "Disrupting class made school more bearable . . . but after school—that longed-for part of the day belongs to the kid alone—was what counted for me and the kids of my generation." He begged his mother to get him a tape recorder to practice his act, and he would make fun of authority figures in the neighborhood. He recounted, "Now we'd be called 'delinquents,' 'troubled,' 'alienated,' or worse; certainly some of the guys from the neighborhood later did time. But there was something innocent about running wild on the streets back then."

Carlin quit school in the ninth grade, later recounting, "I had great marks. I was a smart kid, but I didn't care. They weren't teaching what I wanted. I didn't give a shit. It's important in life . . . not to give a shit. It can help you a lot."

When he was 17, Carlin joined the U.S. Air Force. He later proudly recounted: "So that's two court-martials, and four more Article 15s after the first one. . . . A grand total of seven major disciplinary offenses. Pretty fucking impressive." One of his court-martials happened overseas, drunk in his barracks celebrating his beloved Brooklyn Dodgers beating the Yankees in the World Series. His sergeant yelled at him, "Shut up, Carlin!" to which Carlin tells us, "I replied with my standard 'Go fuck yourself, cocksucker!'" By luck, he eventually received a 3916 discharge, which Carlin recounted, "was like a no-fault divorce." Gaining an early exit without dishonorable discharge for Carlin meant, "I absolutely beat the game."

While still in the air force, Carlin began working as a radio disc jockey. In 1959 at age 22, Carlin teamed up with Jack Burns, and in February 1960, they headed to Hollywood, dreaming of performing on the *Tonight Show*. With good luck and some connections, they were on that show by the end of the year.

"The sixties were my nice years," Carlin recounted, "my nice suit, my nice collar, my nice tie, my nice haircut—and my nice material." Though at that time still tame himself, Carlin had enormous respect for the edgier Lenny Bruce and Mort Sahl, "They were challenging authority. That's what comedy is supposed to do." Bruce and Sahl liked Carlin, and they helped him with career connections.

By the end of 1960s, Carlin was disgusted with his "mainstream dream" and "people pleaser job." He began coming to terms with who he really was: "I got kicked out of three different schools. I got kicked out of the Air Force. I got kicked out of the choir. I got kicked out of the altar boys. I got kicked out of summer camp. I got kicked out of the Boy Scouts. . . . I was a pot smoker when I was 13. We broke the law. . . . I swam against the tide of what is expected and what the establishment wants from us. But I didn't know that about myself . . . because this dream blinded me." He began to recognize that he was a rebel who wanted to artistically project ideas.

In the 1970s, a new countercultural Carlin emerged with a beard and long hair. He recorded the album *Class Clown* with his now famous "Seven Words You Can Never Say on Television," and in 1972, he got arrested in Milwaukee for performing it. Luckily for Carlin, it was the 1970s, and so unlike Lenny Bruce, the case was dismissed with the judge declaring that Carlin's language was indecent but that he hadn't broken the law. However, as the counterculture began to diminish, Carlin lost much of his audience and faced another existential crisis.

In the 1980s, Carlin's life was a mess, "Throughout the eighties I had outbursts of anger. It kept building up and festering. Anger at myself for getting myself in this tax mess, for being such a cokehead I didn't have the sense to avoid the tax mess." Married to Brenda since 1961 and a father since 1963, Carlin also was angry with himself for his failings in his marriage and his parenting. But Carlin used his crisis for ideological and artistic transformation.

"The [1980] election of Ronald Reagan," Carlin recounted, "might've been the beginning of my giving up on my species. Because it was absurd." The absurdity of the Reagan years, Carlin recalled, helped him to find "an authentic position to speak from." Carlin started reading Alexander Cockburn, Noam Chomsky, Hunter S. Thompson, and Gore Vidal, and acknowledged, "I had a left-wing, humanitarian, secular humanist, liberal inclination," but added, "Liberal orthodoxy was as repugnant to me as conservative orthodoxy."

Carlin ultimately came to major realizations such as: "*Laughter is not the only proof of success.* Boy, what a liberating recognition that was! . . . Getting laughs all the time *wasn't my only responsibility*. My responsibility was to engage the audience's mind" [Carlin's emphasis].

While Noam Chomsky's quiet voice and unchanging facial expressions gives his anti-authoritarian messages a certain power for some audiences, when Carlin began delivering Chomsky-like messages, he was able to reach a larger audience that needed to be entertained while prodded to think. A few Carlin examples:

"America's manhood problem was typified by the teenage sexual slang we use about war. In Vietnam we didn't 'go all the way.' We 'pulled out.' Very unmanly. When you fuck an entire people you have to keep fucking and fucking them—women and children too—till they're all dead."

"I don't feel about war the way we're supposed to, the way we're told to by the United States government. A large part of which is the United States military, whose business is war. So the military is telling us how to feel about war—so *they* can stay in business. Something is fucked up here."

"Forget the politicians. The politicians are put there to give you the idea that you have freedom of choice. You don't. You have no choice! You have owners! They own you. They own everything. They own all the important land. They own and control the corporations. They've long since bought and paid for the Senate, the Congress, the statehouses, the city halls. They got the judges in their back pockets and they own all the big media companies, so they control just about all of the news and information you get to hear. They got you by the balls."

As with all the anti-authoritarians in this book, Carlin was far from a perfect human being, especially with regard to self-destructive behaviors, most notably with his severe substance abuse. But with some luck, maturation, humility, and eventually moderation and ultimately abstinence, Carlin's substance abuse did not kill him before he became an anti-authoritarian prophet.

Given the friends Carlin grew up with, the nature of the entertainment industry especially during his formative years, the counterculture drug influence, and the general societal hypocrisy around drugs that made it easy for any anti-authoritarian to disregard drug admonitions, it's understandable how Carlin almost destroyed himself and his family with his substance abuse. Carlin, even after he stopped abusing drugs, had positive memories about hallucinogenic drugs, "Took some acid and mescaline. Didn't overdo it. I had a couple of trips that weren't the best. But I had a lot of great trips. . . . Fuck the drug war. Dropping acid was a profound turning point for me, a seminal experience. I make no apologies for it."

For Carlin, it took some time to separate drug realities from authoritarian propaganda. For example, with respect to the amphetamine-like Ritalin, Carlin recounted, "I'd always used Ritalin. My Ritalin habit didn't make me crazy. I used to take half a Ritalin, or at most one and a half (I had a doctor's prescription for the stuff). That was my speed during my so-called straight years: the groundwork was laid early on for my attraction to cocaine."

Carlin's maturation, humility, moderation, and ultimately complete abstinence was a gradual process. He recounted that in 1972, "I was already using enough cocaine that I had to think consciously about not using it to record an album." Between Carlin's cocaine abuse and his wife's alcohol abuse, their marriage became chaotic and violent, and on a 1973 family vacation, they brandished knives at each other, terrifying their ten-year-old daughter Kelly. Carlin started to gradually mature, "My own drug use, post-Brenda-sober, fell off. . . . Pot I still saw as benign."

As Carlin began caring about being more than just an entertaining comic, and as he became increasingly consumed by being an artist, he realized, "During my drug period, the only thing that was important was getting high—and fulfilling dates when I could. I don't recall these feelings of pursuing and appreciating artistry, the increasing ability to create. I'm sure the drugs blocked that sort of thing out." In 2004, Carlin entered rehab. "For a long time—since giving up pot in the late eighties—I'd been addicted to an opiate called wine-and-Vicodin. . . .I couldn't control it and I needed help. . . . I developed a new appreciation of the AA techniques . . . whatever skepticism I'd had about them. . . . Although I can do without that Higher Power stuff."

At age 67, Carlin recounted, "I put an end to five decades of substance abuse." However, after a lengthy history of cardiac problems including three heart attacks in 1978, 1982, and 1991, Carlin died of heart failure at age 71 in 2008.

Carlin knew that in order to engage audiences, he needed to connect with them on an emotional level, and he effectively connected with increasingly cynical U.S. audiences. In his 1997 book *Brain Droppings*, he wrote: "I frankly don't give a fuck how it all turns out in this country—or anywhere else, for that matter . . . . My motto: Fuck Hope! . . . I view my species with a combination of wonder and pity, and I root for its destruction." Ironically, the arc of Carlin's life provides hope for anti-authoritarians that their lives need not be tragic ones.

We Don't Need No Badges:
Depression, Relationships, Mutual Aid, and Parenting

This final chapter offers some general ideas with respect to depression, relationships, mutual aid, and parenting. In all these areas, what I learned in my schooling and "badges acquisition" has been of little value. However, I have learned a few things in my direct experiences with anti-authoritarians who are struggling to survive and thrive.

Depression

Anti-authoritarians, by nature, assess the legitimacy of authority before taking that authority seriously, and they don't take seriously any authority with a consistent record of hypocrisies and an absence of basic common sense—this covers mainstream mental health authorities as well as the mainstream media.

In July 2017, *Time* magazine ran a lengthy article, "New Hope for Depression" which reported: "The biggest development has been the rediscovery of a promising, yet fraught, drug called ketamine. It's best known as a psychedelic club drug that makes people hallucinate, but it may also have the ability to ease depression—and fast."

Ketamine or "Special K," as it's called on the street, is classified as a "dissociative anesthetic," routinely used as a veterinary anesthetic drug. Adverse effects include numbness, depression, amnesia, hallucinations, and potentially fatal respiratory problems. And the Foundation for a Drug Free World adds, "Ketamine users can also develop cravings for the drug. At high doses, users experience an effect referred to as 'K-Hole,' an 'out of body' or 'near-death' experience. Due to the detached, dreamlike state it creates, where the user finds it difficult to move, ketamine has been used as a 'date-rape' drug."

While psychiatry and the mainstream media are currently excited about the date-rape drug ketamine, this drug is by no means the first "promising new depression medication" in the history of psychiatry. Sigmund Freud was depressed as a young man and started using cocaine, cheerfully proclaiming, "I am just now busy collecting the literature for a song of praise to this magical substance. . . . You perceive an increase of self-control and possess more vitality and capacity for work. . . . Absolutely no craving for the further use of cocaine appears after the first, or even after repeated taking of the drug." The next miracle antidepressant drugs were amphetamines, with Benzedrine created in 1936 (today, amphetamines such as Adderall and Vyvance are used for ADHD).

Beginning in the late 1980s, the "miracle antidepressants" were the SSRIs (selective serotonin reuptake inhibitors) such as Prozac, Paxil, and Zoloft; yet, these SSRIs turned out to be far less effective than initially proclaimed. That same 2017 *Time* article reported the following about the SSRIs and other antidepressants: "The largest, longest study conducted on depression treatments, called the STAR*D trial, found that after people tried four antidepressants over the course of five years. . . . 30% of patients don't experience remission at all." But the failure rate reality is actually far worse. Taking relapse rates into account, according to an *American Journal of Psychiatry* editorial that accompanied the STAR*D report, there was actually a 57% long-term failure rate in STAR*D—but even this analysis turned out to be overly optimistic. Later analyses of STAR*D data by psychologist Ed Pigott and medical reporter Robert Whitaker revealed that less than 3% of the entire group of depressed patients who began the STAR*D study were ascertained as having a sustained remission (participated in the final assessment without relapsing and/or dropping out).

The United States is home to a drug culture in which both authoritarians and anti-authoritarians participate. Some authoritarians seek drugs that can turn large profits and that maintain the status quo by facilitating compliance. Some anti-authoritarians, especially early in life, prize a drug that makes them less compliant to authority and that blissfully connects them with the universe. Some people swear by Prozac or Zoloft, while others swear by marijuana or LSD.

Anti-authoritarians, for the most part, are not opposed to the informed use of drugs, but they are opposed to prescription/illegal drug hypocrisies and misinformation about drug effectiveness and adverse effects.

What about talk therapy? Some people swear by it, but for others it's a waste of time. Psychologist Bruce Wampold reviewed the psychotherapy outcome literature, examining hundreds of studies for his 2001 book *The Great Psychotherapy Debate*. Wampold found that no therapy techniques are any better than any other, but what is highly associated with therapy effectiveness is the nature of the alliance between therapist and client, including a client's confidence in the therapy and in the therapist. "Simply stated," Wampold concludes, "the client must believe in the treatment or be led to believe in it."

Be it antidepressant drugs or talk therapy, the effectiveness of treatment largely depends on faith in the treatment, and this can be problematic for anti-authoritarians who don't easily have faith. What, then, are wise and unwise strategies and techniques for depressed anti-authoritarians?

Depression is fueled by overwhelming pain, and there are many unwise ways to distract ourselves from pain that may work in the short term but are dangerous in the long term. For example, some people cut themselves to distract themselves from emotional pain. I admit to temporarily having latched on to another unwise strategy that unfortunately worked for a while. When I was depressed in graduate school, I accidentally walked out of a chain supermarket without paying for a six-pack of beer that was on the bottom rack of the shopping cart. In the parking lot, when I realized what I had done, I discovered the antidepressant effects of shoplifting. I got a little addicted to the shoplifting buzz and did this same maneuver a few more times. But one day, I noticed that the supermarket had installed mirrors so that the cashier could see the bottom rack. That shook me up. I recall thinking that I was already humiliating myself everyday by remaining in graduate school, and that I didn't need the extra humiliation of getting arrested for shoplifting. So I achieved shoplifting sobriety.

Lots of other poor choices "work" temporarily but not in the long term. It's likely that the chronically depressed Alexander Berkman got a euphoric buzz in planning the assassination of Henry Clay Frick with his cousin and Emma Goldman. But Berkman's assassination attempt resulted in 14 depressing years of hard time in prison, lifelong physical health problems, bouts of depression, and suicidality. Similarly, I can see how the idea of assassinating McKinley could give an anarchist a buzz; however, while doing that deed didn't result in a long life of misery and depression for Leon Czolgosz, that's only because less than two months after shooting McKinley, he was electrocuted by the state with 1800 volts, multiple times.

When overwhelmed by pain, some people consider and/or attempt suicide. Mental health authorities such as the National Alliance on Mental Illness proclaim, "Research has found that about 90% of individuals who die by suicide experience mental illness." However, anti-authoritarian suicidologist David Webb, who attempted suicide several times and was psychiatrically treated, ultimately concluded that it was unhelpful to view feeling suicidal as a consequence of mental illness. In his book *Thinking About Suicide*, Webb criticizes the "mental illness approach" as medicalizing what he views as a "sacred crisis of the self."

For Webb, if being suicidal is viewed as a symptom of mental illness then "talking about your suicidal feelings runs the very real risk of finding yourself being judged, locked up and drugged." So many critically-thinking suicidal anti-authoritarians don't reach out. Society stigmatizes mental illness, so how can one expect a person overwhelmed by emotional pain not to self-stigmatize once they've been labeled as mentally ill? And this stigma creates more pain and hopelessness. In contrast, what was helpful for Webb and helpful for many other anti-authoritarians is validation that their pain is evidence of their soul and their humanity.

Overwhelming pain—be it financial, physical, relationship, school, other incarcerations, or from other sources—is the fuel of depression. So the commonsense question is: How do you reduce pain and increase joy in a way that doesn't make matters worse in the long run?

Mainstream mental health professionals, especially those involved in chemical dependency treatment, may deride the "geographical cure" of simply exiting a miserable situation. But Frederick Douglass and Harriet Tubman certainly did not deride the geographical cure, and Edward Snowden seems a lot better off with his geographical cure than having his health destroyed in federal prison as was the case with Eugene Debs.

In our moneyed society, financial pains can be lethal, and were especially so for Lenny Bruce, Alexander Berkman, and also many non-famous anti-authoritarians who I've known. In our economic system, it is difficult to make a living doing what one believes in, and young anti-authoritarians are often tough on themselves in this regard, adding more pain to their lives. Many anti-authoritarians today often have little choice but low-wage slavery. One can try to escape, but sometimes that's difficult. If life circumstances such as an ailing parent or child-custody requirements keep one stuck in a small town where the only employer is a prison, self-flagellation does no one any good; being the kindest prison guard possible does do some good. And if one is mired in student-loan debt and the only survival option is being a teacher in an authoritarian school, one can try to get some satisfaction by perhaps not forcing students to raise their hands to take a dump.

In our economic system, few of us are not prostituting ourselves to some extent, and so, for those unskilled at denial of this reality, the only real antidote to this pain is a sense of humor. One of my favorite Emma Goldman stories is about her attempt to sexually prostitute herself to raise money for Berkman's assassination expedition. She initially scolds herself, "Sasha is giving his

life, and you shrink from giving your body, miserable coward."
The 23-year-old Goldman then composed herself, convinced
herself that she could attract customers ("my curly blond hair
showed off well with my blue eyes"), and she proceeded on a
Saturday evening in 1892 to walk up and down Fourteenth Street
in Manhattan. Finally, she got what she thought was a customer,
but instead of buying sex, he told her that she didn't have the
knack for it, gave her $10, and told her to go home. This provided
a revelation for Goldman, who recounted that previously, "I had
met two categories of men: vulgarians and idealists . . . . This
man . . . seemed an entirely new type." Sometimes, as Goldman
discovered, we learn something new by our prostitution efforts,
especially if we have retained our sense of humor.

Relationships are critical to depression. Before pharmaceutical companies annexed psychiatry, the obvious importance
of relationships to depression was common sense even among
mental health professionals. *The Interactional Nature of Depression*, edited by psychologists Thomas Joiner and James Coyne,
documents hundreds of studies on the interpersonal nature of
depression. In one study of unhappily married women who were
diagnosed with depression, 60% of them believed their unhappy
marriage was the primary cause of their depression. In another
study, the best single predictor of depression relapse was found
to be the response to a single item: "How critical is your spouse
of you?" Criticism from one's spouse is painful and potentially
depressing unless one doesn't care about one's spouse, and if that
is the case, that can be even more depressing.

A key to overcoming immobilizing depression is to take seriously something besides one's depression, one's mood, and oneself. This is the message of the Buddha, Spinoza, and many other
wise thinkers. If, unlike Thomas Paine, one lacks the energy to
start a couple of revolutions but is passionate about politics, it
is still possible to hang out with like-minded people—an instant
antidepressant for Emma Goldman. Or if one has given up on
changing the world, then one can also hang out with like-minded
people—or, like George Carlin, make a buck entertaining them.

Relationships

There is no more important variable in determining tragedy or triumph for anti-authoritarians than their relationships.

All the anti-authoritarians profiled in this book who hurt themselves, others, or the cause of anti-authoritarianism were pained by their relationships or by their isolation. Phil Ochs, Lenny Bruce, and Ida Lupino had troubled marriages. Leon Czolgosz and Ted Kaczynski lacked any intimates. And Alexander Berkman, from his early family life to lengthy prison time, had great pain in this area as well.

In contrast, the profiled anti-authoritarians who helped themselves and the anti-authoritarian cause had satisfying relationships. Jane and Robert Jacobs as well as Scott and Helen Nearing had long-term mutually affectionate marriages, in which they complemented one another in terms of personality traits and finances and teamed together politically. Carol Chomsky, married to Noam Chomsky for 59 years until her death, was a fellow linguist, had similar political views, and volunteered to go back to school to become the family breadwinner in the event that Noam became incarcerated for his activism.

Anna Murray Douglass, married to Frederick Douglass for 44 years until her death, financed his escape, helped support their family in the early going, was involved in the abolitionist movement, and remained a loyal supporter even though their closeness diminished. The 36-year marriage of Brenda and George Carlin had periods of chaos due to mutual substance abuse, but George generally viewed them as a "good team," especially in support of his career which provided their income.

When Harriet Tubman's attempt to rescue her first husband failed because of his disloyalty to her, she didn't try again; and she would later remarry a more loyal man. In contrast, Ida Lupino repeatedly attempted to rescue her disloyal husband, and the relationship pain of this marriage contributed to her alcohol abuse.

Helen Keller never married but had hugely supportive people in her life, including her 49-year relationship with Anne Sullivan, another lengthy friendship with Polly Thomson, as well as other friends and family. Likewise, Henry David Thoreau had no spouse, but he had a supportive community of loyal friends and family.

In the United States, we are socialized to fail at relationships. Consumer culture and advertising propagandizes us to obsess over our needs, and it manipulates the invention of needs. Consumer culture sells the belief that life is all about a selfish pursuit of needs, and Americans have many self-absorbed "success models" in business and politics. A self-absorbed obsession over one's needs makes satisfying relationships impossible. School teaches us to aggressively compete with the kid sitting next to us rather than cooperating together to solve problems. And it is the highly unusual child who has been taught that even the best of relationships create tensions, and who learns how to nonviolently resolve those tensions.

There are anti-authoritarians who have rejected the authority of consumer culture and who have ideals that could make satisfying relationships more likely, but many of these anti-authoritarians have their own set of relationship problems.

Anti-authoritarians often have conflicts with one another. Alexander Berkman created tension with his fellow anarchists by criticizing them for not being as materially self-denying as he was. Even though anti-authoritarians might have similar ideologies, they can often focus on their differences, resulting in tension, hostility, and estrangement. A famous falling out occurred between abolitionists Frederick Douglass and William Lloyd Garrison over several issues (including Garrison's contention that the U.S. Constitution was a pro-slave document that needed to be abolished, a view that Douglass came to oppose; as well as the Douglass creation of an alternative abolitionist newspaper that competed with Garrison's). After being invaluable to one another and a great team, Garrison and Douglass never healed their relationship fracture.

Anti-authoritarian activists can have so much rage over injustice and feel so powerless that their passions can get in the way of wisdom. As noted, Emma Goldman, Alexander Berkman, and his cousin Modska fed off each other's rage in their ill-advised assassination conspiracy that put Berkman in prison, which created lifelong guilt for the other two, hurt the labor union strike and the cause of anarchism, and created public sympathy for the authoritarian Henry Clay Frick.

Activism can be a source of tension for romantic partners who may not share the same degree of ideological passion or commitment. While Betty Shabazz, after Malcolm X's death, would describe her marriage to him as "the greatest thing in my life," the reality, according to Malcolm X's biographer Manning Marable, was that their marriage was a troubled one. Marable notes, "She had come to resent the fact that for Malcolm, the work of the Nation always came first."

The conflict between Eugene Debs and his wife Kate Debs was made famous by Irving Stone's biographical novel *Adversary in the House*. While Kate may not have been quite as ideologically adversarial as Stone suggests (Kate once loyally told a reporter doing a story on her husband, "Indeed I am a Socialist"), Debs biographer Ray Ginger does report tension caused by Debs's political activism: "She sometimes remarked to small groups of Socialists that her husband was killing himself for people who did not appreciate it. She began to be cold and formal to Socialists who called at her home. She wanted Eugene to be more a husband and less a Socialist, to pay some attention to his health and the family income." Ginger tell us that "Kate would never have cared about the labor movement" had it not been for her husband's personality, as she was "drawn by his candor and persuasiveness." However, because she was not a political activist, Kate was often lonely, resulting in sadness for her and tension in the marriage.

While Ralph Nader maintains close relationships with his siblings and their families, he does not see it possible for a dedicated activist to have a spouse. His sister Laura Nader recounted, "People always used to say, 'Why didn't you get married?' And he would always say, 'What wife would want to tolerate this, my working 18 hours a day?'" And friend and fellow activist Gene

Karpinski recounted, "He gave me a line I'll never forget: 'Gene, there are two kinds of people in this world, the hard-core and the spouse-core. You gotta decide which side are you on.'"

Minimizing resentments and resolving them before they become lethal are critical to relationships. Resentments occur when people feel discounted, disrespected, used, abused, or coerced. Coercion is intrinsic to Western culture's employment, schooling, and parenting. In Western culture, compared to many indigenous cultures, there is little effort at minimizing resentment, and people are routinely unskilled at resolving small resentments before they turn into unresolvable poisons. In Western culture, the decision-making continuum ranges from complete authoritarian control (as in the military) to majority rule (in elections), resulting in many people being discounted and resentful.

In many indigenous cultures, great time and energy is spent in achieving consensus in which nobody feels discounted and resentful. And if resentments do occur, there is great time and energy given to resolving them. Moreover, there is an understanding that if resentments cannot be avoided or resolved, it is better for all involved to separate rather than utilizing coercions to force compliance.

Many anti-authoritarians are well aware that coercion results in resentments that destroy relationships. However, even with this awareness, anti-authoritarians often still fail to effectively minimize and resolve resentments. Anti-authoritarians often have a great deal of pain, which fuels anger and depression, making it difficult to have the time, patience, and energy to prevent or resolve resentments.

Thus, to reduce the fuel for unwise compulsive reactions, anti-authoritarians need to make all efforts to reduce unnecessary pain and increase joy. Anti-authoritarians need to pay attention to their "pain fuel level," recognizing that when it gets too high, they are vulnerable to unwise compulsive reactions.

A key to satisfying relationships is how dissent—and the tension it creates—is dealt with. If one ignores or pathologizes dissent, then one is behaving as an authoritarian, even if one considers oneself otherwise. Non-hypocritical anti-authoritarians take seriously dissent in their personal relationships, and they engage in dialogue to resolve it.

Mutual Aid

Some anti-authoritarians attempt to attain complete self-sufficiency as a way of exiting coercive hierarchies. Other anti-authoritarians attempt as much self-sufficiency as possible but also embrace mutual aid—cooperation without coercion.

In mutual-aid groups, joining and participation is voluntary and an absence of coercion is the goal of organization. In practice, mutual-aid groups are nonhierarchical and egalitarian, distinguished by consensus decision making and participatory democracy.

While a great number of people see value in the mutual aid of Alcoholics Anonymous, many of them would be surprised to discover that the concept of *mutual aid* was popularized in the early twentieth century by the Russian anarchist Prince Peter Kropotkin (1842–1921) with his 1902 book *Mutual Aid*. And many AA participants might be shocked to discover that AA co-founder Bill W. esteemed the "gentle Russian prince" Kropotkin and saw value in nonviolent anarchism.

In *Alcoholics Anonymous Comes of Age*, Bill W. pointed out how attractive the noncoercive nature and freedom of AA is for newcomers, "We cannot be compelled to do anything. In that sense this society is a benign anarchy. The word 'anarchy' has a bad meaning to most of us. . . . . But I think that the gentle Russian prince who so strongly advocated the idea felt that if men were granted absolute liberty and were compelled to obey no one in person, they would then voluntarily associate themselves in a common interest. Alcoholics Anonymous is an association of the benign sort the prince envisioned." Anarchist writer Logan Marie Glitterbomb points out that AA's Twelve Traditions are replete with anarchist mutual-aid principles: stressing unity and solidarity; no governing leaders; and self-supporting and autonomous groups. Anti-authoritarian George Carlin embraced AA but added, "I can do without that Higher Power stuff." Many anti-authoritarians agree, and *Alcoholics Anonymous Comes of Age* recounts AA founders' consideration of not using the word *God* in AA's "Twelve Traditions" and their "Twelve Steps." They ultimately chose to use *God* but to make clear that the term was open to individual interpretation.

The beauty of a mutual-aid group is that while individuals may join for a specific goal—in AA, to stop drinking—the non-coercive nature of a mutual-aid group can be so satisfying that it becomes a vehicle to build community, including career contacts, friends, and lovers.

Mutual aid occurred in the slave abolitionist groups and among those involved with the Underground Railroad. Historian Henry Louis Gates reports that while the vast majority of runaway slaves were young males who absconded alone and then later received help, "The Underground Railroad and the abolition movement itself were perhaps the first instances in American history of a genuinely interracial coalition . . . predominantly run by free Northern African Americans . . . with the assistance of white abolitionists, many of whom were Quakers." Scholars estimate the number of slaves who escaped range from 25,000 to 100,000. Beyond helping facilitate escape, the mutual aid of the Underground Railroad and the abolitionist movement also created fertile grounds for community.

Vital communities have also been created in mutual-aid workplaces, labor unions, and political activist groups. For U.S. anarchists in the late nineteenth and early twentieth century, there was certainly individual tragedy and political failure, however, historians Paul Avrich and Karen Avrich capture in *Sasha and Emma* these anarchists' rich community. In major U.S. cities, there existed a network of informal mutual assistance among anarchists to provide housing and other necessities. Immediately prior to Berkman's assassination attempt on Frick, the Emma-Sasha-Modska trio partnered in a successful worker-collective lunchroom-ice cream parlor in Worcester, Massachusetts, in order to financially support themselves.

The mutual-aid groups with which I am most personally familiar with are those created by ex-psychiatric patients, for example, MindFreedom and the Western Mass Recovery Learning Community. These mutual-aid groups vary in funding, autonomy, decision making, and the variety of mutual assistance offered. Members of these groups are routinely anti-authoritarians who have questioned and challenged the legitimacy of mainstream professional authorities and have resisted them, creating their own alternatives. Through these and other mutual-aid groups, former psychiatric patients—though often previously labeled by mental health professionals as socially unskilled—find friends and a close-knit community.

Mutual-aid groups are a threat to authoritarians, and so authoritarians will attempt to co-opt them, diverting them from their original role and adopting them for their own purposes. What makes AA attractive as a mutual-aid group is voluntary participation, but when court systems coerce people to attend meetings, the non-coercive culture is destroyed; and when hospitals use AA groups as part of a profit-making enterprise, this also subverts the essence of AA. Similarly, the value of mutual aid among former psychiatric patients has been subverted by the co-opting of peer support. Such co-opting occurs when so-called "peer specialists"—ex-psychiatric patients hired in psychiatric hospitals or other institutions—are positioned at the bottom of the workplace hierarchy and used to persuade current patients to accept their treatments.

Authoritarians in power and their like-minded subordinates believe that hierarchy is the only way that human beings can be organized, and that without such hierarchy there is only chaos. And so, if authoritarians cannot eliminate mutual aid, they will attempt to co-opt it to maintain their own control. For this reason, anti-authoritarians should always be prepared for rejection by authoritarians of any true mutual aid. And if mutual-aid efforts prove successful, anti-authoritarians should always be watchful against authoritarian subversion or co-optation.

Parenting

In psychology classes, I was taught that taking away enjoyable stuff from mice or kids in order to get them to learn is called "negative reinforcement," which along with "positive reinforcement" and "punishment" are elements of "behavior modification." This certainly works to control most mice and even some kids—but not anti-authoritarian kids.

Nowadays, these negative behavioral-modifications are routinely called "consequences" but in my day, parents called them punishments. I didn't get punished much since I did well in school, but when I did, the punishment was usually "no television," and I remember my immediate response to it. When my mother said, "No television for a week," I said, "Make it two weeks, I don't care." When she responded, "Then two weeks it is," I said, "I don't care, make it a month." It progressed to years, decades, and centuries. I think by 2567, I will have served my time. So I have some empathy for how a young Alexander Berkman's bravado bought himself a lengthier prison sentence than if he had employed a competent lawyer.

Professionally, I have worked with kids for whom the coercions of parents, teachers, and other adults failed to control behaviors but succeeded in creating resentments. These kids, like me, were not going to allow adults to use knowledge of their joys and pains for purposes of control, so they learned to hide their true joys and pains. They learned to be guarded about their true self so as it would not be used against them. Some kids learn that it's easier to hide themselves from the adult world if they hide from themselves, and so these kids lose awareness of who they are—and some of them need to, later in life, "crack up" for rediscovery.

Life is filled with ironies and occasional pleasant surprises. Ironically, my "stinkin' badges" have given me access to parents of anti-authoritarian kids. And a pleasant surprise for me has been how infrequently I've been fired by these parents. Only rarely has an authoritarian parent dragged their anti-authoritarian kid into my office with expectations that I would provide "treatment" to make their child unquestioningly obedient. The vast majority of parents I have worked with are more of what I would call *normies* than Nazis.

Normies buy into societal norms. They take seriously PhDs and licensing badges of authority. Normie parents may intellectually understand that people can be so overwhelmed by pain that they become self-destructive or violent, but it is easier for normies to compartmentalize such people as mentally ill. Normie parents want to do the "right thing" with their kids; but unfortunately, taking seriously professional badges often turns out to be the wrong thing. The vast majority of mental health professionals are not anti-authoritarians, so they often give advice that can turn a resolvable problem into a tragedy.

While coercions work to control the behavior of many mental health professionals themselves, coercions don't work on anti-authoritarians. While normies get a positive buzz by pleasing authorities and receiving good grades, anti-authoritarian kids get no such buzz for compliance. For anti-authoritarian kids, coercions only create resentments. Resentment destroys relationships and eliminates the possibility for dialogue that can solve problems.

Anti-authoritarian children and teenagers are often taken by parents to a mental health professional because they are underachieving in standard schools. These young people resist all coercions that demand giving attention to subjects that bore them, doing homework for which they see no value, or staying inside a building that feels sterile and suffocating. All anti-authoritarian kids do not have the same temperaments, so such coercions result in some different outcomes—all unpleasant ones.

Some gentler anti-authoritarian kids resist coercions but worry that their resistance will result in dire life consequences. They worry that performing poorly in school will mean "flipping burgers" for the rest of their lives. Their anxiety and pain of failure is exacerbated by their parents' anxiety over failure, and these kids become hopeless, believing that all of life will be as miserable as school. This can result in debilitating anxiety and immobilizing depression. On many occasions I've seen school

failure and the threat of not graduating high school make a teenager suicidal. It is routine for doctors to medicate these kids with
an array of psychiatric drugs, and if parents and professionals
become anxious about suicide, these kids are often psychiatrically
hospitalized, though hospitalization is no guarantee of safety (as
6% of all American suicides occur in hospitals).

In psychiatric hospitalizations, suicidal young people are
routinely told that they are mentally ill. This makes many anti-
authoritarian kids even more hopeless. Anti-authoritarians are
rarely employed in these institutions—where they could offer
young people validation for their common experience, for example, of pain over authoritarian schooling. That validation can both
reduce pain and increase hope—and open them up for dialogue,
which can help young people gain perspective, reduce pain, and
act with greater wisdom.

Anti-authoritarian kids will often question the legitimacy of
mental health authorities whose interventions appear ludicrous
to them. One such intervention is the "no-suicide contract" in
which the patient agrees not to attempt suicide and to seek help if
unable to honor the commitment. Signing such a contract is often
a requirement for release from a psychiatric hospital. For many
patients, it is obvious that these contracts don't prevent suicide
(confirmed by research) and serve only to reduce the anxiety of
the hospital staff.

Other anti-authoritarian kids with less gentle temperaments don't take seriously their schooling or admonitions from
authorities that their rebellious behavior will doom them. They
feel justified in resisting coercion. Their resistance is routinely
labeled by mental health professionals as "acting out," and they
are diagnosed with various disruptive disorders. Their parents
often attempt punishments, which don't work to break these
kids' resistance. Parents become frustrated and resentful that
their child is causing them stress. Children feel parental frustration and resentment and may come to believe their parents do
not like them. So these kids stop liking their parents, stop caring
about their parents' feelings, and seek out peers who they believe

do like them, even if these peers are engaged in criminal behaviors. If parents have financial resources, these kids are often sent to "therapeutic boarding schools" where they associate with kids who may be even angrier than they are, and from whom they learn even more harmful criminal behaviors.

Although these kids are often accused of having "authority issues," it has been my experience that many anti-authoritarian young people labeled with psychiatric disorders don't reject *all* authorities, only those whom they've assessed to be illegitimate. Often these young people are craving a mutually respectful relationship with an adult who can help them navigate the authoritarian society around them. Anti-authoritarian young people assess adults before taking them seriously, and while they will challenge and resist adult authorities who they deem to be illegitimate, they are receptive toward authorities who prove legitimate. Honesty and sincerity are necessary for an authority to be considered legitimate. Young anti-authoritarians must also sense that an adult has both affection and respect for their anti-authoritarian nature.

People engage with those who make them feel good. Normie professionals and parents routinely fail to engage young anti-authoritarians because their frustration, anger, punishments, incongruence, and pathologizing are unpleasant for these kids. What feels good is affection, respect, empathy, nurturance, humor, and mutual fun. When young anti-authoritarians feel that they are liked, understood, and are not being manipulated, most are open to a dialogue about how best to navigate the world without self-destructive or destructive behaviors.

Normie mental health professionals and normie parents routinely fail to help destructive and self-destructive young anti-authoritarians because they are incapable of seeing anti-authoritarians' anger as legitimate and valid. Normies cannot adequately empathize with the painfulness of coercion and how such pain fuels destructive behavior. Invalidated pain can cause some young anti-authoritarians to become completely hopeless and others to become completely enraged.

With young anti-authoritarians' overwhelming pain, hopelessness, and rage, there is no dialogue—no space to think or reflect. With genuine validation of their pain, empathy for hopelessness and rage, and affection and respect for their anti-authoritarian nature, dialogue becomes possible—and wisdom can replace compulsive destructiveness.

Finally, some parenting advice from George Carlin on the blindness of some anti-authoritarian parents. He was so annoyed by his own controlling mother that, like many anti-authoritarians, he took a laissez-faire approach to parenting his own daughter, Kelly, who began smoking marijuana in her early teens and went to school stoned, though at first continuing to receive excellent grades. Kelly eventually hung out with kids who occasionally stole things from her father, and George recalled thinking, "But what could I do? Like the drug situation, I could hardly bitch about it, having been a dedicated felon myself at their age." But then Kelly got involved in a relationship with one of these kids, a boyfriend who emotionally and physically abused her. This resulted in Kelly cutting school, adding cocaine and Quaaludes to her drug use, and becoming depressed, unbeknown to George, who had mistakenly assumed that constantly checking in or asking children how they were doing would lead to resentment. "My own parent's fearsome need to control me scared me off any behavior like that," he said.

Ultimately, George Carlin recognized that what he had needed in his own youth was not what his daughter needed in hers. At that point, he first went to her boyfriend's father and told him to make sure the boy did not come around anymore. The boy defied this, and George recounted what happened next: "I got my baseball bat. I showed him the bat and said: 'I don't play baseball. Neighborhood I come from, we use bats a different way. To change a person's behavior. . . . He got the point. Never came near Kelly again. Later she told me it was the first time in her life she felt I'd done a real traditional fatherly thing. She was shocked, she said. And very proud."

It is common for many parents to give their children what they believe that they needed from their own parents. However, to love children means recognizing each child's unique personality and individual needs.

Conclusion

While there are certainly societies less free than the United States, what makes life difficult for U.S. anti-authoritarians are the mixed messages that they receive. From the Declaration of Independence, to the Bill of Rights, to the Statue of Liberty, the United States gives the appearance of welcoming those who resist illegitimate authority. Moreover, the United States is a place where immigrant anti-authoritarians such as Thomas Paine and Emma Goldman became celebrities. However, when anti-authoritarian resistance truly threatens powerful U.S. authoritarians, the rug is pulled out—often violently so.

Some U.S. anti-authoritarians have been punished with prison and deportation for merely exercising their First Amendment right of "free speech." However, U.S. anti-authoritarians are not routinely marginalized in these ways. Authoritarians need only ensure that anti-authoritarians not be heard in order to marginalize them.

Scott Nearing, indicted by the U.S. government for stating his beliefs, was luckily not convicted in his 1919 trial but was by other means effectively marginalized. He wrote in 1972 that for the past half-century, "I have had the 'right' to speak, write, print, publish, but my words dropped into a deep well of oblivion. I have the 'right' to teach, but no university or school in the country would accept me. I could speak, but few public forums would allow me on their platforms. I could write, but my books were not published by recognized firms, nor were they reviewed in magazines or papers or stocked in book stores." Many anti-authoritarians resonate with Nearing's anger over being disregarded and discarded.

Authoritarians realize that simply ignoring opposition is often an effective way to marginalize it, whether that opposition comes from the voice of a single anti-authoritarian or the majority of the people. In 2014, political scientists Martin Gilens and Benjamin Page, in a study published in *Perspectives on Politics*, empirically established how average U.S. citizens are almost completely ignored by U.S. governmental authorities in terms of public policies. Reviewing U.S. public opinions of policy issues, along with examining 1,779 different enacted public policies between 1981 and 2002, they determined that "even when fairly large majorities of Americans favor policy change, they generally do not get it." They conclude, "The central point that emerges from our research is that economic elites and organized groups representing business interests have substantial independent impacts on U.S. government policy, while mass-based interest groups and average citizens have little or no independent influence."

When dissent—be it through public opinion polls, protest demonstrations, or otherwise—becomes impotent in changing policy, this is an indicator of living under authoritarian rule. If a society is not authoritarian, then the tension that dissent creates is resolved so that dissenters experience their grievances being taken seriously, as evidenced by policy changes. In an authoritarian society, dissenters—even when in the majority—routinely feel impotent and helpless.

Dissent without disobedience is essentially no threat to authoritarians in power. Clever authoritarians welcome dissent without disobedience, since it can be easily ignored and provides the illusion of a free and democratic society. Only disobedience can threaten authoritarians.

If anti-authoritarian voices prove difficult to ignore, authoritarians will resort to overt assaults. For such assaults, authoritarians will often rely on the work of "professional authorities," including the legal system to criminalize disobedience; mental health professionals to pathologize anti-authoritarian behavior; and teachers and the media, who label disobedience as immature.

It is no wonder that people who disobey illegitimate authority often feel such intense anger. Anti-authoritarians cannot be understood if we deny, water down, or pathologize their anger.

This anger may be a result of their dissent being ignored. Or it may be a result of overt assaults on them for challenging and resisting illegitimate authority. Or it may be caused by witnessing such assaults on their anti-authoritarian friends. Or their anger may come from resentment over being forced into constant vigilance against authoritarian assault. The manner in which anti-authoritarians deal with their anger—and how others who care about them deal with it—is critical to tragedy or triumph.

Contempt for coercion and tolerance for eccentricity are the norms in the anti-authoritarian groups that I have studied and among those with which I have personally been involved. I have found striking similarities between the individual personalities within these groups: Thoreau and his Concord buddies in the 1840s and 1850s; New York City anarchists living between 1880 and 1918; and modern so-called "psychiatric survivors." Today, anti-authoritarians with unconventional behaviors who create tension are often marginalized as mentally ill. That makes these modern anti-authoritarians especially angry, so angry that they are likely to create even more tension for others.

In my work as a psychologist, I have been lucky to hang out with teenage anti-authoritarians with the intelligence and spirit of a young Phil Ochs, Jane Jacobs, Noam Chomsky, Malcolm X, Alexander Berkman, George Carlin, and Edward Snowden. I have also been involved in the mental health reform movement comprising former psychiatric patients and dissident mental health professionals. In this movement, I have gotten to know people with personalities that resemble those of Thomas Paine, Frederick Douglass, Harriet Tubman, Henry David Thoreau, Emma Goldman, Helen Keller, Ida Lupino, and Ralph Nader. In movement gatherings and conferences, there are routinely some people who are as kind as Eugene Debs or as playful as Lenny Bruce, and who treat fellow anti-authoritarians resembling the socially awkward Leon Czolgosz as if they are socially adept—and sometimes they become so.

Recall that Stanley Milgram, reporting on his research about obedience to authority, concluded that humanity's "fatal flaw" is our capacity to abandon our humanity so as to comply with abusive authority. Those human beings least afflicted with that flaw have, sadly, been marginalized in U.S. society—including psychiatrically marginalized.

Among the most honored members of modern U.S. society are "first responders" to disasters, including natural disasters such as hurricanes and humanmade ones such as mass shootings. Anti-authoritarians are also first responders to disasters. They are the first to question, challenge, and resist illegitimate authority.

While U.S. society has honored some famous anti-authoritarians long after they are dead, these figures have often been marginalized in their own lifetimes. Throughout U.S. history, anti-authoritarians have usually been able to rely only on each other for mutual aid. If this mutual caring diminishes, their triumphs will also diminish. So, while anti-authoritarians need no badges, they do need one another.

References

INTRODUCTION

"Amazon Exclusive: Q & A with Author Susan Cain." 2012. https://www.amazon.com/Quiet-Power-Introverts-World-Talking-ebook/dp/B0074YVW1G.

American Psychiatric Association. *Diagnostic and Statistical Manual of Mental Disorders*: *Diagnostic and Statistical Manual of Mental Disorders, DSM-II*. Washington, D.C.: American Psychiatric Association, 1968.

American Psychiatric Association. *Diagnostic and Statistical Manual of Mental Disorders*: *Diagnostic and Statistical Manual of Mental Disorders, DSM-III*. Washington, D.C.: American Psychiatric Association, 1980.

Boodman, Sandra G. "Antipsychotic Drugs Grow More Popular for Patients without Mental Illness." *Washington Post*, March 12, 2012. https://www.washingtonpost.com/national/health-science/antipsychotic-drugs-grow-more-popular-for-patients-without-mental-illness/2012/02/02/gIQAH1yz7R_story.html.

Cain, Susan. *Quiet: The Power of Introverts in a World that Can't Stop Talking*. New York: Crown, 2012.

Huston, John, director. *The Treasure of the Sierra Madre* (film), 1948.

Levine, Bruce E. "Why Anti-Authoritarians Are Diagnosed as Mentally Ill." *Mad in America*, February 26, 2012. https://www.madinamerica.com/2012/02/why-anti-athoritarians-are-diagnosed-as-mentally-ill/.

Milgram, Stanley. *Obedience to Authority: An Experimental View*. New York: Harper & Row, 1974.

Olfson, Mark, et al. "National Trends in the Office-Based Treatment of Children, Adolescents, and Adults with Antipsychotics."

Archives of General Psychiatry (now *JAMA Psychiatry*), 69, no. 12 (December 2012): 1247–1256.

Snow, C. P. "Either–Or." *Progressive,* February, 1961.

CHAPTER 1: AUTHORITIES—AND MY PATH TO *RESISTING ILLEGITIMATE AUTHORITY*

Frankfurt, Harry. *On Bullshit.* Princeton, NJ: Princeton University Press, 2005.

Orwell, George. "Why I Write," *A Collection of Essays by George Orwell.* Garden City, New York: Doubleday Anchor Books, 1954. First published in 1947.

CHAPTER 2. THE COMPLIANT, THE NONCOMPLIANT, AND THE ANTI-AUTHORITARIAN

Defining Terms

Bakunin, Mikhail. "What is Authority?" *God and the State,* 1871. https://www.panarchy.org/bakunin/authority.1871.html.

Bay, Christian. *The Structure of Freedom.* Stanford, CA: Stanford University Press, 1958.

The Percentage of Americans Who Resist Illegitimate Authority

Burger, Jerry M. "Replicating Milgram: Would People Still Obey Today?" *American Psychologist,* 64, no. 1 (January 2009): 1–11. http://psycnet.apa.org/journals/amp/64/1/1/.

Chomsky, Noam. *Understanding Power: The Indispensable Chomsky,* edited by Peter Mitchell and John Schoeffel. New York: The New Press, 2002.

Doliński, Dariusz et al. "Would You Deliver an Electric Shock in 2015? Obedience in the Experimental Paradigm Developed by Stanley Milgram in the 50 Years Following the Original Studies." *Social Psychological and Personality Science,* 8, no. 8 (January 1, 2017): 927–933. http://journals.sagepub.com/doi/

10.1177/1948550617693060.

"TSA Poll." Harris Interactive Poll, Fielding Period: November 5–7, 2012. http://www.techharbor.com/sites/default/files/TSA.poll_.pdf.

Milgram, Stanley. *Obedience to Authority: An Experimental View.* New York: Harper & Row, 1974.

Milgram, Stanley, director. *Obedience*, 1962. https://www.youtube.com/watch?v=ek4pWJ0_XNo.

Romm, Cari. "Rethinking One of Psychology's Most Infamous Experiments." *The Atlantic*, January 28, 2015, https://www.theatlantic.com/health/archive/2015/01/rethinking-one-of-psychologys-most-infamous-experiments/384913/.

The Authoritarian and Anti-Authoritarian "Personality" and Left-Right Politics

Adorno, Theodor et al. *The Authoritarian Personality.* New York: Harper & Row, 1950.

Altemeyer, Bob. *The Authoritarians.* University of Manitoba, Winnipeg, Canada: Bob Altemeyer (self-published), 2006. http://theauthoritarians.org/Downloads/TheAuthoritarians.pdf.

Duckitt, J. "Authoritarianism and Group Identification: A New View of an Old Construct." *Political Psychology*, 10, no. 1 (March 1989): 63–84.

Goldman, Samuel. "Are Trump Supporters Authoritarians?" *The American Conservative.* February 24, 2016. http://www.theamericanconservative.com/articles/are-trump-supporters-authoritarians/.

Kreml, William. *The Anti-Authoritarian Personality.* Oxford: Pergamon Press, 1977.

Magistad, Mary Kay. "Got An Authoritarian Streak? Study Says Odds Are, You're for Trump." *PRI*, February 25, 2016. https://www.pri.org/stories/2016-02-25/got-authoritarian-streak-study-says-odds-are-youre-trump.

Makinson, David. "Authoritarianism and Anti-Authoritarianism," *Broadsheet.* No. 15. May 1961. https://www.marxists.org/history/australia/libertarians/makinson/anti-authority.htm.

CHAPTER 3: GREAT CONTRIBUTIONS DO NOT PREVENT MARGINALIZATION

Thomas Paine

Cheetham, James. *The Life of Thomas Paine*, quoted in Harvey J. Kaye, *Thomas Paine and the Promise of America*. New York: Hill and Wang, 2005. First published in 1817.

Foner, Eric. *Tom Paine and Revolutionary America*. New York: Oxford University Press, 1976.

Foner, Philip S., ed. *The Complete Writings of Thomas Paine*. New York: Citadel Press, 1945.

Ingersoll, Robert G. "Thomas Paine," *The Works of Robert G. Ingersoll*. New Dresden Edition, XI, 321, 1892. http://www .gutenberg.org/files/38801/38801-h/38801-h.htm#link0004.

Kaye, Harvey J. *Thomas Paine and the Promise of America*. New York: Hill and Wang, 2005.

Lepore, Jill. "The Sharpened Quill: Was Thomas Paine Too Much of a Freethinker for the Country He Helped Free?" *New Yorker*. October 16, 2006. http://www.newyorker.com/ magazine/2006/10/16/the-sharpened-quill.

McKenna, J. H. "Filthy Little Atheist." *HuffPost*, December 22, 2016. https://www.huffingtonpost.com/j-h-mckenna-phd/filthy -little-atheist_b_13803410.html.

Russell, Bertrand. "The Fate of Thomas Paine." *Why I Am Not a Christian and Other Essays on Religion and Related Subjects*. New York: Touchstone, 1957. First published in 1934.

Ralph Nader

Chamberlain, Lisa. "The Dark Side of Ralph Nader." *Salon*, July 1, 2001. http://www.salon.com/2004/07/01/NADER_JACOBS/.

Goldberg, Michelle. "The Folly of Ralph Nader." *Slate*, September 15, 2016. http://www.slate.com/articles/news_and_politics/ the_next_20/2016/09/ralph_nader_and_the_tragedy_of_vote_ as_consumer_politics.html.

Graham, Kevin. *Ralph Nader: Battling for Democracy*. Denver: Windom Publishing Company, 2000.

Green, Mark. "How Ralph Nader Changed America." *The*

Nation. December 1, 2015. https://www.thenation.com/article/how-ralph-nader-changed-america/.

Mantel, Henriette, and Steve Skrovan, directors. *An Unreasonable Man.* 2006. Screenplay and notes at: http://rapeutation.com/anunREASONABLEmanscreenplay.pdf.

Nader, Ralph. *Unsafe at Any Speed: The Designed-In Dangers of the American Automobile.* New York: Grossman, 1965.

Nader, Ralph. "Why Bernie Sanders Was Right to Run as a Democrat." *Washington Post,* March 25, 2016. https://www.washingtonpost.com/posteverything/wp/2016/03/25/ralph-nader-why-bernie-sanders-was-right-to-run-as-a-democrat/.

Malcolm X

Carey, Bendedict. "Drugs Used for Psychotics Go to Youths in Foster Care." *New York Times,* November 20, 2011. http://www.nytimes.com/2011/11/21/health/research/study-finds-foster-children-often-given-antipsychosis-drugs.html.

Handler, M. S. "Malcolm Rejects Racist Doctrine." *New York Times,* October 4, 1964. http://www.nytimes.com/1964/10/04/malcolm-rejects-racist-doctrine.html.

Handler, M. S. Introduction to, *The Autobiography of Malcolm X.* New York: Ballantine Books, 1999. First published in 1965.

Malcolm X, with Alex Haley. *The Autobiography of Malcolm X.* New York: Ballantine Books, 1999. First published in 1965.

Marable, Manning. *Malcolm X: A Life of Reinvention.* New York: Viking, 2011.

Nahem, Ike. "To the Memory of Malcolm X: Fifty Years After His Assassination." *July 26th Coalition,* February 23, 2015. http://july26coalition.org/wordpress/to-the-memory-of-malcolm-x/.

New York Times. Editorial, February 22, 1965, quoted in Marable, Manning. *Malcolm X: A Life of Reinvention,* New York: Viking, 2011.

Shabazz, Attallah. "Foreword," *The Autobiography of Malcolm X.* New York: Ballantine Books, 1999.

Time Magazine. "Death and Transfiguration," March 5, 1965, quoted in Manning Marable, *Malcolm X: A Life of Reinvention,*

New York: Viking, 2011.

CHAPTER 4: CRIMINALIZATION OF ANTI-AUTHORITARIANS

Emma Goldman

Avrich, Paul, and Karen Avrich. *Sasha and Emma: The Anarchist Odyssey of Alexander Berkman and Emma Goldman*. Cambridge, MA: Belknap Press of Harvard University Press, 2012.

Bucklin, Mel, director. "Emma Goldman: An Exceedingly Dangerous Woman," *American Experience*, 2003.

Drinnon, Richard. *Rebel in Paradise: A Biography of Emma Goldman*. Chicago: University of Chicago Press, 1961.

Goldman, Emma. "Anarchism: What It Really Stands For." *Anarchism and Other Essays*. New York: Mother Earth Publications, 1910.

Goldman, Emma. *Living My Life, Volume One and Volume Two*. New York: Dover, 1970. First published in 1931.

Eugene Debs

Debs, Eugene V. "How I Became a Socialist." *New York Comrade*, April, 1902. https://www.marxists.org/archive/debs/works/1902/howi.htm.

Ginger, Ray. *The Bending Cross: A Biography of Eugene Victor Debs*. New Brunswick: Rutgers University Press, 1949.

Sanders, Bernie (documentary writer and producer). *Eugene V. Debs Trade Unionist, Socialist, Revolutionary*, 1979. https://www.youtube.com/watch?v=w82pFvUq3o8 (transcript at: http://media.smithsonianfolkways.org/liner_notes/folkways/FW05571.pdf).

Shannon, David A. "Eugene V. Debs: Conservative Labor Editor." *Indiana Magazine of History*, 47, no. 4 (1951), 357–364. https://scholarworks.iu.edu/journals/index.php/imh/article/view/8079/9871.

St. Clair, Jeffrey. *Bernie & the Sandernistas: Field Notes from a Failed Revolution*. Petrolia, CA: CounterPunch, 2016.

Zinn, Howard. "Eugene V. Debs and the Idea of Socialism." *Progressive*, 63, no. 1 (January 1999). https://www.marxists.org/archive/debs/bio/zinn.htm.

Edward Snowden

Ellsberg, Daniel. "Snowden Would Not Get a Fair Trial—and Kerry is Wrong." *Guardian*, May 30, 2014. https://www.theguardian.com/commentisfree/2014/may/30/daniel-ellsberg-snowden-fair-trial-kerry-espionage-act.

"Free Snowden: In Support of Edward Snowden." Courage Foundation website 2017. https://edwardsnowden.com/.

Gillespie, Nick. "Amash, Conyers, and the Mavericks Fighting for Your Civil Liberties." *Daily Beast*, July 25, 2013. http://www.thedailybeast.com/amash-conyers-and-the-mavericks-fighting-for-your-civil-liberties.

Greenwald, Glenn. *No Place to Hide: Edward Snowden, the NSA, and the U.S. Surveillance State.* New York: Picador, 2014.

Greenwald, Glenn, Ewen MacAskill, and Laura Poitras. "Edward Snowden: The Whistleblower Behind the NSA Surveillance Revelations." *Guardian*, June 11, 2013. https://www.theguardian.com/world/2013/jun/09/edward-snowden-nsa-whistleblower-surveillance.

MacAskill, Ewen. "How Would Snowden Vote? Republican Debate Shows Limited Options." *Guardian*, December 16, 2015. https://www.theguardian.com/us-news/2015/dec/16/edward-snowden-vote-republican-debate-2016-election.

Nelson, Steven. "Edward Snowden Unpopular at Home, A Hero Abroad, Poll Finds." *US News and World Report*, April 21, 2015. https://www.usnews.com/news/articles/2015/04/21/edward-snowden-unpopular-at-home-a-hero-abroad-poll-finds.

New York Times. "Edward Snowden, Whistle-Blower." *New York Times*, January 1, 2014. https://www.nytimes.com/2014/01/02/opinion/edward-snowden-whistle-blower.html.

CHAPTER 5: GENOCIDE OF AN ANTI-AUTHORITARIAN PEOPLE: NATIVE AMERICANS

Capriccioso, Rob. "A Sorry Saga: Obama Signs Native American Apology." *Indian Country Today*, January 21, 2010. https://indiancountrymedianetwork.com/news/a-sorry-saga-obama-signs-native-american-apology/.

Chrisjohn, Roland D., and Shaunessy M. McKay. *Dying to Please You: Indigenous Suicide in Contemporary Canada.* Penticton, BC: Theytus Books, 2017.

Churchill, Ward. *Acts of Rebellion: The Ward Churchill Reader.* New York: Routledge, 2002.

"Definition: Convention of the Prevention and Punishment of the Crime of Genocide." United Nations Office on Genocide Prevention and the Responsibility to Protect, 2017. http://www.un.org/en/genocideprevention/genocide.html.

D'Errico, Peter. "Native American Genocide or Holocaust?" *Indian Country Today*. January 10, 2017. https://indiancountrymedianetwork.com/news/opinions/native-american-genocide-holocaust/.

Foner, Eric. *Give Me Liberty! An American History*, Fourth Edition. New York: W.W. Norton & Company, 2013.

"H. R. 3326–2." One Hundred Eleventh Congress. Washington D.C.: Government Publishing Office, January 6, 2009. https://www.gpo.gov/fdsys/pkg/BILLS-111hr3326enr/pdf/BILLS-111hr3326enr.pdf.

Jawort, Adrian. "Genocide by Other Means: U.S. Army Slaughtered Buffalo in Plains Indian Wars." *Indian Country Today*, April 10, 2017. https://indiancountrymedianetwork.com/news/environment/genocide-by-other-means-us-army-slaughtered-buffalo-in-plains-indian-wars/.

Nash, Gary. B. *Red, White and Black: The Peoples of Early America.* Englewood Cliffs, New Jersey: Prentice-Hall, 1974.

Nerburn, Kent. *Chief Joseph and the Flight of the Nez Perce.* New York: HarperCollins, 2005.

Rutecki, Gregory. "Forced Sterilization of Native Americans: Late Twentieth Century Physician Cooperation with National

Eugenic Policies." *The Center for Bioethics & Human Dignity*, October 8, 2010. https://cbhd.org/content/forced-sterilization-native-americans-late-twentieth-century-physician-cooperation-national-.

Walker, David. "Quantitative Mental Health & Oppression, Part Two: The Case of the 'American Indian.'" *Mad in America*, February 11, 2015. https://www.madinamerica.com/2015/02/quantitative-mental-health-oppression-part-two-case-american-indian/.

CHAPTER 6 PSYCHIATRIC ASSAULT AND MARGINALIZATION: NOT JUST FRANCES FARMER

American Psychiatric Association. *Diagnostic and Statistical Manual of Mental Disorders: Diagnostic and Statistical Manual of Mental Disorders, DSM-IV.* Washington, D.C.: American Psychiatric Association, 1994.

American Psychiatric Association. *Diagnostic and Statistical Manual of Mental Disorders: Diagnostic and Statistical Manual of Mental Disorders, DSM-5.* Washington, D.C.: American Psychiatric Association, 2013.

Carey, Benedict. "Mental Stress Training Is Planned for U.S. Soldiers." *New York Times*, August 17, 2009. http://www.nytimes.com/2009/08/18/health/18psych.html.

Cartwright, Samuel. "Report on Diseases and Physical Peculiarities of the Negro Race," to Louisiana Medical Association, quoted in Gould, Stephen Jay, *The Mismeasure of Man*, New York: Norton, 1981. First published in 1851.

Chrisjohn, Roland D., and Shaunessy M. McKay. *Dying to Please You: Indigenous Suicide in Contemporary Canada*. Penticton, BC: Theytus Books, 2017.

Cohen, David. "It's the Coercion, Stupid!" *Mad in America*, October 21, 2014. https://www.madinamerica.com/2014/10/coercion-stupid/.

Colaianni, Alessandra. "A Long Shadow: Nazi Doctors, Moral Vulnerability and Contemporary Medical Culture." *Journal of*

Medical Ethics, 38, no. 7. (May 3, 2012): 435–438. http://jme
.bmj.com/content/38/7/435.

Cosgrove, Lisa, and Sheldon Krimsky. "A Comparison of DSM-
IV and DSM-5 Panel Members' Financial Associations with
Industry: A Pernicious Problem Persists." *PLOS Medicine*,
March 13, 2012. http://journals.plos.org/plosmedicine/article
?id=10.1371/journal.pmed.1001190.

Evans, Matt. "Burn All the Liars." *The Morning News*, February 22,
2012. https://themorningnews.org/article/burn-all-the-liars.

Farmer, Frances. *Will There Really Be a Morning*. London: Fon-
tana, 1983.

Frances, Allen. *Saving Normal: An Insider's Revolt Against Out-
of-Control Psychiatric Diagnosis, DSM-5, Big Pharma, and the
Medicalization of Ordinary Life*. New York: William Morrow,
2014.

Friedman, Richard. "A Call for Caution on Antipsychotic
Drugs." *New York Times*, September, 25, 2012. http://www
.nytimes.com/2012/09/25/health/a-call-for-caution-in-the-
use-of-antipsychotic-drugs.html.

Ginger, Ray. *The Bending Cross: A Biography of Eugene Victor
Debs*. New Brunswick: Rutgers University Press, 1949.

Greenwald, Glenn. *No Place to Hide: Edward Snowden, the NSA,
and the US Surveillance State*: New York: Picador, 2014.

Hotchner, A. E. "Hemingway, Hounded by the Feds." *New York
Times*, July 1, 2011. http://www.nytimes.com/2011/07/02/
opinion/02hotchner.html.

Hotchner, A. E. *Papa Hemingway: A Personal Memoir*. New York:
Random House, 1966.

Insel, Thomas. "Post by Former NIMH Director Thomas Insel:
Transforming Diagnosis." *National Institute of Mental Health*
website, April 29, 2013. https://www.nimh.nih.gov/about/
directors/thomas-insel/blog/2013/transforming-diagnosis
.shtml.

LaFraniere, Sharon and Dan Levin. "Assertive Chinese Held in
Mental Wards." *New York Times*, November 11, 2010. http://
www.nytimes.com/2010/11/12/world/asia/12psych.html.

Levine, Bruce E. "Psychiatry Now Admits It's Been Wrong in Big Ways—But Can It Change?" *Truthout*, March 5, 2014. http://www.truth-out.org/news/item/22266-psychiatry-now-admits-its-been-wrong-in-big-ways-but-can-it-change.

Levine, Bruce E. "Why Anti-Authoritarians Are Diagnosed as Mentally Ill." *Mad in America*, February 26, 2012. https://www.madinamerica.com/2012/02/why-anti-authoritarians-are-diagnosed-as-mentally-ill/.

Metzl, Jonathan. *The Protest Psychosis: How Schizophrenia Became a Black Disease.* Boston: Beacon Press, 2010.

Metzl, Jonathan. "Why Are the Mentally Ill Still Bearing Arms?" *The Lancet*, 377, no. 9784 (June 25, 2011): 2172–2173. http://www.thelancet.com/journals/lancet/article/PIIS0140-6736(11)60950-1/.

"Medicating the Military—Use of Psychiatric Drugs Has Spiked; Concerns Surface about Suicide, Other Dangers." *Military Times*, March 29, 2013. http://www.militarytimes.com/story/military/archives/2013/03/29/medicating-the-military-use-of-psychiatric-drugs-has-spiked-concerns/78534358/.

Meyers, Jeffrey. *Hemingway: A Biography.* Boston: Da Capo Press, 1999.

Olfson, Mark, et al. "National Trends in the Office-Based Treatment of Children, Adolescents, and Adults with Antipsychotics." *Archives of General Psychiatry* (now *JAMA Psychiatry*), 69, no. 12 (December 2012): 1247–1256.

Oshinsky, David. *Worse Than Slavery: Parchman Farm and the Ordeal of Jim Crow Justice.* New York: Free Press, 1997.

Pies, Ronald. "Psychiatry's New Brain-Mind and the Legend of the 'Chemical Imbalance.'" *Psychiatric Times*, July 11, 2011. http://www.psychiatrictimes.com/blogs/psychiatry-new-brain-mind-and-legend-chemical-imbalance.

Rush, Benjamin. *Medical Inquiries and Observations, Volume 1.* Philadelphia: J. Conrad & Company, 1805.

Russell, Thaddeus. *A Renegade History of the United States.* New York: Free Press, 2010.

Schwarz, Alan. "Idea of New Attention Disorder Spurs Research,

and Debate." *New York Times*, April 11, 2014. https://www
.nytimes.com/2014/04/12/health/idea-of-new-attention-
disorder-spurs-research-and-debate.html.

Spiegel, Alix. "When It Comes To Depression, Serotonin Isn't The
Whole Story." *NPR Morning Edition*, January 23, 2012. http://
www.npr.org/sections/health-shots/2012/01/23/145525853/
when-it-comes-to-depression-serotonin-isnt-the-whole-story.

Whitaker, Robert. *Anatomy of an Epidemic: Magic Bullets, Psychiatric Drugs, and the Astonishing Rise of Mental Illness in America*. New York: Random House, 2010.

Whitaker, Robert. *Mad in America: Bad Science, Bad Medicine, and
the Enduring Mistreatment of the Mentally Ill*. Cambridge,
MA: Perseus Publishing, 2001.

Whitaker, Robert, and Lisa Cosgrove. *Psychiatry Under the Influence: Institutional Corruption, Social Injury, and Prescriptions
for Reform*. New York: Palgrave Macmillan, 2015.

CHAPTER 7: SCHOOLING'S ASSAULT ON YOUNG ANTI-AUTHORITARIANS

Barsky, Robert F. *Noam Chomsky: A Life of Dissent*. Cambridge,
MA: MIT Press, 1997.

Cain, Susan. *Quiet: The Power of Introverts in a World that Can't
Stop Talking*. New York: Crown, 2012.

Carlin, George. "The American Dream," *Life is Worth Losing*, 2006.
http://scrapsfromtheloft.com/2016/12/28/george-carlin-life
-is-worth-losing-transcript/.

"Children, Teens, and Reading," Common Sense Media website,
May 12, 2014. https://www.commonsensemedia.org/research/
children-teens-and-reading.

Chomsky, Noam. *Understanding Power: The Indispensable
Chomsky*, edited by Peter Mitchell and John Schoeffel. New
York: The New Press, 2002.

Clark, Ronald. *Einstein: The Life and Times. New York:* The World
Publishing Company, 1971.

Gatto, John Taylor. "Why Schools Don't Educate," text of a speech
by John Taylor Gatto accepting the New York City Teacher

of the Year Award. January 31, 1990. www.naturalchild.org/guest/john_gatto.htm.

Goertzel, Victor, and Mildred George Goertzel. *Cradles of Eminence, 2nd Edition.* Edited and updated by Ted George Goertzel, and Ariel M.W. Hansen. Scottsdale, AZ: Great Potential Press, 2004.

Holt, John. "How Children Fail," edited by Ronald and Beatrice Gross, *Radical School Reform,* New York: Simon & Schuster, 1969.

Kasenbacher, Michael. "Noam Chomsky on How He Found His Calling." *Alternet,* December 29, 2012. http://www.alternet.org/education/noam-chomsky-how-he-found-his-calling.

Kozol, Jonathan. *The Night is Dark and I am Far Away from Home.* Boston: Houghton Mifflin, 1975.

Levine, Bruce E. "8 Reasons Young Americans Don't Fight Back: How the US Crushed Youth Resistance." *Films for Action,* August 4, 2011. http://www.filmsforaction.org/news/8-reasons-young-americans-dont-fight-back-how-the-us-crushed-youth-resistance/.

Levine, Bruce E. *Get Up Stand Up: Uniting Populists, Energizing the Defeated, and Battling the Corporate Elite.* White River Junction, VT: Chelsea Green Publishing, 2011.

McDonald, Duff. *The Golden Passport: Harvard Business School, the Limits of Capitalism, and the Moral Failure of the MBA Elite.* New York: Harper Business, 2017.

Milgram, Stanley. *Obedience to Authority: An Experimental View.* New York: Harper & Row, 1974.

Nader, Ralph. "Schooling for Myths and Powerlessness." *CounterPunch,* May 18, 2017. https://www.counterpunch.org/2017/05/18/schooling-for-myths-and-powerlessness-2/.

Project on Student Debt. "Student Debt and the Class of 2015." The Institute for College Access and Success. https://ticas.org/content/pub/student-debt-and-class-2015.

CHAPTER 8: LESSONS FROM ANTI-AUTHORITARIANS WHO HAVE HURT THEMSELVES, OTHERS, OR THE CAUSE

Phil Ochs

Bowser, Ken, director. *Phil Ochs: There But For Fortune*. 2010.

Kamiya, Gary. "Lenny Bruce Died for Our Sins." *Salon*, August 26, 2003. http://www.salon.com/2003/08/26/lennybruce.

Shumacher, Michael. *There But For Fortune: The Life of Phil Ochs*. New York: Hyperion, 1996.

Lenny Bruce

Bruce, Lenny. *How to Talk Dirty and Influence People: An Autobiography of Lenny Bruce*. New York: Simon & Schuster, 1992. First published in 1963.

Carlin, George, with Tony Hendra. *Last Words*. New York: Free Press, 2009.

Goldman, Albert. *Ladies and Gentleman: Lenny Bruce!!* New York: Random House, 1974.

Love, Matthew. "50 Best Stand-Up Comics of All Time." *Rolling Stone*, February 14, 2017. http://www.rollingstone.com/culture/lists/50-best-stand-up-comics-of-all-time-w464199/lenny-bruce-w464260.

Ida Lupino

Donati, William. *Ida Lupino: A Biography*. Lexington, Kentucky: University Press of Kentucky, 1996.

Rosenzweig, Torrie. "Ida Lupino," *Through the Lens Documentary, A & E Biography*. 1997. https://www.youtube.com/watch?v=-RApabc49C0.

Alexander Berkman

Avrich, Paul. *Anarchist Portraits*. Princeton, NJ: Princeton University Press, 1988.

Avrich, Paul, and Karen Avrich. *Sasha and Emma: The Anarchist Odyssey of Alexander Berkman and Emma Goldman*. Cambridge, MA: Belknap Press of Harvard University Press, 2012.

Berkman, Alexander. *Now and After: The ABC of Communist Anarchism*. New York: Vanguard Press, 1929. http://assets .zinedistro.org/zines/pdfs/116.pdf.

Berkman, Alexander. *Prison Memoirs of an Anarchist*. New York: New York Review of Books, 1999. First published in 1912.

Ward, John William. "Violence, Anarchy, and Alexander Berkman," *New York Review of Books*, November 5, 1970. http:// www.nybooks.com/articles/1970/11/05/violence-anarchy-and -alexander-berkman/.

Leon Czolgosz

Briggs, L. Vernon. *The Manner of Man That Kills: Spencer-Czolgosz-Richeson*. Boston: R. G. Badger, 1921.

Ted Kaczynski

Chase, Alston. "Harvard and the Making of the Unabomber." *The Atlantic Monthly*, June, 2000. https://www.theatlantic .com/magazine/archive/2000/06/harvard-and-the-making -of-the-unabomber/378239/.

Chase, Alston. *A Mind for Murder—The Education of the Unabomber and the Origins of Modern Terrorism*. New York: W. W. Norton and Company, 2004.

Green, Sam, and Bill Siegel, directors. *The Weather Underground*. 2002.

McFadden, Robert. "Prisoner of Rage—A Special Report; From a Child of Promise to the Unabom Suspect." *New York Times*, May 26, 1996. http://www.nytimes.com/1996/05/26/us/prisoner -of-rage-a-special-report-from-a-child-of-promise-to-the- unabom-suspect.html.

CHAPTER 9: POLITICAL, SPIRITUAL, PHILOSOPHICAL, AND PSYCHOLOGICAL LENSES FOR ANTI-AUTHORITARIANS

Anarchism

Berkman, Alexander. *Now and After: The ABC of Communist*

Anarchism. New York: Vanguard Press, 1929. http://assets.zine distro.org/zines/pdfs/116.pdf.

Berkman, Alexander. *Prison Memoirs of an Anarchist.* New York: New York Review of Books, 1999. First published in 1912.

Goldman, Emma. "Anarchism: What It Really Stands For." *Anarchism and Other Essays.* New York: Mother Earth Publications,1910.https://theanarchistlibrary.org/library/emma-goldman-anarchism-and-other-essays.a4.pdf.

Kohn, Alfie. *Punished by Rewards: The Trouble With Gold Stars, Incentive Plans, A's, Praise, and Other Bribes.* Boston: Houghton Mifflin, 1993.

Levine, Bruce E. "Living in America Will Drive You Insane—Literally." *Salon,* July 31, 2013. http://www.salon.com/2013/07/31/living_in_america_will_drive_you_insane_literally_partner/.

Lopez, Ricardo. "Most Workers Hate Their Jobs or Have 'Checked Out,' Gallup says." *Los Angeles Times,* June 17, 2013. http://www.latimes.com/business/la-fi-mo-employee-engagement-gallup-poll-20130617-story.html.

Wilson, Michael. "Noam Chomsky: The Kind of Anarchism I Believe in, and What's Wrong with Libertarians." *AlterNet,* May 28, 2013. http://www.alternet.org/civil-liberties/noam-chomsky-kind-anarchism-i-believe-and-whats-wrong-libertarians.

Buddhism

Conze, Edward. *Buddhism: Its Essence and Development.* New York: Harper & Row, 1959.

Pratt, James B. *The Pilgrimage of Buddhism and a Buddhist Pilgrimage.* New York: The Macmillan Company, 1928.

Smith, Huston. *The Religions of Man.* New York: Harper & Row, 1958.

Trungpa, Chögyam. *The Myth of Freedom and the Way of Meditation.* Boston: Shambhala, 1988.

The God of Spinoza and Einstein

Durant, Will. *The Story of Philosophy: The Lives and Opinions of the Greater Philosophers.* New York: Simon and Schuster, 1926.

Gilmore, Michael. "Einstein's God: Just What Did Einstein Believe About God?" *Skeptic*, 5, no. 2 (1997): 62–64. https://web.archive .org/web/20020126112239id_/http://www.skeptic.com/ archives50.html.

Isaacson, Walter. *Einstein: His Life and Times.* New York: Simon & Schuster, 2007.

Martin, Bernard. *Great 20th Century Jewish Philosophers.* New York: The Macmillan Company, 1970.

New York Times. "Einstein Believes in 'Spinoza's God,'" April 25, 1929.

Ratner, Joseph. *The Philosophy of Spinoza.* New York: The Modern Library, 1927.

Spinoza, Baruch. *The Ethics of Spinoza*, edited by Dagobert Runes. Secaucus, NJ: The Citadel Press, 1976.

The Enneagram

Palmer, Helen. *The Enneagram: Understanding Yourself and the Others in Your Life.* San Francisco: Harper & Row, 1988.

Riso, Don Richard. *Personality Types: Using the Enneagram for Self-Discovery.* Boston: Houghton-Mifflin Company, 1987.

Riso, Don Richard. *Understanding the Enneagram: The Practical Guide to Personality Types.* Boston: Houghton-Mifflin Company, 1990.

Rohr, Richard, and Andreas Ebert. *Discovering the Enneagram: An Ancient Tool for a New Spiritual Journey.* New York: Crossroad, 1990.

CHAPTER 10. LESSONS FROM ANTI-AUTHORITARIANS WHO HAVE HELPED THEMSELVES AND THE CAUSE

Henry David Thoreau

Harding, Walter. *The Days of Henry Thoreau: A Biography.* Princeton, NJ: Princeton University Press, 1992.

Purdy, Jedediah. "In Defense of Thoreau," *Atlantic*, October 20, 2015. https://www.theatlantic.com/science/archive/2015/10/in

-defense-of-thoreau/411457/.

Schulz, Kathryn. "Pond Scum: Henry David Thoreau's Moral Myopia." *New Yorker*, October 19, 2015. http://www.newyorker
.com/magazine/2015/10/19/pond-scum.

Thoreau, Henry David. *Walden and Civil Disobedience*. New
York: Airmont Publishing Company, 1965. *Walden* first published in 1854; *Resistance to Civil Government* (*Civil Disobedience*) first published in 1849.

Scott Nearing

Coleman, Melissa. *This Life Is in Your Hands: One Dream, Sixty
Acres, and a Family Undone*. New York: HarperCollins Publisher, 2011.

Hamer, John Faithful. "The Forest Farm Romance." *Committing So-
ciology*, May 17, 2015. https://committingsociology.com/2015
/05/17/the-forest-farm-romance/.

Hay Bright, Jean. *Meanwhile, Next Door to the Good Life*. Dix-
mont, ME: Brightberry Press, 2003.

Joseph, Stanley and Lynn Karlin. *A Maine Farm: A Year of Country
Life*. New York: Random House, 1991.

Nearing, Helen. *Loving and Leaving the Good Life*, White River
Junction, VT: Chelsea Green, 1993.

Nearing, Scott. *The Making of a Radical: A Political Autobiography*. Harborside, ME: Social Science Institute, 1972.

Nearing, Scott, and Helen Nearing. *Living the Good Life: How
to Live Sanely and Simply in a Troubled World*. New York:
Schocken Books, 1970. First published in 1954.

Nearing, Scott, and Helen Nearing. *Continuing the Good Life:
Half a Century of Homesteading*. New York: Schocken Books,
1979.

Frederick Douglass

Douglass, Frederick. *Life and Times of Frederick Douglass*. Boston:
De Wolfe & Fiske Co., 1892.

Douglass, Frederick. *A Narrative of the Life of Frederick Douglass,
an American Slave*. Boston: The Antislavery Office, 1845.

Stauffer, John, et al. *Picturing Frederick Douglass: An Illustrated Biography of the Nineteenth Century's Most Photographed American.* New York: Liveright, 2015.

Harriet Tubman

Foner, Eric. *Gateway to Freedom: The Hidden History of the Underground Railroad.* New York: W. W. Norton & Company, 2015.

Larson, Kate Clifford. *Bound for the Promised Land: Harriet Tubman, Portrait of an American Hero.* New York: Ballantine Books, 2004.

Larson, Kate Clifford. "Five Myths about Harriet Tubman." *Washington Post*, April 22, 2016. https://www.washingtonpost.com /opinions/five-myths-about-harriet-tubman/2016/04/22/b9 f3a270-07f0-11e6-b283-e79d81c63c1b_story.html.

Helen Keller

Jones, Josh. "Mark Twain & Helen Keller's Special Friendship: He Treated Me Not as a Freak, But as a Person Dealing with Great Difficulties." *Open Culture*, May 13, 2015. http://www. openculture.com/2015/05/mark-twain-helen-kellers-special-friendship.html.

Keller, Helen. *The Story of My Life.* New York: Doubleday, 1903.

Nielsen, Kim E. *The Radical Lives of Helen Keller.* New York: New York University Press, 2004.

Rosenthal, Keith. "The Politics of Helen Keller: Socialism and Disability." *International Socialist Review*, no. 96 (Spring 2015). http://isreview.org/issue/96/politics-helen-keller.

Jane Jacobs

Alexiou, Alice Sparberg. *Jane Jacobs: Urban Visionary.* New Brunswick, NJ: Rutgers University Press, 2006.

Caro, Robert. *The Power Broker: Robert Moses and the Fall of New York.* New York: Random House, 1974.

Gopnik, Adam. "Jane Jacobs's Street Smarts." *New Yorker*, September 26, 2016. http://www.newyorker.com/magazine/2016 /09/26/jane-jacobs-street-smarts.

Gratz, Roberta Brandes. "The Genius of Jane Jacobs, Who Changed the Way We Think About Cities." *Nation*, June 8, 2016. https://www.thenation.com/article/the-genius-of-jane-jacobs-who-changed-the-way-we-think-about-cities/.

Jacobs, Jane. *The Death and Life of Great American Cities*. New York: Random House, 1961.

Noam Chomsky

Achbar, Mark, and Peter Wintonick, directors. *Manufacturing Consent: Noam Chomsky and the Media*, 1992.

Barsky, Robert F. *Noam Chomsky: A Life of Dissent*. Cambridge, Massachusetts: MIT Press, 1997.

Chomsky, Noam. *Understanding Power: The Indispensable Chomsky*, edited by Peter Mitchell and John Schoeffel. New York: The New Press, 2002.

Goodman, Amy. "The Life and Times of Noam Chomsky," *Democracy Now*, November 26, 2004. https://chomsky.info/20041126/

Herman, Edward S., and Noam Chomsky. *The Manufacture of Consent: The Political Economy of the Mass Media*. New York: Pantheon, 1988.

MacFarquhar, Larissa. "The Devil's Accountant." *The New Yorker*, March 31, 2003. https://www.newyorker.com/magazine/2003/03/31/the-devils-accountant.

Smith, Courtenay. "Reader's Digest Trust Poll: The 100 Most Trusted People in America" *Reader's Digest*, May 2013. https://www.rd.com/culture/readers-digest-trust-poll-the-100-most-trusted-people-in-america/.

George Carlin

Carlin, George. *Brain Droppings*. New York: Hyperion, 1997.

Carlin, George, with Tony Hendra. *Last Words*. New York: Free Press, 2009.

"George Carlin Archive Interview." Archive of American Television: Academy of Television Arts & Science Foundation. Henry Colman and Jenni Matz conducted interview, December 17,

2007. https://www.youtube.com/watch?v=L8a7cUDJEtU.

Love, Matthew. "50 Best Stand-Up Comics of All Time." *Rolling Stone*, February 14, 2017. http://www.rollingstone.com/culture/lists/50-best-stand-up-comics-of-all-time-w464199/george-carlin-w464261.

CHAPTER 11: WE DON'T NEED NO BADGES

Depression

Goldman, Emma. *Living My Life, Volume One.* New York: Dover, 1970. First published in 1931.

Joiner, Thomas and James C. Coyne. *The Interactional Nature of Depression. Washington DC: The American Psychological Association,* 1999.

"Ketamine," Foundation for a Drug Free World website, 2017. http://www.drugfreeworld.org/drugfacts/prescription/ketamine.html.

Levine, Bruce E. "Anti-Authoritarian Options for Suicidal Anti-Authoritarians." *CounterPunch.* April 18, 2017. https://www.counterpunch.org/2017/04/18/anti-authoritarian-options-for-suicidal-anti-authoritarians/.

Levine, Bruce E. *Surviving America's Depression Epidemic: How to Find Morale, Energy, and Community in a World Gone Crazy.* White River Junction, VT: Chelsea Green Publishing Company, 2007.

National Alliance on Mental Illness. "Risk of Suicide." NAMI website. 2017. https://www.nami.org/Learn-More/Mental-Health-Conditions/Related-Conditions/Suicide.

Nelson, J. Craig. "The STAR*D Study: A Four-Course Meal That Leaves Us Wanting More." *American Journal of Psychiatry*, 163, no. 11 (November 2006): 1864–66. http://ajp.psychiatryonline.org/doi/full/10.1176/ajp.2006.163.11.1864.

Oaklander, Mandy. "New Hope for Depression." *Time Magazine*, July 27, 2017. http://time.com/4876098/new-hope-for-depression/.

Pigott, H. Edmund, et al. "Efficacy and Effectiveness of

Antidepressants: Current Status of Research." *Psychotherapy and Psychosomatics*, 79, no. 5 (August 2010): 267–279.

Wampold, Bruce. *The Great Psychotherapy Debate: Models, Methods, and Findings*. Mahweh, NJ: Lawrence Erlbaum, 2001.

Webb, David. *Thinking About Suicide*. Herefordshire, UK: PCCS Books, 2010.

Whitaker, Robert. "The STAR*D Scandal: A New Paper Sums It All Up," *Psychology Today Blog*, August 27, 2010. http://www.psychologytoday.com/blog/mad-in-america/201008/the-stard-scandal-new-paper-sums-it-all.

Relationships

Avrich, Paul, and Karen Avrich. *Sasha and Emma: The Anarchist Odyssey of Alexander Berkman and Emma Goldman*. Cambridge, MA: Belknap Press of Harvard University Press, 2012.

Ginger, Ray. *The Bending Cross: A Biography of Eugene Victor Debs*. New Brunswick: Rutgers University Press, 1949.

Levine, Bruce E. "The More a Society Coerces Its People, the Greater the Chance of Mental Illness." *AlterNet*, April 26, 2013. http://www.alternet.org/personal-health/more-society-coerces-its-people-greater-greater-chance-mental-illness

Marable, Manning. *Malcolm X: A Life of Reinvention*, New York: Viking, 2011.

Mantel, Henriette, and Steve Skrovan, directors. *An Unreasonable Man*. 2006. Screenplay and notes at: http://rapeutation.com/anunREASONABLEmanscreenplay.pdf.

Stone, Irving. *Adversary in the House*. New York: Doubleday & Company, 1947.

Mutual Aid

Alcoholics Anonymous. *Alcoholics Anonymous Comes Of Age: A Brief History of A. A.* New York: Alcoholics Anonymous World Services, Inc., 1957.

Avrich, Paul, and Karen Avrich. *Sasha and Emma: The Anarchist Odyssey of Alexander Berkman and Emma Goldman*. Cambridge, MA: Belknap Press of Harvard University Press, 2012.

Gates, Henry Louis Jr. "Who Really Ran the Underground Railroad." *The Root*, March 25, 2013. http://www.theroot.com/who-really-ran-the-underground-railroad-1790895697.

Glitterbomb, Logan Marie. "Anarchism for a Mainstream Audience." *Center for a Stateless Society*, July 14, 2016. https://c4ss.org/content/45683.

Parenting

Carlin, George, with Tony Hendra. *Last Words*. New York: Free Press, 2009.

Knoll, James L., IV. "Inpatient Suicide: Identifying Vulnerability in the Hospital Setting." *Psychiatric Times*, May 22, 2012. http://www.psychiatrictimes.com/suicide/inpatient-suicide-identifying-vulnerability-hospital-setting.

Sachmann, Edward S. J., and M. D. Sachmann "No-Suicide Contracts, No-Suicide Agreements, and No-Suicide Assurances: A Study of Their Nature, Utilization, Perceived Effectiveness, and Potential to Cause Harm." *Crisis*, 31, no. 6 (January 2010): 290–302.

CONCLUSION

Gilens, Martin, and Benjamin I. Page. "Testing Theories of American Politics: Elites, Interest Groups, and Average Citizens." *Perspectives on Politics*, 12, no. 3 (September 2014): 564–581.

Index

AK Press is small, in terms of staff and resources, but we also manage to be one of the world's most productive anarchist publishing houses. We publish close to twenty books every year, and distribute thousands of other titles published by like-minded independent presses and projects from around the globe. We're entirely worker-run and democratically managed. We operate without a corporate structure—no boss, no managers, no bullshit.

The Friends of AK program is a way you can directly contribute to the continued existence of AK Press, and ensure that we're able to keep publishing books like this one! Friends pay $25 a month directly into our publishing account ($30 for Canada, $35 for international), and receive a copy of every book AK Press publishes for the duration of their membership! Friends also receive a discount on anything they order from our website or buy at a table: 50% on AK titles, and 20% on everything else. We have a Friends of AK ebook program as well: $15 a month gets you an electronic copy of every book we publish for the duration of your membership. You can even sponsor a very discounted membership for someone in prison.

Email FRIENDSOFAK@AKPRESS.ORG for more info, or visit the Friends of AK Press website: HTTPS://WWW.AKPRESS.ORG/FRIENDS.HTML.

There are always great book projects in the works—so sign up now to become a Friend of AK Press, and let the presses roll!